Dickens
Interviews and Recollections

Volume 2

Also by Philip Collins

A Christmas Carol: The Public Reading Version (*editor*)
A Dickens Bibliography
Charles Dickens: *David Copperfield*
Charles Dickens: The Public Readings (*editor*)
Dickens and Crime
Dickens and Education
Dickens's *Bleak House*
Dickens: The Critical Heritage (*editor*)
English Christmas (*editor*)
From Manly Tears to Stiff Upper Lip: The Victorian and Pathos
James Boswell
Reading Aloud: A Victorian Métier
The Impress of the Moving Age
Thomas Cooper, the Chartist

DICKENS

Interviews and Recollections

Volume 2

Edited by

Philip Collins

First published 1981 by
THE MACMILLAN PRESS LTD
London and Basingstoke
Companies and representatives
throughout the world

ISBN 0 333 26255 7

Printed in Hong Kong

To Jean and Arthur Humphreys
with love and gratitude

Contents

List of Plates

Acknowledgements

Dr Michael Slater and Dr Andrew Sanders, past and present editors of the *Dickensian*, have been generous in advice and in giving me permission to reprint material from their journal, as have their contributors, Professors K. J. Fielding, Jerome Meckier and John R. DeBruyn. The trustees of the Dickens House Museum have allowed me to publish manuscript material and to reproduce portraits from their collection, and the Curator of Dickens House, Dr David Parker, has been most helpful in giving me access to its riches. Other illustrations appear through the kindness of the Forster Collection (Victoria and Albert Museum), the National Portrait Gallery, and the Mander and Mitcheson Collection.

Other friends and colleagues have helped by answering enquiries or securing material for me: Professor Sylvère Monod, Professor F. W. J. Hemmings, Professor Kathleen Tillotson, Dr John Podeschi, Miss Eva Searl, Mr Iain Crawford, Mr Charles Leahy and Mr Richard Foulkes. Like all students of Dickens, I am much in the debt of the editors of the Pilgrim Edition of *The Letters of Charles Dickens*, the annotation as well as the text of which has been invaluable. The staff of Leicester University Library have been energetic in obtaining materials for me, and the Epsom Library and the Eastgate House Museum, Rochester, have answered enquiries. I salute and thank my predecessors in this biographical field, whose researches have greatly eased mine: notably Frederic G. Kitton, William R. Hughes, Robert Langton and W. J. Carlton. I thank also the patient and skilful typists who have coped with my second and third as well as my first thoughts: Mrs Doreen Butler, Mrs Sylvia Garfield, Miss Anne Sowter, Mrs Pat Taylor and Mrs Brenda Tracy.

For permission to reprint copyright material I thank the editors of *The Times Literary Supplement*, *Harper's Magazine* and *University* (Princeton, N. J.), and the following publishers: Oxford University Press and the Clarendon Press for the extracts from the Pilgrim Edition of *The Letters of Charles Dickens*, ed. Madeline House, Graham Storey and Kathleen Tillotson; *The George Eliot Letters*, ed.

Gordon S. Haight; Arthur A. Adrian's *Georgina Hogarth and the Dickens Circle*; and Gordon N. Ray's *Thackeray: The Age of Wisdom, 1847–1863*; John Murray (Publishers) Ltd for the extracts from James Milne's *A Window in Fleet Street*; Frederick Muller Ltd for the extracts from Gladys Storey's *Dickens and Daughter*; William Heinemann Ltd for the extracts from Sir Henry Fielding Dickens's *The Recollections of Sir Henry Dickens, Q. C.*; Harvard University Press, and Belinda Norman-Butler, literary executor for the Estate of William Thackeray, for the extracts from *The Letters and Private Papers of William Makepeace Thackeray*, ed. Gordon N. Ray; the Belknap Press of Harvard University Press for the extracts from *The Journal of Richard Henry Dana, Jr, 1841–60*, ed. R. F. Lucid.

Every effort has been made to trace all the copyright-holders, but if any have been inadvertently overlooked the publishers will be pleased to make the necessary arrangement at the first opportunity.

'Quite the Best Man I Ever Knew'

MARCUS STONE

(1) from J. W. T. Ley, 'Marcus Stone, R. A.', *Dkn*, XVII (1921) 130; (2) from Stone's unpublished reminiscences, dated internally 1911 (MS, Dickens House); (3) from Stone's 'Some Recollections of Dickens', *Dkn*, VI (1910) 61–4; (4) from 'Mr Marcus Stone, R. A., and Charles Dickens', *Dkn*, VIII (1912) 216–17; (5) from address to the Boz Club, *Boz Club Papers*, 1906, p. 24; (6) from autograph notes by Stone on Dickens (MS, Dickens House). 'The very mention of the name of Charles Dickens is always followed in my case with a certain thrill of inward emotion', Marcus Stone told the Boz Club in 1910; and speaking to them four years earlier he deprecated a critical approach to Dickens's genius – surely, he felt, members would 'rather hear about him, about his great and beautiful life, that sweet life without blemish' (*Boz Club Papers*, 1906, p. 25). A 'honeysuckle' reminiscer, then; but a perceptive witness, who knew Dickens intimately *en famille* from 1851 to 1870. Like his father, Frank Stone, A. R. A. (1800–59), who was one of Dickens's dearest friends, Marcus Stone (1840–1921) was an artist. After Frank Stone's death, Dickens became a second father to the family, especially Marcus, and, among other aids and encouragements, employed Marcus as illustrator for *Our Mutual Friend* (1864–5). During the 1850s, the Stones were neighbours of the Dickenses, and during the 1860s Marcus Stone was a frequent and prolonged visitor at Gad's Hill. J. W. T. Ley has further reminiscences by Marcus Stone in *The Dickens Circle* (1918) – Stone was one of the last survivors from this circle – and extract (1) is from Ley's interview with him when he was very aged, tired, sad, and disillusioned with life; but he perked up when asked about Dickens.

(1) He paused for some minutes, and he was evidently dreaming of old days. Then he reverted to Dickens and the old circle, and for half an hour chatted about the people who composed it, whom he knew so well, in a way that was delightful, and made the period one of the pleasantest half hours of my life. He did not like all the people he named. He disliked Fechter particularly, and told me he had never to that day understood Dickens's infatuation for the actor. Nor did he like Edmund Yates.[1] Mention of Yates' name led to a reference to Dickens's quarrel with Thackeray, and I expressed the opinion that as I knew the story, Dickens's conduct was foolish. 'Of course it was', said Mr. Stone. 'But you must remember that Dickens had been friends with Yates's parents, and for the memory of those early days

he was anxious to serve the young man. And Yates could be very fascinating too. Superficially, mind you. But'–with a gesture indicative of dislike–'The man was no gentleman.'

And then, when I put to him the simple question, 'What sort of man was Dickens?' I was amazed by the vigour and earnestness with which he answered me. I had got up to go. He paused, turned and faced me squarely, put a hand on my shoulder, and looked straight into my eyes. 'He was quite the best man I ever knew', he said. 'Yes; the best man I ever knew. He was such a good man that you put his greatness in the second place when you knew him. He occupied himself daily in some sort of work for somebody. The amount of work that he did, the amount of money that he took out of his pocket, was perfectly amazing. But the personal trouble he took for people who had no sort of claim upon him! He was the most compassionate creature that ever lived–in fact, almost to a ludicrous extent at times. He forgave when he ought not to have done so, and gave very often where he ought to have withheld.'

(2) There is no good portrait of him. The best, which represents him as a young man of twenty seven, many years before I knew him, is that by Maclise. One or two photographs are of value, but as a rule they were curiously unlike. Let me try to describe him.

When I first looked upon him in the back garden of Tavistock House [in 1851], I thought him a short man. I had imagined him previously to be a sort of giant. Standing by the side of the Frank Stone six feet, or more, tended to make him appear shorter than he really was. His actual height was five feet nine, a fair average height. From his constant daily habit of taking long walks in all weathers, he was bronzed and ruddy. A lean man, well proportioned, finely developed limbs. A well set up light body in perfect condition made him admirably fitted for the activity to which he accustomed himself. His carriage was erect, his movements usually alert and flexible. His walking pace was four miles an hour. The afternoon walk was generally a stretch of twelve to fifteen miles, frequently more, he made a practice of increasing his speed when ascending a hill, which practice is opposed to the practice of all mountain climbers. . . .

His hands–of the same ruddy bronze colour as his face–he seldom wore gloves–had that characteristic mobility of the thumb, the bending back of the top joint, generally seen in thumbs of painters and sculptors. In profile the lines of his forehead and nose were almost grecian, having a very slight depression between the brows. This is shown in a pencil sketch by Maclise – given in Forster's *Life*, where Dickens is represented with his wife and her sister – his nostril finely curved, well opened and sensitive, a firmly closed well cut mouth.[2]

His eyes, most impressive and wonderful, were of a colour rarely met with, a sort of green hazel grey – steadfast honest, all seeing eyes. Never the less somewhat short sighted, this slight defect of vision did not seem to trouble him, I only once saw him use a pincenez. When he was his own coachman driving his trap from the station one evening after dark. He held a book when reading at short range. They were not seeing, they were also speaking eyes, they could question you, they could assent and sympathize. They could call your attention to an object of interest, by a quick glance at you and then with an equally rapid glance at that which he wanted you to observe. He moved his eyes without moving his head more than is the habit of most people. Wonderful eyes – how they could laugh, how they could cry. I have been embarrassed by my intimate understanding of this ocular telegraph on occasions, when it would have been indiscreet to laugh. . . .

He was clean shaven when I first saw him. I remember how we and all his friends regretted his adoption of a moustache about 1852, we lamented still more his further delinquency when he added his chin beard, shaving his cheeks only, which arrangement was added to the moustache in a year or two, never afterwards to be changed. His hair was dark brown – which became very scanty in his later years, and sprinkled with grey, but never grey enough to disguise the original colour. But for the disfigurement of his handsome face by his beard and moustache, years made little change in his appearance, of course he looked older as time went on but his figure retained its alertness and activity, he never put on flesh or lost it. He gave the impression of a well preserved, self respecting wholesome man.

In common with all great thinkers, his habitual expression was one of almost severe gravity. How could it be otherwise, the hours he gave to 'quill driving' were few, considering his large correspondence, only three to four hours could have been given daily to his literary labours. There could have been no hours of the day during which the task he was engaged upon, was entirely banished from his mind. This constant mental exertion had deeply lined his face very early in life. I used to wonder how he could have survived with sustained powers the stress and strain of such brain toil. . . . It was not surprising that those who did not know better gave him five or six years more than he had a right to. At thirty nine, his age when I first knew him, he looked at least five and forty. When he was five and forty, I asked an intelligent observer to guess his age, his estimate was without a moment's hesitation 'fifty two'.

The grave expression gave great value to his irresistible and contagious laugh, a genuine natural laugh, beginning with a wheezing gasp then gradually struggling in to a hearty ring. [Stone explains how 'the Dickenses and the Stones were close neighbours for nine years', from 1851, when Dickens moved into Tavistock House (part of which the Stones had previously occupied), until 1860, when he finally moved into Gad's Hill. The Stones took the house next door but one to Tavistock House. During the summer of 1851, while the Dickenses were on holiday, the Stones temporarily lived in Dickens's house, Devonshire Terrace. Young Arthur Stone rejoiced in its 'well stocked library', and Marcus Stone in its works of art.] A charming little collection of pictures adorned the dining room, to which very few additions were made in later years. His own portrait and that of Mrs. Dickens by Maclise, the 'Dolly Varden' and the 'Kate Nickleby' by Frith, a scene from *Used up* containing a portrait of Dickens by Egg, small works by Stanfield and David Roberts, a sketch by David Wilkie, 'Mrs. Squeers administering brimstone and treacle to the boys' by Webster, three or four water colours by Cattermole, one of which was the last that he ever produced, an excellent early Callow, and a lovely William Hunt 'Moss Roses', some portraits of the children by my father and pencil drawings of them by Maclise, a subject picture by the latter, 'A Girl crossing a stream on stepping stones', and a very charming 'Little Nell and her grandfather' by Topham. These art Treasures were arranged on the wall with great discrimination, the owner showed himself to be an excellent 'hanger'. The same scheme of hanging was adopted in his new house and afterwards at Gad's Hill.[3] In the Hall was the stuffed raven, the famous 'Grip'.

The presiding influence of the master was visible all over the house, his love of order and fitness, his aversion to any neglect of attention, even in details which are frequently not considered at all. There was the place for everything and everything in its place, deterioration was not permitted. Both inside and out, all was well cared for, well devised, and adopted with purposeful intelligence and consideration. There was no litter or accumulation of rubbish, no lumber room or glory hole. The Pneumatic cleaner of today [1911] would not have gathered a rich harvest of dust in any house of his. If he was something of a martinet he certainly spared himself less than any body. A Napoleonic commander in chief, he found able and active allies in his sister in law and elder daughter who were geniuses in carrying out his ideas.

It might be presumed that the evidence of such order and precision produced a prosaic primness in the aspect of his dwelling, but such was not the case by any means. The comfort was sumptuous, but without ostentation or display, it was gracious, thoroughly homelike, and welcoming.[4]

(3) What [the friendship of Charles Dickens] has been to me in forming my life it would be difficult for me to convey to you. His enormous influence over a young man in his growing age – or, I should say, first a child, then a young man, then a man in his maturity – was such that it could not help being the most important factor in the formation of the character of that fortunate individual. It was so in my case. I knew him as a child, when, strange to say, I had already read all his books that had then been written. My father had known Dickens when he was twenty-five. I, of course, had learnt from my father so much about Dickens before I first saw him that that impression was as great as it would be to-day if some illustrious personage were to come before your vision. [Stone describes how he met Dickens, when he was ten, and what kindnesses he received from him.]

I should like to sketch one or two little vignettes that come across the mind. We often went for long walks, up by Cobham Woods, Rochester, and down the road to Chatham. And all along that route I see his figure. How brightly the sun shone! I suppose there were gloomy days, but they were not worth remembering. One day I recollect we came down to Cooling. Dickens said, 'You see that church? That is where I saw the pauper's funeral in *Oliver Twist* exactly as it is written in the book. Here is something more interesting still. A few months afterwards I received a letter from the clergyman who behaved in an unseemly way on that occasion, asking me whether I conceived it possible that such a thing could ever occur. I wrote back to him and said, "Thou art the man."'

On another occasion we were walking together, and overtook a tilt-cart with the name of 'Weller' on it. I called his attention to it, and he said, 'Yes; and he is more or less the immortal man; he is a fruiterer who keeps a shop in Chatham Market.'

Another day, in going past the theatre in Rochester, Dickens said, 'You see that low wall with a railing on the top; well, I remember when I was a little chap my dear mother (God forgive her) putting me on that wall and making me cheer the Prince Regent.'

One night he proposed to two of the boys and myself that we should walk down to Rochester and go and see the pantomime. It was a cold night. Dickens wore a cap and muffler; and as he drew near the theatre he said, 'I think I shall keep the muffler on, because people are so apt to pay me compliments if they recognise me.' There were three people in the front row of the pit, and one man – a sailor – in the centre, and he was smoking, although smoking was strictly prohibited. The harlequin was very old and very fat, and he could not get out of the trap without the help of the clown and pantaloon. Dickens did not escape observation, in spite of the muffler, and the clown made a wretched attempt at a gag, but failed; but he managed to bring out the words, 'The great Charles Dickens.' After that we fled. . . .

At Gadshill at Christmas time we had a great deal of nonsense, for that dear man had the greatest delight in nonsense that ever existed.

(4) As a young man I was frequently invited to stay at Gad's Hill, his home in Kent. I spent Christmas at that place every year as long as he lived there, besides paying a visit sometimes in the summer for a month at a time. Such was his thoughtfulness that even when he was away reading in America, by his express instructions, Christmas continued to be celebrated at Gad's Hill, and we who were his intimates assembled there as usual. Of course, the place was not quite the same without him. How we all worshipped him. I really believe a nobler man never lived. He was at times even foolishly generous. I remember that a man whom he employed robbed him abominably. He was advised to prosecute the fellow, but this he declined to do. Instead, he actually started the delinquent in a little business. When remonstrated with on the subject all that large-hearted man would say was: 'Poor fellow, he has lost his character, and will not be able to get another situation.' Sometimes I saw Dickens at the *Household Words* office, in Wellington Street, within a few yards of where the *Morning Post* office now stands. 'Are you for a chop at the office and the theatre afterwards?' he would write to me, and naturally I was not loth to accept the invitation thus conveyed.

It was his great delight to see M. Fechter, that delightful actor, who in those days was the idol of the town.[5]

Speaking of Fechter reminds me of the Swiss châlet which he presented to Dickens, and which was set up in the grounds of Gad's Hill. I was on a visit there when the thing arrived straight from Switzerland. It was a wonderful collection of parts which had to be put together like a puzzle. At that time there was a little French stage carpenter at the Lyceum, where Fechter was acting. His name was Godin, and he was a genius in his way. . . . Like every one else, he had great admiration for Dickens, and he insisted that he should go to Gad's Hill and put up the châlet himself. Dickens accepted the obliging offer, and Godin went down, expecting to be able to finish the work in one day. The puzzle proved more complicated than he thought, however, and when the evening came the structure was still unfinished. Dickens, however, offered him dinner and a bed. The family pointed out that their annual New Year's dinner was to take place that night, and that several noblemen and persons of distinction in the country had been invited to it. 'Never mind,' said Dickens, 'I can find him a suit of evening clothes, and I daresay he will look as well as any one else. How can I, when M. Godin has come down as an act of friendship to me, let him go to the "Falstaff" to sleep?' The little French carpenter dined in good company that night, and I have no doubt that to his dying days it was a proud recollection to him.

Dickens, I may tell you, had nothing of the feeling of class exclusiveness about him. Indeed, he had quite an exaggerated respect for anyone who did any work, no matter how humble it might be. My business relations with Dickens were no less pleasant than my private relations. When I illustrated *Our Mutual Friend* and *Great Expectations* I used to get proofs and select my own subjects.[6] I then sent them on for his approval, and I have no recollection that he ever rejected one, although I was a mere boy at the time. He would send them back with the title written underneath them. His knowledge of all that concerned his characters was remarkable. Sometimes I had to ask him for information with regard to some of them, as of course I was working with him, and had read only part of the story. The cover of *Our Mutual Friend*, with the representation of different incidents in the story, I drew after seeing an amount of matter equivalent to no more than the first two one-shilling monthly parts. Here it is: you will see that I depicted, among other characters, Mr. Silas Wegg. Well, I was aware that Wegg had a wooden leg, but I wanted to know whether this was his right or his left leg, as there was nothing in the material before me that threw light on this point. To my surprise, Dickens said: 'I do not know. I do not think I had identified the leg.' That was the only time I ever knew him to be at fault on a point of this kind, for as a rule he was ready to describe down to the minutest details the personal characteristics, and, I might almost add, the life-history of the creations of his fancy.

(5) Not only did he give me every facility [as illustrator of his novels], but he assisted me also with the most valuable information when I wanted it, and he showed me what an extraordinary grasp he had of the characters he created. He could always tell me much more about them than was written in the book, and when I, as an illustrator, having only a number or two in print, had to ask him for further particulars than were to be found in my proof, he could tell me everything about them as if they were living people.

I found a very great and marked difference with other authors I had to deal with in those early days. I remember a notable instance with Anthony Trollope. I once had to illustrate a book of his which was already completed in manuscript, but the parsimony of a publisher only permitted me to have two numbers in print when beginning my illustrations. In those numbers I found two young ladies whom I had to draw, two of the principal characters in the book, of whose appearance there was not the least description. I applied to Anthony Trollope and said, 'Is Julia dark and Clara fair. How am I to distinguish one from the other?' and he replied, 'I do not know; do what you like.' Having been left to my own devices, I made Julia dark and Clara fair, but afterwards in the book I found there were certain references to Clara's dark hair. It was evident to me that these people were in no way alive to Trollope, whilst in the case of Dickens his people were always living people.[7]

In those blessed days when I passed many and many happy months in the house of Dickens, when he was writing some of those great works so well-known, I have seen him so full of the incidents of his book that he wept when he has had to kill people, and he was sad and moody for days over a tragedy.

(6) [Dickens said:] 'Never make a fair copy of a much corrected manuscript. An MS with few or no corrections is always given to the boy beginner to set up, and you will get a proof full of errors. The

MS which is difficult to decipher is put into the hands of a first rate compositor whose proof will give very little trouble. . . .

'I generally find when I write a line which I believe to be a fresh thought expressed in an original way, that the passage is marked "query" in the proof when it comes from the printers. . . .'

NOTES

1. Charles Albert Fechter (1826–79), actor and dramatist, of German origin, performed in France and Germany before transferring his career to London and New York. Dickens admired, backed and befriended him, and he gave Dickens the famous chalet erected in the grounds of Gad's Hill. On Edmund Yates, see below, II, 205. His parents, mentioned below by Marcus Stone, were the notable actor Frederick Henry Yates and his actress wife Elizabeth, with both of whom Dickens was very friendly.

2. In other descriptions of Dickens, Stone remarked that 'His face was singularly handsome. He had a nose of almost perfect beauty, with a nostril of exquisite curvature and sensitiveness which it is impossible to describe. His eyes also were the most impressive and wonderful eyes I ever saw' – *Dkn*, VI (1910) 64. In 'C. D.'s Appearance' (MS, Dickens House) he describes the nostrils as 'sensitive and mobile' and the eyes as 'of unforgetable beauty. A splendid frankness and honesty shone out of them. Such perception and observation and such rare power of unconscious expression, I have never seen in any other's eyes.'

3. For full particulars of Dickens's artistic possessions, see *Catalogue of the Beautiful Collection of Modern Pictures, Water-colour Drawings and Objects of Art of Dickens, which will be Sold by Messrs. Christie, Manson and Woods* [1870], repr. 1935, ed. J. H. Stonehouse. See also 'Charles Dickens as a Lover of Art and Artists', by his younger daughter [Kate Dickens Perugini], *Magazine of Art*, Jan–Feb 1905, pp. 125–30, 164–9.

4. For further particulars of this and other Marcus Stone manuscript material, see *The Catalogue of the Suzannet Charles Dickens Collection*, ed. Michael Slater (1975) pp. 156–8.

5. Stone's more candid opinion of Fechter appears in extract (1), above.

6. Stone is misleading here. What he says applies to *Our Mutual Friend*, the serial parts of which he illustrated. He also illustrated the Library Edition (1862) of *Great Expectations*, but the novel had been published entire in 1861, so Stone would not be working from proofs.

7. Trollope, however, claimed that, of all his gallery of characters, 'I know the tone of the voice, and the colour of the hair, every flame of the hair, and the very clothes they wear' – *Autobiography* (1883) ch. 12. On novelists' visualising their characters, see Michael Irwin, *Picturing: Description and Illusion in the Nineteenth Century Novel* (1979).

'A Faultless Host' (and a 'Delightful Hostess')

HENRY AND EMMELINE COMPTON

(1) from Mrs Compton's recollections in *Pen and Pencil*, Supplement, pp. 39–40;
(2) from *Memoir of Henry Compton*, ed. Charles and Edward Compton (1879),
pp. 193–6, 311–12. Emmeline Montague (died *c*. 1910), of a theatrical family, made
her London debut in 1839, and was a leading actress for a decade; but, after her
marriage in 1848 to Henry Compton (1805–1877), comedian, and the leading
Shakespearian clown of his generation, she retired from the stage, except that she
played in some of Dickens's theatricals on their provincial tours – Mistress Ford in
The Merry Wives (1848) and the heroine Lucy in *Not So Bad* (1851). Dickens invited
her, without success, to play in *The Frozen Deep* (1857). Presumably to reassure him
that a former professional actress was nevertheless presentable, Dickens told the
Duke of Devonshire that she was 'quite a lady, and of the purest character' (*N*, II,
296). Inviting the Comptons to Gad's Hill in 1857, Dickens regarded them as 'old
friends' (*N*, II, 867). Compton's sons record that their father considered Dickens
'the only amateur actor that he could expect to succeed as a professional' (*Memoir*,
p. 161), and another witness recalls Compton's belief that Dickens would have
made his 'fame and fortune' on the stage – S. J. Adair Fitz-Gerald, *Dickens and the
Drama* (1910) pp. 49–50. Long before they met, Compton had admired Dickens's
writings.

(1) My intimacy with the great Novelist commenced before my
marriage, more than forty years ago, at a period when the Stage
occupied a considerable share of his time and attention. It was on
the occasion of one of a series of amateur theatricals instituted by
Dickens. . . . Then, and on many subsequent occasions, I had the
honour of acting with Dickens and his distinguished company, and,
although appearing with 'Amateurs', I always realised that Dickens
was an Actor whose tact, talent, and resource would be equal to any
emergency that might arise. These theatrical tours are among my
most cherished recollections. They were a triumphant success from
beginning to end. I fully concur in all that has been written in praise
of his extraordinary powers both as Actor and Manager, but,
notwithstanding this, I do not think that, had he adopted the Stage
as a profession, he would have been a genius like Kemble or
Macready.

With Mrs. Dickens (whom I remember as a delightful hostess) I often came in contact, for during the tours I resided in the same hotel at which she and her distinguished husband stayed. Indeed, I was frequently a guest at their table. Charles Dickens's polite attention to me, and his interest in my welfare, were most marked, and he invariably honoured me with his arm to dinner; even when travelling he would insist upon my utilising his desk as a footstool.

I remember that he was very clever in making a particular kind of punch – gin punch – a beverage which he usually concocted after dinner, being aided in its preparation by Mark Lemon, whose duty was, if I remember rightly, to squeeze the lemons! The ladies who were present were induced to partake of it, and Dickens was highly delighted when they expressed their appreciation thereof.

I frequently had the pleasure of meeting him both in Devonshire Terrace and in Tavistock House, and invariably found him a most kind, genial, and attentive host; one could always feel at home with him. My impression of his personal appearance is that he was somewhat slightly built, and rather under the medium height. His face was not what I should call handsome, but, what is still better, it was decidedly intellectual and full of expression. His eyes were very bright, his complexion ruddy, and his hair so abundant that it would sometimes hang over his forehead, often compelling him to throw it back with his hand.

He was not a man to talk a great deal, but what he said was to the purpose. He was one of the most energetic men I ever saw, and threw himself entirely into whatever he did. In the 'round games', played after dinner, in his own domestic circle, he was as thoroughly in earnest as in the more serious duties of life. As might be expected of such a man, he was both sensitive and irritable, and a restless disposition (another personal characteristic) made him desirous of continually *doing* something.

(2) My father [Henry Compton] had made Dickens's acquaintance shortly before his marriage, and they afterwards became intimate. He frequently visited at Dickens's house, where he met the most celebrated men of the day. The dining-tables were purposely made very narrow, to facilitate opposite guests talking with one another. Sometimes the end of the table touched a mirror, which reflected the whole scene, and increased the brilliance of its appearance. 'These dinner-parties,' he said, 'were very enjoyable.' Dickens himself was a faultless host, and knew the art of putting his guests at

their ease, so that each appeared at his best. The example of their host's brilliance and animation aroused the energies of this company, causing each individual to exert his powers of entertainment and conversation to their utmost. The effect was what would be expected from the entertainer and his friends. Every subject of the day came under the discussion of the men best fitted to discuss it; politics, literature, and the drama were each treated with a felicity of phrase, a practical knowledge, and a subtlety of discrimination seldom met with. A rare humour and keen wit were brought to the consideration of every theme, with sometimes a boldness of paradox that refreshed and delighted the company. Altogether, my father said he had been to few parties where the pleasure was more exquisite and more sustained. It was always a matter of regret to him that the domestic affairs of the great humorist should have interrupted an intercourse productive of the intellectual enjoyment he preferred to any other amusement. . . .

Speaking of Dickens, he said that his powers of observation were wonderful. He (Mr. Compton) had many opportunities of witnessing his marvellous facility in this respect, and also of his wit in describing his impressions. On one occasion some of them were with Dickens, watching a man in the simple operation of grooming a horse, and making the peculiar hissing noise so necessary, it would appear, to the completion of this operation. No one could find a word expressive of this noise till Dickens at once described it as 'effervescing'.

Office-staff Memories

WILLIAM EDRUPT AND ANOTHER

(1)   'Dickens's Amanuensis: An Interesting Talk with the Man who Used to Write for Charles Dickens', *Tit-Bits*, 2 Sep 1882, p. 320; (2) Catherine Van Dyke, 'A Talk with Charles Dickens's Office Boy, William Edrupt of London', *Bookman* (New York), Mar 1921, pp. 49–52. The amanuensis interviewed is unnamed. Edrupt, the former office boy, was eighty when interviewed in 1920–1. In an earlier and briefer interview he described Dickens as 'a very gentlemanly man, very dressy, and always looked just as though he had come out of a bandbox' – *Dkn*, XIV

(1918) 66. This being the first of a series of items by Dickens's journalistic colleagues, a word on this important aspect of his career may be useful. No other English author of his stature has given such continuous attention, during twenty years of his prime, to magazine editing. *Household Words* (1850–9) and its almost identical successor *All the Year Round* (begun 1859, and still running when he died) were notably successful ventures, largely because of his journalistic flair and his energetic activity. Reminiscences of him as 'Conductor' of these weeklies abound, since his collaborators, whether staff members or occasional contributors, were all of course ready with their pens. See references in the biographical particulars of contributors in *Household Words: . . . Table of Contents*, ed. Anne Lohrli (1973), and the 'Selective Biography' in *Charles Dickens' Uncollected Writings from Household Words*, 2 vols, ed. Harry Stone (1968). See also the standard bibliographies for recent studies, notably by Harry Stone, Gerald G. Grubb, Philip Collins and K. J. Fielding. Unfortunately, Dickens's right-hand man from 1850 to 1869, W. H. Wills (1810–80), left no reminiscences, and his few published letters to or about Dickens are not specially revealing: see *Charles Dickens as an Editor: Being Letters Written by Him to William Henry Wills*, ed. R. C. Lehmann (1912) and Lady Priestley, *The Story of a Lifetime* (1904) for examples. The journals' most prolific contributor, and the only university graduate on their staff, Henry Morley (1822–65), offers an affectionate, respectful but critical view: Dickens 'had not a sound literary taste', he 'has great genius, but not a trained and cultivated reason. I can never answer for his opinions . . . .' But on Dickens's death he realised 'the strength of the regard that had grown up so quietly' – 'nineteen years of goodwill between us that time has deepened, and in all our intercourse never an unpleasant word'. Later, as a Professor of English, Morley was reluctant to lecture on Dickens; when he did, he nearly broke down in tears – Henry Shaen Solly, *Life of Henry Morley* (1898) pp. 149, 163, 279, 261.

(1) 'Yes; I did shorthand work for Mr. Dickens for eighteen months. I did not take dictations for any one of his novels – only his fugitive pieces.[1] He dictated to me most of his articles in *All the Year Round*. He was a very kind man to those under him. He always treated me very well indeed. Most people seem to think Dickens was a ready writer. This was by no means the case. He used to come into his office in St. Catherine-street about eight o'clock in the morning and begin dictating. He would walk up and down the floor several times after dictating a sentence or a paragraph, and ask me to read it. I would do so, and he would, in nine cases out of ten, order me to strike out certain words and insert others. He was generally tired out at eleven o'clock and went down to his club on the Strand. A very singular thing was that he never dictated the closing paragraphs of his story. He always finished it himself. I used to look in the paper for it, and find that he had changed it very greatly from what he had dictated to me.

'Dickens had a very odd habit of combing his hair. He would

comb it a hundred times in a day. He seemed never to tire of it. The first thing he did on coming into the office was to comb his hair. I have seen him dictate a sentence or two, and then begin combing.[2] When he got through he dictated another sentence. He was very careful about his writings. He wanted every sentence to be as perfect as possible before letting it go to press.

'Dickens was an odd fellow regarding the company he sought. I have known him, while I was employed by him, to go down to the Seven Dials, about the worst place in London, and sleep and eat there. He roasted his herring where the rest did, and slept with the poorest. He loved low society. He never seemed so happy as when seated in a poor coffee house, with a crowd of the lower classes talking around him. He never missed a word that was said, and was the closest observer I ever saw. Nothing escaped him. When I was working for him he was at the zenith of his fame, just before his death; and even then he loved these careless, rollicking rounds among the poor better than a high-toned dinner.'

'Was he as great a drinker as he has the reputation of being?'

'I never saw him drunk myself. I have seen him several times exhilarated, however. He only drank the best of wine, but he drank that very freely. Sherry was his especial favourite, and he never refused a glass of fine old sherry. He was an insatiable cigarette-smoker, and when dictating to me always had a cigarette in his mouth. He was a very spruce man, too. He brushed his coat frequently, and changed his collars several times in a day. He was every bit as humorous in his speech as in his writings. When he was in a peculiarly fine humour he could keep you laughing by the hour with his witty talk. He was not one of those men who are above those they employ; he chatted as freely with me as with any member of his club on the Strand. . . . '

(2) [William Edrupt began work as Dickens's office boy at the age of eight.] 'I grew up in the office, running his errands to printers, carrying his packages – he was always sending off something to somebody. Sometimes I was sent out to fetch ices, of which he ate considerable, though he ate very lightly of everything else. Sometimes when he had written hours without stopping, he would suddenly jump up and bid me go out to the street with him; and then we would walk and walk. I'd stand it as long as I could! Then I'd tell him my legs ached and we would come right home and have a cake.

'I think Mr. Dickens was a man who lived a lot by his nose. He seemed to be always smelling things. When we walked down by the Thames he would sniff and sniff – "I love the very smell of this", he used to say.

'Now, I am not a reading man myself, but I think Mr. Dickens liked my not being one. "Have you read anything of mine yet, William my boy?" he used to ask me. "No, Sir", I'd answer, and he would slap me on the back and laugh every time. One day he asked me, "William do you know what a jinnee is?"

' "Yes, Sir", I answered proudly; "they say *you* are one." Mr. Dickens threw back his head and laughed and laughed and then rushed out to tell a friend. I did not know till long after that what I had heard people call him was a *genius* and not a *jinnee*. . . .

'I went to Mr. Dickens's first at the office of *All the Year Round* in Wellington Street. He had a bedroom fitted up there and used sometimes to spend the night when he lectured or took part in theatricals. He did that often, but I don't think he ever spent a night away from home when he could help it, for no man loved his home better.

'When Mr. Dickens wrote *Mrs. Lirriper's Lodgings* three hundred thousand copies were sold in the magazine – a great sale in those days. The street in front of the office was crowded with folks wanting to know the end of the story. There were big posters up all over the town, and I was fairly bursting with pride, for I knew how hard Mr. Dickens worked at it. I loved all his successes, though I don't think he cared anything about them so long as his work was done. Sometimes he would scarcely eat or sleep when beginning a new book. But when the pages covered with writing began to pile up, I knew that pretty soon he would ease off considerably. Sometimes after Mr. Dickens had written for hours I would get him a bucket of cold water, and he would put his head into it and sometimes his hands. Then he would dry his head with a towel and go on writing.

'Well, folks everywhere were betting considerably on the end of *Mrs. Lirriper's Lodgings*.[3] It came out at Christmas time. One real sharp man tried to have me get Mr. Dickens to tell the end of the story. He intended to sell out the news and make bets on it. I asked Mr. Dickens and he, knowing I had never read the story, questioned me until I told him the man had offered me sixpence to try and find out what was going to happen.

'Mr. Dickens gave me three shillings a week, and every time my Ma had a new baby (which was often) he advanced me a shilling, but having to rive it home, I could only keep twopence a week for myself. My master knew this, and that the sixpence the man offered to me for telling the end of the story meant a lot to me; but when I told him the man wanted to sell out the happenings to others, he said, "Come here William, boy", and he took me on his knee. "I'll give you sixpence now for yourself, and I'll give you this penny with a hole in it if you promise me to keep it for good and ever, but you tell that scoundrel that I say the end of the story is *this – they all die sooner or later.*"

'Mr. Dickens's looks? He was one of the best dressed men you could ever see, downright stylish. Everything he had was always of the very best, and he took the greatest care of his things in every way. I never saw a spot on anything, his clothes or his desk. I used to think his gloves beautiful as any lady's. I used to tidy up his desk; but it was always tidier before I touched it, I think. His notes and books and papers were always left just right. He wrote with a quill. I was not allowed to sharpen it.

'I never saw Mr. Dickens angry with anyone who dealt fair with others, though he could get in a terrible rage over anyone who did a mean thing. He could remember everything in a really wonderful way. Sometimes gentlemen would tell me addresses to bring parcels to and I would forget them, but even if it were a week after Mr. Dickens heard them in the office he could name the street and number. He was also very prompt – never a moment late in anything; and when I was late I got scolded for it.

'Mr. Dickens's family often came to the office. I remember Mrs. Dickens well. She was very stout and could hardly get her crinoline through the door. My master loved his children. He loved all children, but his own he fair adored; he would stop work and turn right round and spend his whole afternoon with them. Sometimes he'd take me, and we'd all go on an outing.

'Many people ask if Mr. Dickens was a great eater, as they say he always put such a lot of things in his books about eating – all sorts of feasts and good dinners, they tell me. He wasn't but a light eater himself.'

NOTES

1. Dickens never (it would seem) dictated his novels, and very rarely dictated letters. Apart from these journalistic 'fugitive pieces', most of which he never reprinted, he is only known to have dictated *A Child's History of England*: see above, I, 123.

2. His daughter Katey remarked on Dickens's liking 'a tidy head'; if his hair got dishevelled by the wind in the garden, and he saw himself in one of the many mirrors around the house, he would 'fly for his hairbrush' – Gladys Storey, *Dickens and Daughter* (1939) p. 78. See also below, p. 339.

3. Edrupt speaks as if *Mrs Lirriper* was a serial, but it was not.

'My Master in Letters'

GEORGE AUGUSTUS SALA

(1) from his *Charles Dickens* [1870] pp. 9–15, 27–8; (2) from *Things I Have Known* (1894) 1, 72–9, 94–5, 103–9, 126, 131–2. Sala (1828–96), special correspondent, novelist, miscellaneous author, and 'the most active and successful journalist of the Victorian era', as his old enemy the *Saturday Review* acknowledged (16 Feb 1895, p. 223), was a brilliant and prolific if erratic and unreliable contributor to Dickens's weeklies, and always acknowledged him as 'my master; and but for his friendship and encouragement, I should never have been a journalist or a writer of books' (*Charles Dickens*, p. vi). One of the flashiest and most conspicuous of 'Mr Dickens's young men', he aped his master in many ways, duly using 'Stephens's dark blue writing fluid . . . the ink specially favoured by Dickens. . . . Moreover, Dickens's young men were, to a certain extent, constrained to imitate the diction of their chief, and I fell in with the trick as deftly as perhaps my colleagues did' – *Life and Adventures of George Augustus Sala* (1895) 1, 398, 436, a book which contains further reminiscences of his *Household Words* years. Forster, citing him from his *Charles Dickens* (reprinted below) as 'an authority on London streets', remarks that, 'of all the writers, before unknown, whom *Household Words* helped to make familiar to a wide world of readers, he had the strongest personal interest in Mr. Sala, and placed at once in the highest rank his capabilities of help in such an enterprise' (*Life*, xi, iii, 836; vi, iv, 513). Through his mother, a well-known actress and singer, Sala as a boy and a lad saw Dickens in 1836 and 1843, but first met him as a journalistic colleague in 1851. A vulgarian, he was shrewder about Dickens than many more sophisticated commentators.

(1) [Writing a few days after Dickens's death, Sala remarks on how familiar and recognisable a figure his was; there were] few last week who would have been unable to point out the famous novelist, with his thought-lined face, his grizzled beard, his wondrous searching eyes, his bluff presence and swinging gait as, head aloft, he strode now through crowded streets, looking seemingly neither to the right nor the left, but of a surety looking at and into everything – now at the myriad aspects of London life, the ever-changing raree-show,

the endless round-about, the infinite kaleidoscope of wealth and pauperism, of happiness and misery, of good and evil in this Babylon; – now over the pleasant meads and breezy downs which stretched around his modest Kentish demesne hard by the hoary tower of Rochester.

Just as the Kentish farmers and peasants would greet with simple, rural courtesy the neighbour they knew so well, and esteemed so highly for his frank and cordial bearing, so would London folks draw aside as the great writer – who seemed always to be walking a match against Thought – strode on, and, looking after him, say, 'There goes Charles Dickens!' The towering stature, the snowy locks, the glistening spectacles, the listless, slouching port, as that of a tired giant, of William Makepeace Thackeray, were familiar enough likewise in London, a few years since, but, comparatively speaking, only to a select few. He belonged to Club-land, and was only to be seen sauntering there or in West-end squares, or on his road to his beloved Kensington, or in the antique hall at Charterhouse on Founders' Day, or on Eton Bridge on the Fourth of June, or sometimes, haply, on the top of a Richmond omnibus, journeying to a brief furlough at Rose Cottage.

Thackeray in Houndsditch, Thackeray in Bethnal Green or at Camden Town, would have appeared anomalous; as well could we picture Carlyle at Cremorne, or Tennyson at Garraway's; but Charles Dickens, when in town, was ubiquitous. He was to be met, by those who knew him, everywhere – and who did not know him? Who had not heard him read, and who had not seen his photographs in the shop-windows? The omnibus conductors knew him, the street-boys knew him; and perhaps the locality where his recognition would have been least frequent – for all that he was a member of the Athenæum Club – was Pall Mall. Elsewhere he would make his appearance in the oddest places, and in the most inclement weather: in Ratcliff Highway, on Haverstock Hill, on Camberwell Green, in Gray's Inn Lane, in the Wandsworth Road, at Hammersmith Broadway, in Norton Folgate, and at Kensal New Town.

A hansom cab whirled you by the Bell and Horns at Brompton, and there was Charles Dickens striding, as with seven-leagued boots, seemingly in the direction of North-end, Fulham. The Metropolitan Railway disgorged you at Lisson Grove, and you met Charles Dickens plodding sturdily towards the Yorkshire Stingo. He was to be met rapidly skirting the grim brick wall of the prison in

Coldbath Fields, or trudging along the Seven Sisters' Road at Holloway, or bearing, under a steady press of sail, through Highgate Archway, or pursuing the even tenor of his way up the Vauxhall Bridge Road. He seemed to prefer for mere purposes of exercise the lengthy thoroughfares of our exterior boulevards to narrow and intricate streets. They offered, perhaps, a better opportunity for fair and honest walking, and for the performance of that self-appointed task of pedestrianism which for so many years he had undertaken daily, and which well-nigh undeviatingly, and wherever he was – in London, at home at Gadshill, in France, in Italy, or in America – he performed to the last rood and furlong of a mentally-measured route. It was one of Mr. Dickens's maxims that a given amount of mental exertion should be counteracted by a commensurate amount of bodily fatigue; and for a length of years his physical labours were measured exactly by the duration of his intellectual work. . . .

The photographic portraits of Charles Dickens form a legion; and the more recent ones give a life-like resemblance of him as he seemed to the present generation – a bronzed, weather-worn, hardy man, with somewhat of a seaman's air about him. His carriage was remarkably upright, his mien almost aggressive in its confidence. He was one of the few men whose individuality was not effaced by the mournful conventionality of evening dress. . . . His appearance in walking dress in the streets, during his later years, was decidedly 'odd', and almost eccentric, being marked by strongly-pronounced colours, and a fashioning of the garments which had somewhat of a sporting and somewhat of a theatrical guise.

To those who did not know that he was Charles Dickens, he might have been some prosperous sea-captain home from a long voyage, some Western senator on a tour in Europe, some country gentleman of Devon or of Yorkshire who now and then bred a colt or two, and won a cup, but never betted. But those who could look far back remembered when Charles Dickens was in countenance, like Milton in his youth, 'eminently beautiful', and when in attire he was, next to Count D'Orsay, the choicest and most tastefully dressed dandy in London. For the similitude of the elderly Dickens we must rely upon the wonderfully faithful photographic portraits lately published; for the Dickens of middle age, we must refer to the noble portrait by Mr. Frith, or to the grand, but somewhat dusky, picture by Ary Scheffer, or to the engraving from the delicate miniature by Margaret Gillies, prefixed to Mr. Horne's *New Spirit of the Age*; but for the Dickens of thirty years since, for the 'unknown young man' who, as his greatest critic and admirer, Mr. Thackeray, said, 'calmly and modestly came and took his place at the head of English literature', we must turn to the portrait by his early friend, Daniel Maclise. . . .

He was a great traveller. We are not alluding to his two journeys to the United States, to his long residence in Italy, to his frequent excursions to France, or even to his prolonged explorations – now on business, now on pleasure – of his own country. Where he had travelled longest, where he had looked deepest and learned most, was in inner London. He is no Regent Street lounger: he scarcely ever mentions Pall Mall; he rarely alludes to Piccadilly; he is not much at home in fashionable squares; he is not to be found in the Ladies' Mile; he is out of his element at Brompton, or in the Regent's Park, or in Great Gaunt Street, or at Greenwich, or Richmond, or in any of the localities so well beloved by Thackeray. But he knew all about the back streets behind Holborn, the courts and alleys of the Borough, the shabby sidling streets of the remoter suburbs, the crooked little alleys of the City, the dank and oozy wharfs of the water-side. He was at home in all lodging-houses, station-houses, cottages, hovels, Cheap Jacks' caravans, workhouses, prisons, school-rooms, chandlers' shops, back attics, barbers' shops, areas, back yards, dark entries, public-houses, rag-shops, police-courts, and markets in poor neighbourhoods.

(2) [Sala made a brilliant début in *Household Words*, 6 Sep 1851, with his much-admired essay 'The Key of the Street', and followed this up with further pieces on London.] I had written, perhaps, half a dozen papers for *H. W.* when I received a note from Dickens saying that he would like to see me on a given forenoon at the office in Wellington Street. Rarely have I been more surprised – I may almost say more amazed – than I was when, in the little editorial sanctum with the bow-window of the house of Wellington Street, I was again presented to Charles Dickens – this time by Mr. William Henry Wills, the assistant editor and general manager of the paper. . . . I was overcome with astonishment at the sight of the spare, wiry gentleman who, standing on the hearthrug, shook me cordially by the hand – both hands, if I remember aright – and said kind things about my writings – things which I am proud to remember and too proud to repeat.

But, ah! how changed was the illustrious compeller of smiles and tears. He was then, I should say, barely forty; yet to my eyes he seemed to be rapidly approaching fifty. The silky locks had thinned, and were grizzling; the slight side-whiskers had been replaced by a moustache and spade-shaped short beard. The eyes had lost nothing of their searching sweetness – eyes that have always seemed to follow one about like those of the so-called Beatrice Cenci in Guido's deathless canvas; but the brows and cheeks were deeply lined; and trouble, as well as thought and intensity of literary application, had had, perhaps, something to do with those premature furrows and wrinkles. . . . Although outwardly aged beyond his years, it was nevertheless the selfsame Charles Dickens of 1836 and 1843 with whom I held converse in the little room in Wellington Street in 1851; and touching that converse I may say just thus much. To talk to Dickens was a vastly different thing from talking to Thackeray. The author of *Vanity Fair* was a master of anecdote, *persiflage*, and repartee; he was a varied and fluent linguist; he was a lover and practitioner of art; he was saturated with seventeenth and eighteenth century literature, both French and English; and he could hold his own with such masters of conversation as Abraham Hayward and Richard Monckton Milnes (Lord Houghton), and with such a formidable epigrammatist and wit as Douglas Jerrold.

Dickens, on the other hand, seldom talked at length on literature, either of the present or the past. He very rarely said anything about art; and, for what is usually termed 'high art', I think that he had that profound contempt which is generally the outcome of lack of learning. Indeed, when I first visited Venice and wrote for him an article called 'A Poodle at the Prow' [*All the Year Round*, 11 July 1863] – my text being a gondola on the Grand Canal and the gondolier's dog – he expressed himself as especially pleased with my production on the ground that it contained 'no cant about art'. What he liked to talk about was the latest new piece at the theatres, the latest exciting trial or police case, the latest social craze or social swindle, and especially the latest murder and the newest thing in ghosts. He delighted in telling short, droll stories, and occasionally indulging in comic similes and drawing waggish parallels. He frequently touched on political subjects – always from that which was then a strong Radical point of view, but which at present [1894] I imagine would be thought more Conservative than Democratic; but his conversation, I am bound to say, once for all, did not rise above the amusing commonplaces of a very shrewd, clever man of the world, with the heartiest of hatred for shams and humbugs. . . .

All of the young men who gathered round him – Blanchard Jerrold, Sydney Blanchard, W. Moy Thomas, Walter Thornbury, and, later, John Hollingshead and James Payn – were, to a greater or a smaller extent, imitators of the style of their Chief; and they were . . . proud of following his lead. . . . Dickens was the presiding and the predominating influence in *Household Words*. He did not often have to suggest articles for me, because in process of time I discovered that I could fix upon acceptable subjects myself. But the manuscript once handed in, I seldom, if ever, saw a proof thereof. First, Mr. W. H. Wills was the carefullest of proof-readers, and did everything necessary in the way of cutting down; and, next, Dickens took the revises in hand himself, and very often surprised me by the alterations – always for the better – which he made, now in the title, and now in the matter, of my 'copy'.

For example, I lived for many months in seclusion at a little village called Erith, in Kent, which has now become, I believe, quite a fashionable place. In the paucity of my inventiveness I gave to Erith the blunderingly transparent disguise of 'Sherith'; but Dickens, with happy boldness, changed the name to 'Dumbledowndeary'. Again, in a description of a visit by the possessor of a 'tasting-order' to the wine-cellars of the London Docks, I incidentally hinted that on the return journey the visitor, if he travelled on the top of an omnibus, sometimes experienced very queer sensations; to which Dickens added in the revise the remark, 'particularly when the bow of your cravat slides to the back of your head and hangs there like a bag-wig'. These thoroughly Dickensian touches, added purely by his own autocratic will, did, I am convinced, a great deal of good to the productions of his young men; but, at the same time, the frequency of Dickensian tropes, illustrations, and metaphors, interpolated in the articles of his disciples, led to their being taunted with being slavish imitators of their leader. . . .

The last guest [at the regular *Household Words* dinners] whom I will mention was a clean-shaven, farmer-like, elderly individual, Inspector Field, of the Detective Force. There was something, but not much, of Dickens's Inspector Bucket about Inspector Field; and I venture to think that he was a much acuter and astuter detective in *Bleak House* than he was in real life. On the whole, he reminded me forcibly of one of the old Bow Street runners, with more than one of whom I was on friendly terms in my harum-scarum youth; and Bow Street runners of the old days have been crystallised by Dickens in the Blathers and Duff in *Oliver Twist*. Dickens had a curious and almost morbid partiality for communing with and entertaining police officers. . . .

With the exception of William Cobbett, I doubt whether there has ever been, among modern English writers, a more thoroughly typical example of the plain, downright Englishman than Charles Dickens. One of the best characteristics of his simple, manly, ringing English prose is the entire absence of Gallicisms therefrom. . . . Thorough, vigorous, stubborn English sentiments are rarely absent from Dickens's miscellaneous essays; nor, when in his fictions you are reading the episodes of Continental life which occur in *Dombey and Son*, in *Little Dorrit*, and in *Our Mutual Friend*, can you easily divest yourself of the impression that Dickens had, on the whole, a good-humoured contempt for foreigners – a contempt due, perhaps, in some measure to the fact that he was born in an epoch when an implacable war was raging between England and France, and that his earliest years were passed among persons in whose minds the memory of that war still lingered. . . . This contempt, in Dickens's *Pictures from Italy*, is aggravated into something like savage and ignorant ridicule. The *Pictures from Italy* is not by any means a good-natured book. Dickens had not the slightest knowledge, or love, or even respectful appreciation, of what is called 'High Art', and indeed his acquintance with art of any kind beyond the illustrations to his own works, and a sympathetic admiration for his congener Hogarth, was extremely limited; and because he could not understand the pictorial and plastic masterpieces which he saw in Rome and in other Continental cities, he sneered at the artists themselves, and derided the people who could understand and did admire the immortal productions of Italian art. Clarkson Stanfield and Daniel Maclise were also among his intimate friends; so was Marcus Stone, and he was an early patron of Mr. W. P. Frith, R. A., whose delightful picture of 'Dolly Varden' found a purchaser in Dickens. *Oliver Twist* and the *Sketches by Boz* naturally brought him in contact with George Cruikshank. Through the *Old Curiosity Shop* he made the acquintance of George Cattermole; and his early relations with Hablot K. Browne ('Phiz') were of the friendliest kind. Still, although throughout his career he had numerous artistic friends, I am persuaded that he cared for them much more as social companions than as masters of their art.

Notwithstanding his lack of comprehension or of affection for pictures and statues, and his being provided into the bargain with an ample stock of the soundest of old John Bull prejudices – prejudices which he has himself slily laughed at in his sketch of Mr. Podsnap – the great novelist was fond of Continental travel; his taste for which may have been, no doubt, to a considerable extent, cultivated and enhanced by his close association with Wilkie and Charles Collins, both of whom had passed nearly the whole of their boyhood in Rome. Dickens's long residence in Genoa; the frequent journeys which he made to different cities in the Peninsula, rarely in search of the picturesque or the romantic, but always in sedulous quest of the humorous, the odd, and the grotesque; his subsequent sojourns in Switzerland and in Paris, all served to nourish within him a liking for wandering; not indeed very far afield, but over well-trodden tourists' routes, where he could find tolerably comfortable accommodation, and amusing surroundings. He seems, by hard application, to have become a fair French scholar: so at least I gather from sundry evidences in Mr. Forster's *Life*. I never heard him *speak* French, and am consequently no judge whatever of his proficiency in the pronunciation of that language; but I have seen letters written by him in very fair colloquial French, and I have no doubt that he could hold his own in conversation with Frenchmen. . . .

It is possible . . . that Dickens may have read the more prominent works of Victor Hugo and of Alexandre Dumas; but of any extensive familiarity with French literature or men of letters he was practically destitute; nor have I ever known him quote any well-known passage from a standard French author, or heard him ask any questions about the personality or the idiosyncrasies of any of the historic men and women who have been the glory of French literature. . . .

Dickens was, as I have more than once hinted, strongly conservative in a good many social matters, and [when confronted with the new American and French systems of 'grand hotels'] he rather leaned towards the old-fashioned English hotel, with its old port, its old sherry, its old landlord and landlady, its old bill of fare, its sirloin of beef, leg of mutton, boiled fowl and broiled veal cutlet, and its old scale of charges. . . .

[In Paris during the 1850s, Dickens would sometimes go to one of the great Boulevard *cafés* after dinner, but] more frequently we would repair to the theatre. I suppose there never was a more assiduous playgoer than Charles Dickens. . . . [But the] tragedies performed at the Théâtre Français and the Odeon were not much to

Dickens's taste. He preferred the light operatic burlesques at the Bouffes Parisiens. Offenbach was then in all his glory. . . .

Another of 'Mr Dickens's Young Men'

EDMUND YATES

From *Edmund Yates: His Recollections and Experiences* (1885 edn) pp. 175, 296–309, 321. Yates (1831–94), journalist, novelist and one-man-show performer, was employed at the General Post Office, 1847–72. Son of the actors Frederick and Elizabeth Yates, old friends of Dickens, he first met the novelist in 1854: 'There was no one in the world for whom I had so much admiration, or whom I so longed to know' (ibid., p. 174). He contributed to *Household Words*, 1856–7, and extensively to *All the Year Round*, and soon became a very close friend. It was over him that the tumultuous 'Garrick Club affair' occurred in 1858, involving a quarrel between Dickens and Thackeray and their respective parties. 'Contemporary opinion concerning Yates ranged from that of Richard Renton, who thought Yates "that prince of journalists", to that of Swinburne, who regarded him as a blackguard and "*cochon sublime*"' – *Household Words: . . . Table of Contents*, ed. Anne Lohrli (1973) p. 474. Certainly no one ever called Yates refined; and he, together with Percy Fitzgerald, must have been among the people Forster had most in mind when, describing Dickens's social circle in his later years, he remarked with ponderous restraint that, 'if any one should assert his occasional preference for what was beneath his level over what was above it, this would be difficult of disproof' (*Life*, VIII, ii, 635). Yates is the authority, second-hand, for one very interesting (alleged) confession by Dickens. The American actor Otis Skinner (1858–1942), in an interview (Boston *Sunday Herald*, 21 Mar 1915), reported him as saying that Dickens had once 'admitted that it was the keenest disappointment of his life not to have been a successful actor. When Yates replied: "But, Charles, you are a great novelist", he retorted, "That's all very well, but I would rather have been a great actor and had the public at my feet"'–*Dkn*, XI (1915) 134. P. D. Edwards, *Edmund Yates 1831–1894* (University of Queensland, 1980) usefully surveys the man and his work.

There were no photographs of celebrities to be purchased in those days [1854], and I had formed my idea of Dickens's personal appearance from the portrait of him, by Maclise, prefixed to *Nickleby*: the soft and delicate face, with the long hair, the immense stock, and the high-collared waistcoat. He was nothing like that. Indeed my mother, who saw him shortly after this, and who had not met him for fifteen years, declared she should not have recognised him, for, save his eyes, there was no trace of the original Dickens about him. His hair, though worn still somewhat long, was beginning to be sparse; his cheeks were shaved; he had a moustache and a 'door-knocker' beard encircling his mouth and chin. His eyes were wonderfully bright and piercing, with a keen, eager outlook; his bearing hearty and somewhat aggressive. He wore, on that occasion, a loose jacket and wide trousers, and sat back in his chair, with one leg under him and his hand in his pocket, very much as in Frith's portrait. . . .

During the last years of his life, he was so large a feature in mine, his influence over me as a friend, counsellor, companion, and employer, was so powerful, and his regard for me so great, that the record of my career during that period owes much of whatever interest it may possess to his connection with it. . . . My relations with the man, whom since my childhood I had, I may almost say, worshipped, were so close, the intimacy into which, notwithstanding his nineteen years of seniority, he admitted me was so great, in our views and sympathies there was, if I may venture to say it, so much in common, that I was always proud to think he felt my society congenial to him, and permitted me an exceptional insight into his inner life.

The nineteen years' seniority was not reflected in the terms of our companionship or our converse. 'Fancy my being nineteen years older than this fellow!' said he one day to his eldest daughter, putting his hand on my shoulder. The young lady promptly declared there was a mistake somewhere, and that I was rather the elder of the two. And certainly, except in the height of his domestic troubles, Dickens, until within a couple of years of his death – when, even before he started for America, his health was, to unprejudiced eyes, manifestly beginning to break – in bodily and mental vigour, in buoyancy of spirits and keenness of appreciation, remained extraordinarily young.

This, I think, is to be gleaned from the *Letters*, but is not to be found in Forster's *Life*. The fact, I take it, is that the friendship between Dickens and Forster, as strong on both sides in '70 as it was in '37, was yet of a different kind. Forster, partly owing to a natural temperament, partly to harassing official work and ill-health, was almost as much over, as Dickens was under, their respective actual years; and though Forster's shrewd common sense, sound judgment, and deep affection for his friend commanded, as was right, Dickens's loving and grateful acceptance of his views, and though the communion between them was never for a moment weakened, it was not as a companion 'in his lighter hour' that Dickens in his latter days looked on Forster. Perhaps of all Dickens's friends, the man in whom he most recognised the ties of old friendship and pleasant companionship existing to the last was Wilkie Collins; and of the warm-hearted hero-worship of Charles Kent he had full appreciation.

To me, from the first time I saw him, when he grasped my hand at Tavistock House in '54, to the last, when I took leave of him as he was dressing to go out to dinner, in his bedroom in the house in Hyde Park Place which he had hired for the season of '70, he was always affectionate, helpful, and unreserved. . . .

I have heard Dickens described by those who knew him as aggressive, imperious, and intolerant, and I can comprehend the accusation; but to me his temper was always of the sweetest and kindest. He would, I doubt not, have been easily bored, and would not have scrupled to show it; but he never ran the risk. He was imperious in the sense that his life was conducted on the *sic volo sic jubeo* ['my will is my command'] principle, and that everything gave way before him. The society in which he mixed, the hours which he kept, the opinions which he held, his likes and dislikes, his ideas of what should or should not be, were all settled by himself, not merely for himself, but for all those brought into connection with him, and it was never imagined they could be called in question. Yet he was never regarded as a tyrant: he had immense power of will, absolute mesmeric force, as he proved beneficially more than once, and that he should lead and govern seemed perfectly natural to us. . . .

It had been obvious to those visiting at Tavistock House that, for some time, the relations between host and hostess had been somewhat strained; but this state of affairs was generally ascribed to the irritability of the literary temperament on Dickens's part, and on Mrs. Dickens's side to a little love of indolence and ease, such as, however provoking to their husbands, is not uncommon among middle-aged matrons with large families. But it was never imagined that the affair would assume the dimensions of a public scandal.

Dickens, the master of humour and pathos, the arch-compeller of tears and laughter, was in no sense an emotional man. Very far, indeed, was he from 'wearing his heart upon his sleeve', where his own affairs were concerned, though under Mr. Delane's advice he was induced to publish that most uncalled-for statement in *Household Words* regarding his separation, a step which, in the general estimation, did him more harm than the separation itself.[1]

He showed me this statement in proof, and young as I was, and fresh as was then our acquaintance, I felt so strongly, that I ventured to express my feelings as to the inadvisability of its issue. Dickens said Forster and Lemon were of the same opinion – he quarrelled with Lemon and with Messrs. Bradbury and Evans for refusing to publish the statement in *Punch*, and never, I think, spoke to any of them again – but that he himself felt most strongly that it ought to appear; that, on Forster's suggestion, he had referred the matter to Mr. Delane, and by that gentleman's decision he should abide.

There can, I take it, be no doubt that if the matter was referred to any jury composed of men ordinarily conversant with the world and society, the verdict returned would be a unanimous condemnation of the advice tendered to Dickens by Delane. The truth is that this particular episode in Dickens's career is not an appropriate one for indiscriminate investigation, and the mistake which it will be generally held Dickens made was that which is usually known as 'washing dirty linen in public'. Dickens had the faults, as well as the virtues, of the literary character. A man who has given to the world so many distinct creations – creations which will always have their place in English literature, and which have passed into the main currency of the English language – was full of the irritability, the sensitiveness, and the intolerance of dulness which might have been expected. If he had been wholly devoid of a certain bias in the direction of theatrical ostentation – if, in a word, his temperament had been more rigid, more severe; if he had not given such prominence in his thoughts to the link which bound him to the public whom he served so splendidly, he would not, in this particular affair have acted as he did. . . .

Life at Gadshill for visitors, I speak from experience, was delightful. You breakfasted at nine, smoked your cigar, read the papers, and pottered about the garden until luncheon at one. All the morning Dickens was at work. . . .

After luncheon (a substantial meal, though Dickens generally took little but bread and cheese and a glass of ale) the party would assemble in the hall, which was hung round with a capital set of Hogarth prints, now in my possession, and settle on their plans. Some walked, some drove, some pottered; there was Rochester Cathedral to be visited, the ruins of the Castle to be explored, Cobham Park (keys for which had been granted by Lord Darnley) in all its sylvan beauty within easy distance. I, of course, elected to walk with Dickens; and off we set, with such of the other guests as chose to face the ordeal. They were not many, and they seldom came twice; for the distance traversed was seldom less than twelve miles, and the pace was good throughout. . . .

It was during one of these walks that Dickens showed me, in Cobham Park, the stile close by which, after a fearful struggle, Mr. Dadd had been murdered by his lunatic son in 1843.[2] Dickens acted the whole scene with his usual dramatic force. . . .

They were stiff walks for anyone not in full training, as Dickens always was at that time, but to me they never seemed long or fatiguing, beguiled as the time was by his most charming talk. With small difficulty, if the subject were deftly introduced, he could be induced to talk about his books, to tell how and why certain ideas occurred to him, and how he got such and such a scene or character. Generally his excellent memory accurately retained his own phrases and actual words, so that he would at once correct a misquotation; but on more than one occasion I have, in conversation with him, purposely misquoted from one of his books, in order that he might set me right. . . .

Dickens took great interest in theatrical affairs, and was very fond of theatrical society. He had a lifelong affection for Macready, and a great regard for Regnier and Fechter; of the latter he said once to me, 'He has the brain of a man, combined with that strange power of arriving, without knowing how or why, at the truth, which one usually finds only in a woman.' He had also a liking for Phelps, Buckstone, Webster, Madame Celeste, and the Keeleys. He saw most of the pieces which were produced from time to time, but he delighted in the *ir*-regular drama, the shows and booths and circuses. . . .

On the very last outing which we had together, about two months before his death, we went to a circus, where we saw a highly-trained elephant standing on its head, dancing and performing tricks. Dickens was greatly pleased. 'I've never seen anything better!' he said; 'it's wonderful how they teach them to do all this!' Then a moment after his eyes flashed with that peculiar light which always betokened the working of some funny notion of his brain, and he said, 'They've never taught the rhinoceros to do anything; and I don't think they could, *unless it were to collect the water-rate, or something equally unpleasant!*' . . .

[Did Dickens kill himself by over-working?] But the conditions of existence are prescribed by that constitutional fatalism known as temperament. Dickens was not only a genius, but he had the volcanic activity, the perturbed restlessness, the feverish excitability of genius. What he created that he was. His personages were, as readers of his letters know, an integral part of his life.

Nor were the enthusiasm and intensity which he experienced in his daily business less remarkable. The meditative life, the faculty of a judicious resting, the power of self-detachment from contemporary events which enables so many of our octogenarians to be comparatively juvenile, had no charm for him. To him old age would never have brought tranquillity, and therefore it may be said that old age would never have arrived. It was a law of his existence that his foot should be always in the stirrup and his sword always unsheathed. He had, moreover, as I have above explained, a chivalrous regard to the public. He was their devoted servant, and he was anxious to spend his life-blood in their cause. Consequently, even when he knew his power as a novelist was on the wane[3] – according to Forster it had, indeed, been on the wane so far back as the days of *Bleak House* – he determined to seek a new sphere, and one which to his histrionic temperament was singularly congenial, in his readings. This I believe to be the true account of the reasons which weighed with him in selecting that arduous ordeal which brought his life to its premature close. Other reasons of a more melodramatic and sensational character might be cited, but it is my conviction that they would be less to be trusted.

One word more. In regard to the friendship which Dickens vouchsafed me, I have been frequently asked, 'Did he come up to the expectations you had formed of him? Was Dickens the man as lovable as Dickens the author?' And I have always replied, 'Yes; wholly.'

NOTES

1. The publication of Dickens's contentious statement, 'Personal' (*Household Words*, 12 June 1858, p. 601), had been approved by his friend John Delane (1817–79), editor of *The Times*, 1841–77.

2. Richard Dadd, the artist now best remembered for his fairy pictures, had lived in the locality. He spent the rest of his life in lunatic asylums.

3. Modern critics do not regard Dickens's powers as being 'on the wane' in the 1850s – much the reverse – but many reviewers did so at the time: see George H. Ford, *Dickens and His Readers* (1955), and *Dickens: The Critical Heritage*, ed. Philip Collins (1971). Whether Dickens himself thought his powers were on the wane is uncertain, but he did sometimes find writing slower and more difficult in his later years.

A Rod of Iron in his Soul

ELIZA LYNN LINTON

From *My Literary Life* (1899) pp. 55–73. Eliza Lynn (1822–98), wife of the engraver W. J. Linton, was a prolific journalist, novelist and miscellaneous author. She was a protegée, and 'dear daughter', of the poet Walter Savage Landor, at whose house she first met Dickens (c. 1849). From 1853 she was a regular contributor to his weeklies: 'Good for anything [he noted], and thoroughly reliable' – G. S. Layard, *Mrs Lynn Linton* (1901) p. 81. 'I did not know him intimately', she acknowledged; her business relations with his journals were conducted with W. H. Wills, but she also had to do with him when, as executrix of her father's will, she sold Gad's Hill – which had belonged to the Rev. James Lynn – to Dickens (ibid., p. 128). She was famous for a waspish tongue, both about manners – witness her sharp attacks on the behaviour of 'emancipated' young women in the 1860s – and about individuals: George Eliot was one who provoked her special wrath. But she was also one of the most professional of women writers in the second half of the nineteenth century. Her remark, below, about Dickens's loving 'deeply, passionately, madly' presumably hints at the Ellen Ternan affair; but it is not known who she is alleging 'deceived him from start to finish'.

Once, when I was staying with [Landor], he had a small dinner-party, of Dickens, John Forster, and myself. This was my first introduction to both these men. I found Dickens charming, and Forster pompous, heavy, and ungenial. Dickens was bright and gay and winsome, and while treating Mr Landor with the respect of a younger man for an elder, allowed his wit to play about him, bright and harmless as summer lightning. He included me, then quite a beginner in literature, young in years and shy by temperament, and made me feel at home with him; but Forster was saturnine and cynical. . . . I remember George Henry Lewes telling me the difference between Thackeray and Dickens in the way of service to a friend. Dickens, he said, would not give you a farthing of money, but he would take no end of trouble for you. He would spend a whole day, for instance, in looking for the most suitable lodgings for you, and would spare himself neither time nor fatigue. Thackeray would take two hours' grumbling indecision and hesitation in writing a two-line testimonial, but he would put his hand into his pocket and give you a handful of gold and bank notes if you wanted them. I know of neither characteristic personality; but I repeat the illustration as Mr. Lewes gave it.

Talking of Dickens and Thackeray, it is curious how continually they are put in opposition to each other. . . . Both these men illustrated the truth which so few see, or acknowledge when even they do see it, of that divorcement of intellect and character which leads to what men are pleased to call inconsistencies. Thackeray, who saw the faults and frailties of human nature so clearly, was the gentlest-hearted, most generous, most loving of men. Dickens, whose whole mind went to almost morbid tenderness and sympathy, was infinitely less plastic, less self-giving, less personally sympathetic. Energetic to restlessness, he spared himself no trouble, as has been said; but he was a keen man of business and a hard bargainer, and his will was as resolute as his pride was indomitable. In the latter years of his life no one could move him; and his nearest and dearest friends were as unwilling to face as they were unable to deflect the passionate pride which suffered neither counsel nor rebuke. Yet he was as staunch and loyal a friend as ever lived; and, thanks to that strain of inflexibility, he never knew a shadow of turning – never blew hot and cold in a breath. At the same time, he never forgave when he thought he had been slighted; and he was too proud and self-respecting for flunkeyism. He declined to be lionised, and stuck to his own order; wherein he showed his wisdom, and wherefor he has earned the gratitude of all self-respecting *littérateurs* and artists not born in the purple. He knew that in a country like ours, where the old feudal feeling has sunk so deep, and the division of classes has been so marked and is still so real – he knew that the biggest lion of the class 'not born' is never received as an equal by the aristocracy. He is Samson invited to make sport for the Philistines, but he is not one of themselves, and never will be considered one of themselves. Hence Charles Dickens, even in the zenith of his fame, was never to be seen at the houses of the great; and with the exception of Lord Lansdowne and the Baroness Burdett-Coutts he owned no intimate friendships among the Upper Ten.

Thackeray, on the contrary, like Moore, loved the grace and delicacy and inborn amenities of what is called 'good society'. He was no more of a snob than Dickens, no more of a tuft-hunter, but he was more plastic, more frankly influenced by that kind of social sensuality which finds its enjoyment in good living, good manners, pretty women, and refined talk. Dickens had no eye for beauty, *per se*. He could love a comparatively plain woman – and did; but Thackeray's fancy went out to loveliness; and cleverness alone, without beauty – which ruled Dickens – would never have stirred his passions. Both men could, and did, love deeply, passionately, madly, and the secret history of their lives has yet to be written. It never will be written now, and it is best that it should not be.

But, I repeat again what was said before, in each the intellectual appreciation of life and the personal temperament and character were entirely antagonistic. The one, who wrote so tenderly, so sentimentally, so gushingly, had a strain of hardness in his nature which was like a rod of iron in his soul. The other, who took humanity as he found it, who saw its faults and appraised it at its lower value – yet did not despise what he could not admire – was of all men the most loving, the most tender-hearted, the least inflexible.

I did not know either man intimately; but if not the rose itself, I knew those who stood near. Their close friends were also mine, and I heard more than I saw. Many secret confidences were passed on to me, which, of course, I have kept sacred; and both men would have been surprised had they known how much I knew of things uncatalogued and unpublished. . . .

[After Dickens's death, she visited her old home, Gad's Hill.] True to his energetic nature, Dickens had altered much, and spoilt some things while he had improved others. A rosery instead of a cherry and filbert orchard I did not think an improvement, and I missed some of the choicest apple trees – a golden pippin, a nonpareil, a golden russet among the number. But the house was improved; and, when in his occupation, and with his taste in furniture, and the like, it must have been singularly bright and cheerful. His taste was all for bright colours and pleasant suggestions. He liked flower patterns and lively tints, and the greenery-yallery school would have found no disciple in him. He was always fidgety about furniture, and did not stay even one night in an hotel without rearranging the chairs and tables of the sitting-room, and turning the bed – I think – north and south. He maintained that he could not sleep with it in any other position; and he backed up his objections by arguments about the earth currents and positive or negative electricity. It may have been a mere fantasy, but it was real enough to him; and having once got the idea into his mind, it is very sure that he could not have slept with his head to the east and his feet to the west, or in any other direction than the one he had decided on as the best. Nervous and arbitrary, he was of the kind to whom whims are laws, and self-control in contrary circumstances was simply an impossibility.

How bright he was! How keen and observant! His eyes seemed to penetrate through yours into your very brain, and he was one of the men to whom, had I been given that way, I could not have dared to tell a lie. He would have seen the truth written in plain characters behind the eyes, and traced in the lines about the mouth. His look was of the kind which *dévalisé* the mind; and straight as he was in his own character, he would have caught the crookedness of another as by the consciousness of contrasts. And yet I know one cleverer, more astute, less straight than himself, who sailed round him and deceived him from start to finish; who tricked and betrayed him, and was never suspected nor found out.

With Mr. Thackeray, on the contrary, I fancy deception and double-dealing would have had an easy time of it. . . . and if I had wanted a tender and sympathetic father confessor, I would have gone to the creator of Becky Sharp rather than to him who wrote *The Chimes* and *The Christmas Carol*. . . .

Yet Charles Dickens had warm sympathies, too, and his true friends never found him wanting. To those whom he affected he was princely in his helpfulness – always remembering that this helpfulness took other forms than that of pecuniary aid. To Wilkie Collins he was as a literary Mentor to a younger Telemachus, and he certainly counted for much in Wilkie's future success as a *littérateur*. I was told by one who knew, that he took unheard-of pains with his younger friend's first productions, and went over them line by line, correcting, deleting, adding to, as carefully as a conscientious schoolmaster dealing with the first essay of a promising scholar. In his *Rambles beyond Railways*, the hand of the master was ubiquitous and omnipotent, and so in the stories published in *Household Words* and *All the Year Round*. For Dickens was absolutely free from the petty vice of jealousy. He was too self-respecting and withal too conscious of his own powers to be afflicted by the success of others. The antagonism created by the world's fancy between him and Thackeray never existed in reality between the men themselves. . . .

Mr. Landor [depicted by Dickens as Mr Boythorn in *Bleak House*] recognised himself in Dickens' mirror, and I do not think he relished the picture. He did not speak of it to me, but he did speak of Dickens with a certain acerbity of tone different from his first encomiastic manner. I was always sorry about that character, for Landor had been a good friend to Dickens, and loved him in the large way proper to such a nature as his.

Meeting Dickens: 'A Foretaste of Paradise'

JAMES PAYN

From *Some Literary Recollections* (1884) pp. 184–8, 232–3, 263–6. Payn (1830–98), educated at Eton, the Royal Military Academy, Woolwich, and Cambridge, was a prolific journalist and novelist, and editor successively of *Chambers's Journal* and the *Cornhill*. His first prose article appeared in *Household Words*, in 1853, and he was thereafter a regular contributor. Leslie Stephen, in a memoir prefacing Payn's *The Backwater of Life* (1899), remarked that his Radicalism 'was that which is represented by Dickens, and corresponds to the middle-class sentiment of the period – not to any strong democratic or socialist tendency', and that Payn 'believed heartily in the morality of the *Christmas Carol*, and resented any criticisms of Dickens's "sentimentalism"' (p. xxiii). Referring to the one 'sad blot' in Dickens's life – his 'putting away' his wife, 'a public outrage, a blazoned defiance of all ordinary rules of conduct' – and seeking to explain why 'a man of so many good qualities should have so conducted himself', Payn asserted that Dickens 'was in a degree intoxicated with public applause, as well as spoiled by the sycophants who hung about him, and sanctioned his vagaries' (*Chambers's Journal*, 21 Mar 1874, p. 177). Payn's first meeting with him – 'an epoch in my existence' – took place when Dickens was in Edinburgh giving public readings in 1858. They 'laughed all day', Dickens reported (*N*, III, 61), during an expedition to Hawthorden, the birthplace of the poet William Drummond. Politely, he had, in advance, asked Payn if he could 'spare time' to accompany him and his daughters on this expedition.

If I had only twenty-four hours to live I should have 'spared time' for such a purpose, which did not indeed seem to trench upon my earthly span at all, but to be a foretaste of Paradise. Such enthusiasm is unknown in these days, wherein Dickens himself, as an American writer informs us, 'is no longer to be endured', and will doubtless excite some ridicule; but for my part I am not one whit ashamed of it. Nay, contemptible as the confession may appear, I

feel the same love and admiration for Charles Dickens now as I did
then. What indeed astonished even me, I remember, at the time,
was that personal acquintance with him increased rather than
diminished his marvellous attraction for me. In general society,
especially if it has been of an artificial kind, I have known his
manner to betray some sense of effort, but in a company with whom
he could feel at home, I have never met a man more natural or more
charming. He never wasted time in commonplaces – though a lively
talker, he never uttered a platitude – and what he had to say he said
as if he meant it. On an occasion, which many of my readers will call
to mind, he once spoke of himself as 'very human': he did so, of
course, in a depreciatory sense; he was the last person in the world to
affect to possess any other nature than that of his fellows. When some
one said, 'How wicked the world is!' he answered, 'True; and what a
satisfaction it is that neither you nor I belong to it.' But the fact is, it
was this very humanity which was his charm. Whatever there was of
him was real without padding; and whatever was genuine in others
had a sympathetic attraction for him.

The subject, however, which most interested him (and, in a less
degree, this was also the case with Thackeray) was the dramatic –
nay, even the melodramatic – side of human nature. He had stories
without end, taken from the very page of life, of quite a different
kind from those with which he made his readers familiar. There are,
indeed, indications of this tendency in his writings, as in the tales
interspersed in *Pickwick*, in the abandoned commencement of
Humphrey's Clock, and more markedly, in his occasional sketches, but
they were much more common in his private talk.

When visiting the exhibition of Hablot Browne's pictures the
other day I was much struck by the fact that, when indulging his own
taste, the subjects chosen by the artist were not humorous but
sombre and eerie. This, I feel sure, was what made him so
acceptable an illustrator to Dickens. He could not only depict
humorous scenes with feeling, but also such grim imaginings as the
old Roman looking down on dead Mr. Tulkinghorn, and the Ghost
Walk at Chesney Wold. The mind of Dickens, which most of his
readers picture to themselves as revelling in sunshine, was in fact
more attracted to the darker side of life, though there was far too
much of geniality in him to permit it to become morbid.

On the occasion of our first meeting, however, I saw nothing of all
this: he was full of fun and brightness, and in five minutes I felt as
much at my ease with him as though I had known him as long as I

had known his books. . . . Late that night I supped with him – after his reading – at his hotel, alone; after which I discarded for ever the picture which I had made in my mind of him, and substituted for it a still pleasanter one, taken from life. . . .

What Thackeray – a well-qualified critic indeed – wrote of Dickens he also certainly felt. I had once a long conversation with him upon the subject: it was before the shadow (cast by a trivial matter after all) had come between them, but I am sure that would not have altered his opinion. Of course there were some points on which he was less enthusiastic than on others; the height of the literary pedestal on which Dickens stood was, he thought, for some reasons, to be deplored for his own sake. 'There is nobody to tell him when anything goes wrong,' he said; 'Dickens is the Sultan, and Wills is his Grand Vizier'; but, on the whole, his praise was as great as it was generous. . . .

He was himself an excellent man of business, though in early life he made great pecuniary mistakes by an impatience of disposition, a desire to get things settled and done with, which is shared by many men of letters to their great loss; he was painstaking, accurate, and punctual to a fault; and the trouble he took about other people's affairs, especially in his own calling, is almost incredible. . . . The chiefs of our own calling are always ready to give a helping hand to their juniors; but Dickens looked upon it as an imperative duty so to do. Many a time have young would-be contributors called upon me, and produced from their breast-pockets as passport to my attention a letter of rejection, torn and frayed, and bearing tokens of having been read a hundred times, from the Master.

'He wrote me this letter himself', they would say, as though there were but one 'He' in the world. It was generally a pretty long one, though written at a time when minutes were guineas to him, full of the soundest advice and tenderest sympathy. There was always encouragement in them (for of course these were not hopeless cases), and often – whenever, in fact, there seemed need for other help besides counsel – some allusion, couched in the most delicate terms, to 'the enclosed'. Dickens not only loved his calling, but had a respect for it, and did more than any man to make it respected. With the pains he took to perfect whatever proceeded from his own pen everyone who has read his life must be conversant; but this minute attention to even the smallest details had its drawbacks. When an inaccuracy, however slight, was brought home to him, it made him miserable. . . .

In friendship, which in all other points must needs be frank and open, this problem often remains unsolved – namely, the friendship of one's friend for some other man. D. and E. have the most intimate relations with one another, but for the life of him E. cannot understand what D. sees in F. to so endear him to him. This was what many of D.'s (Dickens's) friends, and certainly the world at large, said of F. (John Forster). It is not my business, nor is it in my power, to explain the riddle; I rarely met them together without witnessing some sparring between them – and sometimes without the gloves. On the other hand, I have known Forster pay some compliments to 'the Inimitable' in his patronising way, which the other would acknowledge in his drollest manner. It is certain that Forster took the utmost interest in Dickens, even to the extent of seeing everything he wrote through the press, and as to the genuineness of Dickens's regard for him I have the most positive proof.

The Conductor of *Household Words*

JOHN HOLLINGSHEAD

(1) from *My Lifetime* (1895) 1, 72–3, 96–103, 188, 190; 11, 24; (2) from *According to My Lights* (1900) pp. 9–19. Hollingshead (1827–1904), after experience in commerce, became a journalist, firstly on financial topics, and was from 1857 on the staff of Dickens's weeklies, and a prolific contributor. Later he became a distinguished theatrical manager, running the Gaiety Theatre, 1868–86, and presenting the first English production of Ibsen (*Pillars of Society*, 1880). See also his 'Mr. Charles Dickens as a Reader', *Critic*, 4 Sep 1858, repr. in his *Miscellanies* (1874), and 'Fifty Years of *Household Words*', *Household Words*, Jubilee Number, 26 May 1900.

(1) Charles Dickens was a 'sentimentalist' in finance and taxation. He had very little sympathy with political economy; but, believing that I knew what I was writing about and feeling sure that I was in earnest, he gave me a free hand. Our politics were much alike. When I collected some of these papers, of a purely political and financial character, and published them under the title of *Rubbing the Gilt Off*, I wished to show my admiration for Mr. John Bright by a dedication [and, by permission, did so].

Dickens was pleased with my readiness and versatility. . . . I was now installed as a member of staff – that is to say, I was allowed to send what I wrote to Messrs. 'Bradbury and Evans', the printers. All Dickens's 'young men' were supposed to be imitators of the master, and the master was always credited with their best productions. I hope this was so in my case, but I am afraid it was not. My subjects were not very much à la Dickens, and, bad or good, I had a blunt plain style of my own. Of the many articles I wrote for Dickens – and I wrote a great quantity – having sometimes two, and once at least, three papers in the same number, I can honestly say that Dickens's editorship did not alter six lines in as many years. My faults and merits (if any) were my own. The only paper that Dickens ever suggested in any degree . . . was 'What is a Pound?' – a story of two ignorant dustmen who find a sovereign in a dustbin, and start to spend it. The article was printed 'in proof' and paid for, but never published by Dickens. When he returned it to me, after a time, I took it to the late Doctor Norman Macleod, then editor of Good Words, who accepted it with pleasure, and paid me double the Dickens's scale, which was ample, but not sentimentally liberal. . . .

My rapid success on Household Words in a few weeks produced an invitation to dinner at the office in Wellington Street, Strand, to meet the master for the first time. . . . The party consisted of Wilkie Collins, Mark Lemon, Mr. Wills, the Honourable Mr. Townshend, Charles Dickens and myself. The master, dressed in a velvet smoking coat, as part of his dress suit, received me in a very friendly manner, and made me a companion in five minutes. I noticed, as I thought then, a slight lisp, the deep lines on his face – almost furrows, and the keen twinkling glance of his eye. . . .

Our dinner was simple and good. We began with oysters, brought in fresh from Old 'Rule's' in Maiden Lane. . . . The principal dish was a baked leg of mutton, the bone of which had been taken out, and the space supplied with oysters and veal stuffing. I always understood that this was an invention of Dickens, who, without being a gourmand, was fond of eating and drinking. As I was helped twice to this novel delicacy, I remembered some of the master's descriptions of humble but savoury dishes in two or three of the Christmas books. He saw I was enjoying myself, and appeared to be delighted. The conversation, if not remarkable, was amusing. . . . Theatrical matters were touched upon, and Dickens, complaining of the star system, and the spread of scratch companies, said he almost regretted that he took a leading part in the abolition of the patent theatre monopoly. Dickens's principles were sound, but they were not deeply rooted, and he was swayed by every breath of feeling and sentiment. He was a Liberal by impulse, and what the 'DRYASDUST' school would have called a 'wobbler'.

When the cloth was removed, Dickens treated us to another of his table inventions – his celebrated 'Gin Punch'. This was another *Christmas Carol* production, and I believe he was as proud of it as he was of *Pickwick*. The preparations for this drink were elaborate and ostentatious. The kettle was put on the fire; lemons were carefully cut and peeled; a jug was produced, and well rubbed with a napkin, inside and out; glasses were treated in the same manner; the bottle was produced, the gin tasted and approved of, and the brew then began. The boiling water was poured in, the sugar, carefully calculated, was added, the spirit, also carefully calculated, was poured in, the lemon was dropped on the top, the mouth of the jug was then closed by stuffing in the napkin rolled up like a ball, and then the process of perfect production was timed with a watch.

Dickens's manner all this time was that of a comic conjurer, with a little of the pride of one who had made a great discovery for the benefit of humanity. It was this interest in common things – this enjoyment of life – this absence of all apparent knowledge of his commanding position amongst the world's greatest authors, which gave Dickens one of his principal charms. No man, in his inner mind, felt so sure of Westminster Abbey and immortality, and no man kept that inner mind more carefully concealed. He lived above and beyond the opinion of his contemporaries, and was always a cheery companion for young and old. When the grog or Punch was served out, he waited, with a wink in each eye, for the verdict, which was favourable. 'What do you think of it?' he asked, addressing me, as if he would be glad to have a new opinion for what it might be worth. . . .

When Dickens lived in Tavistock House he developed a mania for walking long distances, which almost assumed the form of a disease. He suffered from lumbago, and I have always thought that this was brought on by monotonous pedestrianism – the determination to do a certain distance every day, generally from two in the afternoon till seven in the evening, one mile every quarter-of-an-hour, measured by the milestones. He did his literary work mostly in the morning, from nine till about two, and usually wrote his letters at night. When he was restless, his brain excited by struggling with incidents or characters in the novel he was writing, he would frequently get up and walk through the night over Waterloo Bridge, along the London, New Kent and Old Kent Roads, past all the towns on the old Dover High Road, until he came to his roadside dwelling. His dogs barked when they heard his key in the wicket-gate, and his behaviour must have seemed madness to the ghost of Sir John Falstaff.

Once, in these early morning excursions, he went into a roadside inn near his house for some refreshment, and tendered a half-crown for payment, which had become greasy-looking and suspicious by contact with a little piece of French chalk which he had in his pocket. The man did not know his customer, and the hour being suspicious and the roads much infested with tramps, he refused the coin with indignation, and made the great author understand that 'smashing' was a game not popular in that district. Dickens was staggered at first, and amused afterwards; and when he really made himself known – which he had some difficulty in doing, as he was covered with the dust of a twenty-eight mile walk, and was not at first sight a trustworthy person – he was smothered with apologies. . . .

He hesitated long and painfully before he gained courage to go to America [for a Readings tour, in the 1860s]. He was not disinclined to admit that he had done some little injustice to the United States in his *American Notes*. The same might have been said of Italy and his *Pictures* from that country. With all his great and commanding genius, he had many prejudices, and was somewhat 'parochial' in his sympathies, except on abstract questions of personal liberty. He was an inspired Cockney. I use the word in no depreciating spirit, but as a brand of character. . . .

My work and my recreations brought me into contact with a number of men and a few women connected with literature, science, and art – all interesting and worthy objects of study. As a rule, I found their affability increased in proportion to their celebrity; it was only the smaller fry who put on airs of self-importance. One or two of the big scientific men, like Professor Owen, I met with some little diffidence, as I had written superficial articles for *Household Words* on subjects which they had studied for a lifetime. It was less my fault than Charles Dickens's. He wanted 'readable' papers. 'Let Hollingshead do it,' he said, more than once. 'He's the most ignorant man on the staff, but he'll cram up the facts, and won't give us an encyclopædical article.' . . .

Dickens was an admirer and an old patron of Mr. Toole, and he saw Mr. Henry Irving for the first time. He made no remark about Irving's acting, except that it was very good, and that the character of Mr. Chevenix was evidently modelled upon Dombey.[1] Dickens was a little 'cranky' in his dramatic criticism. I remember him telling me that he preferred Mr. John E. Owens – a clever impersonator of a Western American farmer, who appeared at the Adelphi – to Mr. Joe Jefferson. In this, as in some other things, his judgement was faulty.

(2) A short, upright man of spare figure, who held his head very erect and had an energetic, industrious, not to say bustling, appearance [is how Hollingshead remembered Dickens]. He was very methodical, and he looked it. . . . [Though his sub-editor W. H. Wills greatly helped him, his weeklies] were really edited by Dickens, who also took a large part in their trade management. He selected his contributors, interviewed them when necessary, and examined many details which Thackeray left to Mr. George Smith, his publisher. Dickens was a born trader, with a considerable power of organisation, and his plans were laid down with financial prudence. 'Fancy prices' for magazine work in the early fifties were neither demanded nor expected. . . . The tariff for writing on *Household Words* and its successor, *All the Year Round*, was never at any time a sentimental tariff; but extra work, as distinguished from English composition, was paid for when demanded. . . .

His walks were always walks of observation, through parts of London that he wanted to study. His brain must have been like a photographic lens, and fully studded with 'snap-shots'.[2] The streets and the people, the houses and the roads, the cabs, the buses and the traffic, the characters in the shops and on the footways, the whole kaleidoscope of Metropolitan existence – these were the books he studied, and few others. He was a master in London; abroad he was only a workman. . . .

He was a clever amateur actor (he could do nothing badly), but I can hardly agree with many of his friends who looked upon him as a second Edmund Kean. . . .

He had no doubts about his rightful position in the world of letters. For the last twelve of fifteen years of his life he never read any notices of his writings. He knew and felt that he had earned his tombstone in Westminster Abbey. That he returned to this resting-place as soon as he did I fully believe was mainly due to his mechanical walks, and the exhaustion and excitement caused by his 'dramatic readings'. A day or two before he died, I am told on good authority, he was found in the grounds of Gadshill, acting the murder scene between Sikes and Nancy.

NOTES

1. In the winter of 1869–70, when Hollingshead was managing the Gaiety Theatre, Dickens went there to see Henry J. Byron's drama *Uncle Dick's Darling*, in which J. L. Toole played a Cheap Jack and the young Henry Irving played Mr Chevenix. 'I gave him the Royal Box', Hollingshead recalled, 'and received him with all the honours of Royalty.'

2. Dickens uses just this 'photographic' image – but with the crucial addition 'fanciful' – in a notable letter about his imaginative perception. Traversing some unfamiliar country in 1858, 'I . . . made a little fanciful photograph [of it] in my mind [and] I couldn't help looking upon my mind as I was doing it, as a sort of capitally prepared and highly sensitive plate' which it was 'really a pleasure to work with', since it 'received the impression so nicely' (*N*, III, 58). Few of his exiguous remarks about his art are more suggestive.

'This Most Charming of Men'

PERCY FITZGERALD

(1) from *Recreations of a Literary Man* (1882) I, 51–5, 77, 88, 97–101, 131, 139–40; (2) from *Boz Club Papers* (1908) pp. 18–20; (3) from *Life of Charles Dickens* (1905) II, 145, 182–3, 210–11, 247–8; (4) from *Memories of Charles Dickens* (1913) pp. 42–4, 105, 111–12, 160, 171. Fitzgerald (1834–1925), prolific Irish journalist, novelist and biographer, probably wrote more about Dickens, biographically and otherwise (notably on *Pickwick*), than any contemporary or successor. A constant contributor of essays and stories to Dickens's weeklies from 1856, and acquainted with him from 1858, he often proclaimed himself 'a favourite' of the great man, and not without justice; at least Dickens felt 'grievously disappointed' when his unmarried daughter Mamie could not be 'induced to think as highly of him as I do' (*N*, III, 478). A biographer of Boswell, he had some of Boswell's less admirable characteristics but lacked his accuracy and literary judgement. His superabundant writings on Dickens are repetitious, garrulous, uncritical and factually unreliable. But, while trading long and unblushingly on his friendship with Dickens, he served the Immortal Memory after his fashion, founding the Boz Club (1900), becoming

the first President of the Dickens Fellowship (1902), etc. There is pathos in his
response to the attacks – which included a parody in *Punch* – on his *Life of Dickens*: 'I
suppose I have laid myself open to it all, but I did know Dickens and I did love him,
and an old man garrulous about old happy days and old happy loves ought not to
be an object of ridicule' – *Dkn*, xxii (1926) 23–4. Tiresome and inaccurate, he did
indeed know Dickens well, and was liked by him – a fact which inclines one to
question either Dickens's powers of judgement or one's own. The following extracts
minimise his tiresomeness. In the first, he has been describing Dickens's regular
walks up the Strand, from Charing Cross Station (the terminus from Higham) to
his magazine's office in Wellington Street, and his familiarity with the local
shopkeepers.

(1) It was always pleasant to see what pride tradesmen took in
having him for a customer, and what alacrity they showed in serving
him or in obliging him in any way. This I believe was really owing to
his charming hearty manner, ever courteous, cordial, and zealous;
his cheery fashion of joking or jest, which was irresistible. The
average tradesman has small sympathy or intelligence for the
regular literary man. He is sometimes *caviare* indeed to him. Our
writer, however, was a serious personality of living flesh and blood,
and would have made his way in life under any condition. His
extraordinary charm of manner, never capriciously changed, the
smile and laugh always ready – that sympathy, too, which rises
before me, and was, really unique – I can call no one to mind that
possessed it or possesses it now in the same degree. Literary men, as a
rule, have a chilliness as regards their brethren. . . .

It is in his relations with writers in his periodical, and, indeed, in
all connections with his 'literary brethren', as he modestly called
them, that this amiable and engaging man appears to the most
extraordinary advantage. As I read over his many letters on those
points, I am amazed at the good-natured allowance, the untiring
good humour, the wish to please and make pleasant, the almost
deference, the modesty in one of his great position as head, perhaps,
of all living writers – to say nothing of his position as director of the
periodical which he kindled with his own perpetual inspirations.
There was ever the same uniform good nature and ardour, the
eagerness to welcome and second any plan, a reluctance to dismiss
it, and this done with apologies; all, too, in the strangest contrast to
the summary and plain-spoken fashion of the ordinary editor. I
fancy this view has scarcely been sufficiently brought out in all the
numerous estimates of this most charming of men. And, at the risk of
some intrusion of my own concerns, I shall be enabled to show him
in even a more engaging and attractive light. The various accounts

have scarcely been concerned with this side of his character. . . .

It will now be characteristic [Fitzgerald remarks, after giving instances of Dickens's editorial vigilance and helpfulness] to see what pains were taken – how heads were laid together to improve and make good – all under the master's directions and inspirations, who, as he said often, always gave to the public his best labour and best work. This constancy always seemed to me wonderful. He never grew fagged or careless, or allowed his work to be distasteful to him. This is a most natural feeling, and comes with success; and there is a tendency to 'scamp' work when the necessity for work is less. Mr. Thackeray confessed to this sense – in the days when he became *recherché* – and found a sort of distaste to his work almost impossible to surmount. . . .

I have many proof-sheets by me, corrected by his own hand in the most painstaking and elaborate way. The way he used to scatter his bright touches over the whole, the sparkling word of his own that he would insert here and there, gave a surprising point and light. The finish, too, that he imparted was wonderful; and the 'dashes', stops, shiftings, omissions, were all valuable lessons for writers.[1] . . .

There never was a man so unlike a professional writer: of tall, wiry, energetic figure; brisk in movement; a head well set on; a face rather bronzed or sunburnt; keen, bright, searching eyes, and a mouth which was full of expression, though hidden behind a wiry moustache and grizzled beard. Thus the French painter [Ary Scheffer's] remark that 'he was more like one of the old Dutch admirals we see in the picture galleries, than a man of letters', conveyed an admirably true idea to his friends. He had, indeed, much of the quiet resolute manner of command of a captain of a ship. He strode along briskly as he walked; as he listened his searching eye rested on you, and the nerves in his face quivered, much like those in the delicately formed nostrils of a finely bred dog. There was a curl or two in his hair at each side which was characteristic; and the jaunty way he wore his little morning hat, rather on one side, added to the effect. But when there was anything droll suggested, a delightful sparkle of lurking humour began to kindle and spread to his mouth, so that, even before he uttered anything, you felt that something irresistibly droll was at hand. No one ever told a story so drolly, and, what is not so common, relished another man's story so heartily. A man of his great reputation and position might have chosen what company he pleased, and would have been welcome in the highest circles; but he never was so happy as with one or two intimate friends who understood him, who were in good spirits or in good humour. . . .

Nothing was more agreeable than a 'run down' [to Gad's Hill] for a few days, or even from Saturday till Monday, arranged at 'the office' in a hearty cheery style there was no resisting. Even here, his accurate, business-like mode would be shown; the hour and train fixed, or a leaf torn from his little book and the memorandum written down for guidance. His day was mapped out; there was haste but no scramble. . . . I do not recall anything more delightful than one of these holidays. . . .

On another occasion I found myself at Gad's Hill, with the late excellent, worthy George Moore – a simple, earnest man, whose simplicity was, I know, welcome to the host.[2] I recollect telling this gentleman a piece of news about some friend in a distant part of the kingdom, which gave him an agreeable surprise, on which our host shook his head significantly. 'There, again!' he said, 'what I always say: the world is so much narrower and smaller than is believed.' This was a favourite theory of his: that people were more nearly and curiously connected than appeared. He had many of these little theories, illustrated, not by any means solemnly, but with a sort of bright and smiling mystery, and, indeed, they added a charm to his conversation: – to wit, his account of 'averages', such as that a particular number of people *must* be killed on the railways within the year. Once he told me that I had been seen walking by the office, and that I had looked at him fixedly, walked on, and disappeared, at the time being at the other end of the kingdom. He was thus fond of the mysterious in a small way, and had generally a store of something curious in this direction.[3] . . .

One day [on holiday], from breakfast until almost past the afternoon, was spent at the table, when he was in extraordinary spirits and full of enjoyment, and told stories and drew fanciful sketches of droll, far-fetched situations, which he played with and touched and heightened in the most farcical style.[4] In nothing was he more delightful, or 'in his element', as it is called, than in talking of all matters connected with the stage. He delighted in the very scent of the place, and welcomed any bits of news or gossip connected with it. It was enjoyable to watch his keen interest even in the obscurest histrionic elements. On this little expedition, as there was a free evening, it was understood, almost as of course, that we should visit the little local theatre, where he sat out very patiently some rather crude and ancient melodrama. Next morning at

breakfast he was in possession of all local histrionic information –
how the manager's wife engrossed all the leading characters for
herself, and would let no one have any of the 'fat', which was true
almost literally; the manager a patient being. These things were
pleasantly retailed and set off in his own lively way over the tea and
coffee – and these things to hear one did seriously incline – for those
who like the stage can never dismiss this sort of interest and
reverence, and the sight of the meanest country theatre always raises
curiosity and respect. In this view, he enjoyed allusions and stories
connected with the melodramas of old times, and had some good
ones to relate: as of the actor of Rochester Theatre, who forgot his
part and could not attract or hear the prompter. At last, in
desperation, he said to his comrade with deep 'no-meaning', '*I will
return anon!*' and then went off to consult his book.

(2) Charles Dickens, it seems to me, was one of the most engaging
men that one could call to mind or conceive of. 'Engaging' is the
exact word. He was always unspoilt; never subject to any humours,
or changes, or caprices. He was ever the same to his friends; never
what is called 'uppish', which is just what you might expect from a
man of his fine character. Yet you can have no idea of the position he
held from any comparison with the position men occupy at the
present day. I assure you that it would be impossible to supply even
a notion of the extraordinary elevation that he held in the
community. Every eye in the country, indeed in the Empire, was
turned towards him; as well as in foreign parts and the United
States. No one indeed, can even conceive the singular veneration,
admiration and love that was felt for him. . . .

Now, notwithstanding the exalted position that Dickens
occupied, were I asked what was the characteristic of this great man
I should say it was *modesty*. Never was there a more modest man. He
was utterly unspoilt. He never what is called 'put on side' or took
airs; he never had any caprices; he never had any humours; he was
always modest, quiet and unassuming. He ever wished to take the
second place and not the first. He was always willing to listen to
others, and not to speak himself; he was always willing to laugh at
someone else's joke, and not to make his own. He was almost *too*
retiring. I well remember that at a dinner party at which he
attended there was also present a judge – an exceedingly noisy,
talkative person, who engrossed the whole of the conversation, and
almost silenced the great guest, to the indignation of everyone

present. At last he culminated his extravagances by saying, 'Well, I appeal to you, Mr. Dickens. Is there a single modern novelist that can compare with Walter Scott?' – to the horror of every one present. But Dickens said in the gentlest possible manner, 'I perfectly agree with you. I think Walter Scott is the first of all the novelists', and then, having been allowed to get hold of the talk, he proceeded to tell us his opinions of Walter Scott, which of his novels he liked or rather loved best – which I may say was *The Bride of Lammermoor*, and he explained to us how and why he liked it.

And this recalls to me a happy holiday time. He asked me on several occasions – a very great privilege – to travel round with him on one of his reading tours. One day he was rather unwell, and he sent out to a bookseller's to get a novel. The messenger brought him this *Bride of Lammermoor*, and Dickens thereupon proceeded to enter on a most interesting review of the mechanical details of the book, where he thought there were some weak places in it. At the same time he explained to me that he did not do this in any spirit of criticism, but simply said that he thought the book might have been improved in certain places.[5]

(3) Only those who have known him and been much with him can really convey an idea of what he exactly was and how he looked. His wonderful face was so mobile, changeable and protean – like Elia's Munden – that there is no fixity or certainty in the matter. Only those who observed him narrowly could be the judges of likeness. I confess that, for myself, the typical Boz is not the glossy-haired, well-coloured, smartly-dressed, dapper-looking figure the public knows, but the gnarled, deeply-delved, well-worn, but most keen and striking face which we knew in his last days, truly remarkable, with a touch of sadness, presently changing to brightness; the eyelids squeezed together in keen relish; the mouth fashioned into a humorous expression of enjoyment; the cheeks crumpled up by the same sense of pleasure. The Boz that appeared on the platforms to read was not the Boz of private life. . . .

Boz had a warm regard for the old school of players – Buckstones, Websters, Fechters, Harleys, and the like. The friendship with the French actor was based on an exgggerated estimate of his gifts and warm personal attachment, to neither of which did Fechter respond. This amiable magnifying of the merits of persons Boz loved was a little weakness, and I think came of his habit of writing when he had to make telling 'points' at every sentence. It was like his estimate of the detectives, of railway-guards, and other officials, whom he endowed with a sagacity they did not really possess. To the same exaggeration belonged his endowing the poor and the sorrowing with all the heroic virtues, with patience, long-suffering, sweetness. . . .

It is really amazing to find with what an abundance of gifts and equipments Dickens was furnished. For a novelist it seems quite unique. For let us think for a moment – and many have not even a suspicion of it – how many things he was. First, a novelist, one of the greatest. Next a dramatist, and a successful one; an essayist, and a brilliant one. He was a reformer and philanthropist, again a successful one. He was an actor of distinction and power, and wished to go on the stage. He was also a brilliant and effective reader of his own writings, and perhaps the most successful ever known. He was the editor of a most popular weekly journal that enjoyed extraordinary success, and he had been for a time editor of a daily paper. He had been apprenticed to a trade; he had been an out-of-door law clerk; a reporter – one of the best ever known in the 'Gallery'; also a sort of 'special', despatched to the country in the wake of political personages, in which calling he displayed his energy and capacity so as to win the applause of his employers. He was a capable man of business and organizer. He was a stupendous walker to the end of his life, and a great traveller. He was an admirable speaker, and even orator. Here was an extraordinary assemblage of gifts in a story-teller, the more extraordinary when we compare him with other novelists of his rank, who are for the most part languid and easy-going, and known for their writings only. It is obvious that such a combination must, as I have said, operated on his writings as a 'motor force'.

[Turning to 'Other "Motors"' Fitzgerald writes:] In considering Dickens as a novelist or story-teller, there is one unique thing to be taken into account – viz., his vast and overpowering *personality*. This entered into all he wrote. As he entered a room, sat or stood before you, you felt you were in the presence of amazing vitality. He spoke always with warmth and ardour. When he came to write, he brought all this with him; it overflowed into every sentence. Hence it is impossible to look on him as a conventional narrator, calmly reporting what befell his characters; he is really telling of himself and of his feelings and impressions. This wonderful personality of Dickens naturally became a vast force in his writing. It was so full – even, I might say, so tumultuous – that it would have been felt had he never written a line. It also accounts for that actual living movement in the form of walking, riding, travelling by coach or other vehicle, railway excursion, ascent of mountains abroad, travelling over the Continent in diligences or carriages. Everyone familiar with his writings will recognise how he delighted in this motion. . . .

(4) [Fitzgerald describes Dickens's nostalgia for the old melo-dramas such as Pocock's *The Miller and His Men*, which he had seen in his youth.] For he delighted in calling back all his youthful pictures, which seemed to him more dramatic and suggestive than the more brilliant business of actual life. This always seemed to me to furnish a key to his infinitely interesting character. Simple and genuine things – old images, old dreams – were what pleased him.

[He took Fitzgerald to a revival of Pocock's play. Before the show, they dined in the Albion in Drury Lane.] Some familiar, semi-Bohemian followers of the old times came up shyly and yet familiarly, to be received by him in his own genial, cordial way. For he never changed to anyone, and he was ever cordial to the humbler fry of his profession, and not only cordial, but hearty and jovial. We then crossed to Drury Lane Theatre, and were duly installed in a good box. The heavy folds of the old green curtain rolled up slowly, and there were seen the millers bending under their burdens, toiling up the steep towards their mill. How merrily his eye twinkled as he murmured with Grindoff, 'More sacks to the mill!' . . . Alas! the disillusion worked slowly and surely. The whole was stupid, dull, and heavy to a degree, so at last, about the second Act, Boz arose slowly and sadly, and said 'he could stand it no longer'. I really think he was grieved at having his old idol shattered, and perhaps was mortified. . . .

[Forster, Fitzgerald argues, gives inadequate attention in the *Life* to Dickens's] twenty years of arduous, never-ceasing labour and drudgery, pursued from week to week, with scarcely an hour's relaxation – to wit, the 'conducting' or editing of his two great journals. 'Conducting' was the fitting word, for, like the manager of a theatre, he had to find and direct suitable men and characters, study his public, play upon their feelings, follow and divine their humours, amuse and divert by the agency of others, and, when that failed him, by his own. . . . And only fancy it! Twenty years of it – of that never-flagging, never-relaxing weekly work. That editing was ever in his mind, ever before him, from Monday until Saturday; and what characters and intellects, of graduated degrees, did he find; what strange lessons, pictures, adventures of a new life did he not discover?

It is therefore no exaggeration to say that anyone who would calmly take stock of Boz's character and methods must make his laborious way through the forty or fifty volumes of these journals, and follow his Dickens carefully. He will find traces of him on every page. . . . No other instance can be furnished of such intense literary labour. . . , maintained at the same high pressure for twenty years.[6] Twenty years of *weekly editing* rarely interrupted or devolved – proof correcting in galley-slips, on the most lavish scale (most trying to the eyes), all continued for twenty years. All the while the engendering of an expected and necessary novel going on, with the searching for and selection of long serials, and the devising of plans for increasing circulation. Twenty years of such editing! Incredible! There have been but few, if any, instances of so long a course of *weekly* editing by a man of genius. But he had within him this amazing store of energies, which carried him on. And yet this was no rough-shod, hard, unsympathising being, who had not time to be tolerant and gentle. . . .

After a few numbers had been issued, it became easy to recognise the clear and distinct purpose of the work. Its great aim was to supply information on what are called the 'actualities' of surrounding life, to deal with the 'business of pleasure' and the pleasures of business; but all was to be presented in a lively, attractive, and ever humorous fashion. . . . The writers were compelled, owing to the necessity of producing effect, to adopt a tone of exaggeration. Everything, even trivial, had to be made more comic than it really was. This was the law of the paper, and the reader is conscious of it when he takes up the journal after an interval of years. As I can testify from my own experience, this pressure became all but irresistible. A mere natural, unaffected account of any transaction, it was felt, was out of place; it would not harmonise with the brilliant, buoyant things surrounding it. I often think with some compunction of my own trespassings in this way, and of the bad habit one gradually acquired of colouring up for effect, and of magnifying the smallest trifle.[7]

NOTES

1. Elsewhere, acknowledging that on every page of his first novel *Never Forgotten* (serialised in *All the Year Round*, 1864–5) there are 'sentences of [Dickens's] composition, happy little turns, quips and cranks, which pointed the narrative', Fitzgerald comments, 'But a "galley slip" of Boz's was amazing. It suggested a blue network spread over the printed lines, the blank spaces of the sides full of crowded writings, whole paragraphs deleted, all this representing very considerable [printing] cost' – *Memories of Charles Dickens* (1913) p. 225. Fitzgerald was not exaggerating: see Philip Collins's account of Dickens revising a Fitzgerald item, '"Inky Fishing Nets:" Dickens as Editor', *Dkn*, LXI (1965) 120–5.

2. George Moore (1806–76), Evangelical merchant (cf. *Speeches*, p. 432), was supported by Dickens in charitable ventures. See below, p. 341.

3. Fitzgerald often recalls Dickens's 'it's a small world' notion and his conception of averages. In another version Dickens reflects, in November, that another forty or fifty people *must* be killed in London street-accidents before 31 December (*Life of Dickens*, I, 207).

4. 'It is difficult to give an idea of Dickens's "bearing" in conversation; for he regularly acted his stories, and was irresistible. He called up the scene, his eyes became charged with humour, the wrinkles at the corners of his mouth quivered with enjoyment, his voice and richly unctuous laugh contributed, with his strangely grotesque glances, and so he told the tale' (*Life of Dickens*, II, vi, 313).

5. Referring elsewhere to this critique of Scott's novel, Fitzgerald mentions, as being among Dickens's favourite books, R. H. Dana's *Two Years before the Mast*, Michael Scott's *Tom Cringle's Log*, and John Poole's *Little Pedlington* (*Recreations*, I, 141–3).

6. Later, however, Fitzgerald more accurately remarks that, though Dickens never stopped working on his periodicals, he was less interested in and less involved with *All the Year Round* (*Memories*, p. 206).

7. Fitzgerald writes more fully about this in his *Memoirs of an Author* (1894), 'Dickens and *Household Words*' and 'Style, Old and New'.

'So Unlike Ordinary Great Men'

GRACE GREENWOOD

From 'Charles Dickens: Recollections of the Great Novelist', *New York Daily Tribune*, 5 July 1870. 'Grace Greenwood' (Mrs Sara Jane Lippincott, née Clarke, 1823–1904) was a popular American journalist, essayist and poet. In June 1852, she says (but July is more probable), having a letter of introduction from the novelist G. P. R. James, she dined at Tavistock House. The other guests included the German actor Emil Devrient, the poets Landor and 'Barry Cornwall' (B. W. Procter), and Charles Kemble and his daughter Adelaide (the famous soprano Madame Sartoris). She published a brief account in her series 'Greenwood Leaves from over the Sea' (*National Era*, Washington, 12 Aug 1852), but Dickens's death stimulated her to write more fully, adding particulars of later meetings and correspondence. Points made in the earlier account but not the later include Dickens's admiring Hawthorne and Catherine Dickens's being 'in character and manner truly a *gentlewoman*'.

I have in my mind still a perfectly distinct picture of the bright, elegant interior of Tavistock House, and of its inmates – of my host himself, then in his early prime – of Mrs. Dickens, a plump, rosy, English, handsome woman, with a certain air of absent-mindedness, yet gentle and kindly – Miss Hogarth, a very lovely person, with charming manners – and the young ladies, then every young – real English girls, fresh and simple,and innocent-looking as English daisies. I was received in the library. Mr. Dickens – how clearly he stands before me now, with his frank, encouraging smile and the light of welcome in his eyes – was then slight in person, and rather pale than otherwise. The symmetrical form of his head, and the fine, spirited bearing of the whole figure, struck me at once – then the hearty *bonhomie*, the wholesome sweetness of his smile; but more than anything else, the great beauty of his eyes. They were the eyes of a master, with no consciousness of mastery in them; they were brilliant without hardness, and searching without sharpness. I felt, I always felt, that they read me clearly and deeply, yet could never fear their keen scrutiny. They never made you feel uncomfortable. I can but think it a pity that in so many of the pictures we have of him the effect of his eyes is nearly lost by their being cast down. They had in them all the humor and all the humanity of the man. You saw in them all the splendid possibilities of his genius, all the manly tenderness of his nature.

Approaching Mr. Dickens as I did, with what he would have considered extravagant hero-worship, I was surprised to find myself speedily and entirely at my ease. Still, he seemed to put forth no effort to make me feel so. In manner, he was more quiet than I expected – simple and apparently unconscious. In conversation he was certainly not brilliant, after the manner of a professional talker. His talk did not bubble with puns, nor scintillate with epigrams, but it was racy and suggestive, with a fine flavor of originality and satire, and the effect of everything he said was doubled by the expression of those wonderful eyes. They were great listening eyes. When I remember how they would kindle at even my crude criticisms, my awkward attempts to convey to him the ideas and emotions which my visit to the Old World had called out, I can imagine the eager look, the kindred flash with which they must have responded to [more illustrious and brilliant interlocutors]. . . .

So completely in his generous appreciation and hospitable interest did Mr. Dickens seem to pass out of himself, that I had strange difficulty in realizing that he was *he*; that the alert, jaunty figure, dressed with extreme nicety, and in a style bordering on the ornate, and with such elegant and luxurious surroundings, was indeed the great friend of the people; the romancer of common life; that the kindly, considerate host who saw everything, heard everything, was the poetic, dramatic novelist, who, next to Shakespeare, had been for years the 'god of my idolatry'. . . .

At various times during the evening I had with my host little talks, of which I fortunately made some notes. I remember he graciously invited me to assist him in making a claret-punch, and while we were engaged in that serious work – (I stirred in the sugar for my part) – I told him how delighted I was with *Bleak House*, then in its early numbers, and how especially interested I was in Esther Summerson, his first essay at writing in the character of a woman, and to my mind a wonderful instance of mental transmigration. Most writers masquerading in feminine attire, sooner or later, reveal the 'beard under the muffler', the boots beneath the kirtle, but nowhere is any such masculine, illusion-breaking revelation made in this exquisite personation. Mr. Dickens seemed pleased, and confessed that the character of this young lady, as autobiographically evolved, had cost him no little labor and anxiety. 'Is it quite natural,' he asked 'quite girlish?' I replied that if an American woman could speak for English young-womanhood, it certainly was; and when he said he was about to get Esther in love, and hardly knew how he should be able to manage the delicate difficulties of the case, I told him that I was sure he would carry her triumphantly through – and he did.

Then and afterward my host talked with me quite freely, but with singular modesty, of his own productions and modes of study and writing, answering my questions frankly and patiently. I asked if certain characters which I pointed out, generally esteemed very peculiar and eccentric, if not positively unnatural and impossible, were not altogether beings of the mind, pure creatures of his own fancy; and he said explicitly that the most fantastic and terrible of his characters were the most real – the 'unnatural' were the natural – the 'exaggerations' were just those strange growths, those actual human traits he had copied most faithfully from life. Sam Weller, whom everybody recognized as an acquaintance, was not a real but quite an imaginary personage, he said – was only the representative of a class. Afterward, standing by his study table, and observing the exquisite order and nicety of its arrangements, I asked him if he actually did his every-day work there. 'Oh, yes,' he said; 'I sit here and write, through almost every morning.'

'Does the spirit always come upon you at once?' I asked.

'No – sometimes,' he answered, 'I have to coax it; sometimes I do little else than draw figures or make dots on the paper, and plan and dream till perhaps my time is nearly up. But I always sit here, for that certain time.' . . .

Yankee-like, I pursued my interesting investigations, asking him if, in case the flow of inspiration did not come till near the hour for lunch, or exercise, he left that seat when the hour struck, or remained.

'I go at once', he said, 'hardly waiting to complete a sentence. I could not keep my health otherwise. I let nothing deprive me of my tramp.'

Then I asked if the mental work did not go on as he walked, and he said he supposed it always did in some degree, especially when he was alone, yet that he thought he saw almost all there was to be seen in his walks about London and Paris – indeed everywhere he went; that he had trained his eye and ear to let nothing escape him; that he had received most valuable suggestions and hints of character in that way. I remember that he said in this connection that he seldom came upon a group of people standing before a print-shop window without pausing a few minutes to study their faces and listen to their criticisms. Two pointed sayings of his I recorded, one for its wit, the other for its humanity. Speaking of *Uncle Tom's Cabin*, then just out, he said he thought it decidedly a story of much power, dramatic and moral, but scarcely a work of art: he thought too, he said, that Mrs. Stowe had made rather too much of her subject – had overdone in the philanthropic direction. Uncle Tom evidently struck him as an impossible piece of ebony perfection, as a monster of excellence, and other African characters in the book as too highly seasoned with the virtues except for a spice of drollery and occasional perversity. 'Mrs. Stowe', he said, 'hardly gives the Anglo-Saxon fair play. I liked what I saw of the colored people in the States. I found them singularly polite and amiable, and in some instances decidedly clever; but then,' he added, with a droll, half smile, and a peculiar comical arch of his eyebrows, 'I have no prejudice against white people.'

In the course of the evening, I expressed to him my pleasure of seeing that his servants wore no distinctive livery, and he replied: 'I hope you are not surprised; I do not consider that I own enough of any man to hang a badge upon.'

Mr. Dickens was then in the full tide of his brilliant career as an amateur player. I expressed a desire to see him act, and he to have me see him, saying that he believed he had more talent for the drama than for literature, as he certainly had more delight in acting than in any other work whatever. . . .

During the first year succeeding my return from England I wrote a little for *Household Words*, and received some kind notes from its editor, but when, in the Winter of '68, he came to Philadelphia, where we were then living, I thought he must have forgotten me and sorrowfully enough resigned myself to the prospect of merely seeing him once or twice at the reader's desk – till a friend brought me word that he remembered me well, and would be glad to meet me. I went on an appointed day to his hotel. . . . I found indeed that he had not forgotten me, nor any of the circumstances of our slight acquaintance. He mentioned one after another all who were present on that memorable dinner-party – recalled a laughable incident occasioned by the extreme deafness of one of the guests, and even the joint concoction of the punch. . . . Again I found him so genial, simple, and companionable, so unlike ordinary great men, that the old feeling came over me, the old difficulty of realizing that it was Charles Dickens I was talking to, and none other. . . .

He had before spoken to me very pleasantly of my reports of the readings in *The Philadelphia Press*, and invited me to write for *All the Year Round*. What all this was to me, at that time, he could not have guessed – I can hardly tell. I was then in a sad, depressed state of mind, from ill-health and nervous prostration – that dreary, stranded condition, when one looks on one's day as past, on one's life as a failure. Beside *his* life mine should have seemed, perhaps, a yet more pitiful failure – but somehow it didn't. He did not overshadow and stifle one in that way – his genius did not so exhaust all the oxygen from the air around him. He was full of generous, inspiring sympathy, and despised no smallest work, if well done. When, in reply to a question as to what I had been doing since he last heard from me, I said, with an exceeding sense of literary insignificance, 'Oh, Mr. Dickens, I have not done *anything* worth considering. I have been writing for children, principally. I have only fed the lambs.' I shall never forget the earnest way in which he replied to this – 'I hope you do not think lightly of *that* work. You could not have been more nobly employed'. . . .

After Mr. Dickens returned to England, I wrote several times for *All the Year Round*; yet, though he acknowledged my contributions with the utmost kindness, I felt that the personal care he gave to them, slight as it was, was too much for me to impose on him. I could always see some marks of his revision, and knowing that every thing I offered must come under eyes as keenly critical as they were kindly, I could not do my best. I sketched out many things for his paper, but finished few. He liked distinctively American topics. Still one felt obliged to study English tastes in the treatment. His philanthropy if he would have allowed one to use in connection with him, a word so tainted with cant that he hated it – did not I fear, taken an Aboriginal direction. In a letter, dated Christmas Eve, 1868 – after informing me of the publication of a little story, he says: 'I rather doubt "The Poor Indian" as a subject of interest to the public. The wretched creature must pass away. When he comes to the point of stopping steam and scalping engineers, he must be remitted to that "equal sky" where there are no such relaxations.'

The last words of the last letter I ever received from Mr. Dickens were: 'I am happy to report myself quite well, and always faithfully your friend.' I would put no especial emphasis on that word 'friend', traced by his cordial, liberal hand. I know well I can claim nothing on the ground of a most unequal friendship, which gave so much in unconscious generosity and could receive so little return . . . .

NOTE

1. It has been impossible to trace any items by her in *Household Words*. A letter to her, 19 Aug 1869 (MS, Free Library of Philadelphia) mentions an item of hers published in *All the Year Round*, 7 Aug 1869 (n. s., II, 226–8).

Just Like his Books

FRANCESCO BERGER

(1) from his *Reminiscences, Impressions and Anecdotes* (1913) pp. 19–29; (2) from his *97* (1931) pp. 19–22. Berger (1834–1933; his *97* was published on his ninety-seventh birthday), born in England of emigré Italian and German parentage, was a composer and a Professor of Pianoforte at the Royal Academy of Music. While studying at Leipzig, he met Charley Dickens, who was working there, 1853–5. He thus became acquainted with the Dickens family, and was invited to compose the overture and incidental music for Dickens's productions of *The Lighthouse* (1855) and *The Frozen Deep* (1857). As one of the last-surviving friends of Dickens, he wrote various pieces for, or was interviewed in, the *Dickensian* and other journals. In one, he remarks of Dickens that, 'considering how distinguished was his social standing and how far-reaching his personal influence, he was a *modest* man' – *Dkn*, II (1906) 101. Berger was one of the few members of the Dickens circle to mention Ellen Ternan, being reported as saying that 'he knew the Ternan family well, and often during the 'sixties played games of cards at their house with the mother, daughter, and Dickens, on Sunday evenings. This was generally followed by Ellen and Dickens singing duets to his pianoforte accompaniment' – *Notes and Queries*, CLXV (1933) 87.

(1) I think for three months we rehearsed [*The Lighthouse*] twice in each week, so that by the time it was ready, not only was each Actor perfect in his part, but each knew everybody else's as well, and W. H. Wills, the Prompter, had very little to prompt. It is so impressed on my memory that after half a century I could even now repeat whole scenes from it. After every rehearsal, all concerned remained to supper, and it *was* a supper, such as would have

delighted John Browdie. And such grog, or punch! Brewed either by 'the Manager' himself or by 'Auntie' (Miss Hogarth), you may be sure it had the true Dickens flavour!

And here I must remark on a characteristic of Dickens which I think has scarcely been *sufficiently* noted by his biographers, and that is, his *wholeheartedness*. Whatever he did, he did as though *that only* were the principal thing to be done in life. His whole soul, his undivided energies, were in the occupation of the moment. No detail was forgotten, no personal discomfort was allowed to weigh. Whether getting up a 'benefit' for a friend, or acting, or dancing, or brewing punch, it was always the same. . . .

Wilkie Collins [when writing *The Frozen Deep*] consulted 'the Manager' about his Part, and Dickens advised him to write the Play irrespective of making it a 'one-part' Play, and to leave it to him to introduce a scene, or to amplify, if necessary.[1] And this was done. When the Play was put into rehearsal, for many weeks one particular scene was omitted, and when at last Dickens introduced it (it was a scene in which he had the stage all to himself) it was a most wonderful piece of Acting. Anything more powerful, more pathetic, more enthralling, I have never seen.

The Piece was duly produced at 'Tavistock House' and was an enormous success. It was *the* talk of London. Illustrated Papers produced scenes from it. . . . [Berger quotes a critique in *The Leader*, 10 Jan 1857:] 'Mr. Dickens's performance of this most touching and beautiful Part might open a new era for the stage, if the stage had the wisdom to profit by it. It is *fearfully fine* throughout – from the sullen despair in the second Act, alternating with gusts of passion or with gleams of tenderness . . . down to the appalling misery and supreme emotion of the dying Scene. Most awful are those wild looks and gestures of the starved, crazed man; that husky voice, now fiercely vehement, and now faltering into the last sorrow; that frantic cry when he recognizes Clara; that hysterical burst of joy when he brings in his former object of hatred, to prove that he is *not* a murderer; and that melting tenderness with which he kisses his old friend and his early love, and passes quietly away from Life. In these passages, Mr. Dickens shows that he is not only a great Novelist, but a great Actor also. . . . Mr. Dickens has all the technical knowledge and resources of a professed Actor; but these, the dry bones of acting, are kindled by that soul of vitality which can only be put into them by the man of Genius, and the interpreter of the affections. . . . Altogether, the audience return

home from Tavistock House rather indisposed for some time to come
to be content with the time-honoured conventionalities of the public
stage. . . .'

(2) Dickens's taste in all art matters was for the unsophisticated, the
obvious. Art for art's sake, the Art that we spell with a capital A did
not appeal to him. A picture, he said, should tell a story, music
should have a tune, fiction should embody actual or possible events.
As his creed was practical sympathy with the entire human race, so
he held that the object of Art was to add to the comfort and
happiness of the many, rather than to provide æsthetic pleasure for
the few. And to this doctrine I respond with a hearty Amen.

When I once spent a week with him and his family in Boulogne, I
had occasion to notice him in the rôle of devoted parent. One
evening, when he, Wilkie Collins and I visited a fair then in progress
in that quaint old town, he carried his youngest boy on his shoulders
from show to show, that he might see the fun as well as his elders.
And how keenly he sympathised with neglected, ill-used, misunderstood boys, readers of his books do not need to be reminded.

In personal appearance he might have been taken for a well-to-
do country gentleman, for there was nothing Bohemian about him.
He was neither tall nor short, neither fat nor thin. He carried himself
very erect, walking with almost military precision. His complexion
was ruddy, he was close-shaven on the cheeks with a short
'Imperial' beard. His hair was very dark brown, not black, and
getting scanty in places. He was always well dressed, frequently
wearing a black velvet waistcoat, which looked very smart with the
long gold watch-chain that depended from his neck. His voice was
remarkably mellow and capable of great modulation. His laughter
was most hearty and sonorous, quite infectious to the hearer. His
hand-grip made your fingers tingle long after he had released them.
There was no particle of affectation about him, no suspicion of any
'side'.

On the stage, both in drama and in farce, he was absolutely
splendid. His anger was terrible, his pathos heart-breaking, his love-
scenes exquisitely tender, his humour incomparable. He was an
agile dancer, light on his feet and graceful in his movements. I have
played 'Sir Roger' to his dancing until I was exhausted while he
showed no sign of fatigue.

Though I worship the man and his genius, I did not share the
enthusiasm which his 'Readings' evoked. He appeared to me

hampered by the restrictions of platform and evening dress as contrasted with the freedom of the boards and theatrical costume. And he allowed himself certain mannerisms of voice and gesture which, in the theatre, he would not have resorted to. But, of course, nothing could detract from the interest, the absorbing interest of hearing and seeing such a man recite his own pages. . . .

People often say to me: 'So, you knew Dickens. Tell us about him. What sort of man was he?' I can give no better answer than bid them read his books, for in them they will find all there is to know of him. No author ever revealed himself more completely to his readers than Dickens does in his pages. . . .

NOTE

1. As Robert Louis Brannan shows, Dickens was virtual co-author of the play: see his *Under the Management of Mr Charles Dickens: His Production of 'The Frozen Deep'* (1966). Dickens played Richard Wardour, a man crazed with jealousy because he has lost the love of Clara Burnham (Mamie Dickens) to a rival, Frank Aldersley (Wilkie Collins). He swears to kill this rival and, when they are both on a Polar expedition, has the chance to do so; but instead he nobly rescues Aldersley from certain death, deposits him at Clara's feet, and expires in her arms.

Loving Memories of a Very Faithful Follower

CHARLES KENT

(1) from 'Charles Dickens from a Personal Point of View', *Sala's Journal*, 30 Sep 1893, pp. 245–6; (2) from *Charles Dickens as a Reader* (1872; repr. with Introduction by Philip Collins, 1971) pp. 28–36, 72, 96–7, 263–7; (3) from *Pen and Pencil*, pp. 151–6. William Charles Mark Kent (1823–1902), minor poet and miscellaneous writer, editor of the *Sun* newspaper, 1845–71, and of other journals, contributor to many journals including Dickens's weeklies, became acquainted with the novelist in 1848 through Dickens's warm appreciation of his review of *Dombey*: see *Dickens: The Critical Heritage*, ed. Philip Collins (1971), pp. 227–30. They became good friends, and 'my faithful Kent' – as Dickens called him, with graceful allusion to *King Lear* – organised the farewell banquet to him (6 Nov 1867) before his American tour, wrote the authorised account of the public readings (1872), and

compiled anthologies of *The Humour and Pathos of Charles Dickens* (1884) and of *Wellerisms* (1886). He worshipped Dickens, who, as Percy Fitzgerald remarked, 'never had a more faithful follower' than this 'exuberant, affectionate, romantic' admirer.

(1) On being asked to write this paper upon Charles Dickens from a personal point of view, my first impulse was to describe him under the most delightful aspect in which he ever stood in my regard, namely, whenever he welcomed me to the last and brightest of all his charming homes, at Gadshill Place, near Higham, by Rochester. But, on second thoughts, it seemed far more suitable that I should recall him to my recollection in the midst of the surroundings the nearest of all to his own large heart, and the most familiar to everybody in his great fictions, meaning the enormous labyrinth and swarming multitudes of his beloved London. . . . So emphatically had Dickens made London his own that countless parts of it had come to be known generically as 'Dickens's London'. And I perfectly well remember one day, when I was lunching with Matthew Arnold, on my expressing to him my anguish at the rapid disappearance of these historical spots, his saying to me, 'I so perfectly agree with you that I should like to see them all placed carefully under glass.' . . .

In the habit myself, for many years past, of roving through the streets of London at any period of either the night or day, I have often come upon him in what, to those unacquainted with his ways, might have seemed the unlikeliest parts of the capital for him to have thought of penetrating. But never at these times has he appeared before me unexpectedly. For, wheresoever London might extend, there those who knew him best would feel quite sure that, at some moment or another, Charles Dickens might confidently be looked for. His chief studio, in fact, during his nearly forty years of authorship, it may be truly said, was London – that marvellous microcosm, from his keen observation of which as a peripatetic philosopher, he derived his profound knowledge of every type of humanity.

Wherever Dickens appeared in the capital – north, south, east, or west – his presence was instantly recognised. Thanks to his ubiquitous photographs, his identity was perceived – by every chance crowd, by literate and illiterate alike, even by those who had never seen him before – to be that public benefactor who had been for so many years the good genius of their homes. His handsome presence, his noble head, his delightful face won for him the regard of those who were personally strangers to him. This was so even to the very last. As to those who knew him well and were admitted to his intimate friendship, which of them who ever heard the music of his cordial voice, or felt the generous grasp of his hand, but bears them still in their tender remembrance? In [*Dickens as a Reader*], I said of him that 'Among his friends and intimates no great author has ever been more truly or more tenderly beloved.' After the lapse now of twenty-three years since the world was grief-stricken by the sudden announcement of his death, I can only repeat those words with greatly increased emphasis. . . .

As a companion, Dickens's chief charm was that he was so intensely sympathetic. Enjoying throughout life almost perfect health, except towards its close, and twice previously in his earlier days, if he came suddenly upon any one in acute suffering, no one, even a woman, could be a tenderer nurse. The late Vicar of St. Helen's gave me vivid illustration of this in regard to himself on a certain day when he was crossing the Channel on a steamboat, among the passengers on which was, happily for him, Charles Dickens. The sufferer in this instance was hurrying homewards to undergo an operation, when Dickens, coming up behind him and suddenly realising whose was the back of the neck he had just seen, exclaimed, in a kindly but comical way: 'My boy, you *have* got a carbuncle!' From that moment until Dickens landed the Vicar at his own door he never once left him, plying him all the while at intervals with minute doses of brandy, but for which sedulous and careful treatment, as the Vicar's doctor afterwards assured him, his life could not, in all human probability, have been saved.

Another day – it was towards the close of the spring of 1870, and, as the event proved, but a very few weeks before his startlingly sudden death – Charles Dickens, seeing that I was under profound depression of spirits, at once swept aside all his own, some of them weighty, preoccupations so that he might devote himself forthwith, and until after nightfall, to cheering me up with his delightful companionship. He sketched out upon the instant for our guidance the programme of an excursion which insured us several hours' enjoyment together, including a *tête-à-tête* dinner, and one of those long rambles in which, even over the most familiar ground, he always so thoroughly delighted. It proved to be the last walk through London we were ever to have exclusively to ourselves. Though the end was then only too rapidly drawing near, it was, happily for me, not by any means the last day I was with him. It is one, however, that is almost sacred in my remembrance, coupled as it is with some of my tenderest recollections of one of the dearest friends I ever possessed.

(2) [In *Dickens as a Reader*, Kent premises that the Public Readings were notable as 'supplementary, and certainly as very exceptional, evidences of genius on the part of a great author', and 'a wholly unexampled incident in the history of literature'. Never before had a great author thus gone out to meet his public; and the 'affectionate admiration' felt for him, as well as his works, was unique, being so widespread and of such long standing. Moreover it was one of Dickens's most remarkable characteristics that, 'while he was endowed with a brilliant imagination, and with a genius in many ways incomparable, he was at the same time gifted with the clearest and soundest judgment, being, in point of fact, what is called a thoroughly good man of business'. Kent describes the history of the Readings and gives an account of every item he performed. The following extracts describe his manner of reading.] Whatever scenes he described, those scenes his hearers appeared to be actually witnessing themselves. He realised everything in his own mind so intensely, that listening to him we realised what he spoke of by sympathy. Insomuch that one might, in his own words, say of him, as David Copperfield says of Mr. Peggotty, when the latter has been recounting little Emily's wanderings: 'He saw everything he related. . . . ' While, on the one hand, he never repeated the words that had to be delivered phlegmatically, or as by rote; on the other hand, he never permitted voice, look, gesture, to pass the limits of discretion, even at moments the most impassioned; as, for example, where Nancy, in the famous murder-scene, shrieked forth her last gasping and despairing appeals to her brutal paramour. The same thing may be remarked again in regard to all the more tenderly pathetic of his delineations. His tones then were often subdued almost to a whisper, every syllable, nevertheless, being so distinctly articulated as to be audible in the remotest part of a vast hall like that in Piccadilly. . . .

Attending his Readings, character after character appeared before us, living and breathing, in the flesh, as we looked and listened. It mattered nothing, just simply nothing, that the great author was there all the while before his audience in his own identity. His evening costume was a matter of no consideration – the flower in his button-hole, the paper-knife in his hand, the book before him, that earnest, animated, mobile, delightful face, that we all knew by heart through his ubiquitous photographs – all were equally of no account whatever. We knew that he alone was there all the time before us, reading, or, to speak more accurately, re-creating for us, one and all – while his lips were articulating the familiar words his hand had written so many years previously – the most renowned of the imaginary creatures peopling his books. Watching him, hearkening to him, while he stood there un-mistakably before his audience, on the raised platform, in the glare of the gas-burners shining down upon him from behind the pendant screen immediately above his head, his individuality, so to express it, altogether disappeared, and we saw before us instead, just as the case might happen to be, Mr. Pickwick, or Mrs. Gamp, or Dr. Marigold, or little Paul Dombey, or Mr. Squeers, or Sam Weller, or Mr. Peggotty, or some other of those immortal personages. . . .

Even the lesser characters – those which are introduced into the original works quite incidentally, occupying there a wholly sub-ordinate position, filling up a space in the crowded tableaux, always in the background – were then at last brought to the fore in the course of these Readings, and suddenly and for the first time assumed to themselves a distinct importance and individuality. Take, for instance, the nameless lodging-housekeeper's slavey, who assists at Bob Sawyer's party, and who is described in the original work as 'a dirty, slipshod girl, in black cotton stockings, who might have passed for the neglected daughter of a superannuated dustman in very reduced circumstances'. No one had ever realised the crass stupidity of that remarkable young person – dense and impenet-rable as a London fog – until her first introduction in these Readings, with 'Please, Mister Sawyer, Missis Raddle wants to speak to *you!*' – the dull, dead-level of her voice ending in the last monosyllable with a series of inflections almost amounting to a chromatic passage. Mr. Justice Stareleigh, again! – nobody had ever conceived the world of humorous suggestiveness underlying all the words put into his mouth until the author's utterance of them came to the readers of *Pickwick* with the surprise of a revelation. Jack Hopkins in like manner – nobody, one might say, had ever dreamt of as he was in Dickens's inimitably droll impersonation of him, until the lights and shades of the finished picture were first of all brought out by the Reading. Jack Hopkins! – with the short, sharp, quick articulation, rather stiff in the neck, with a dryly comic look just under the eyelids, with a scarcely expressible relish of his own for every detail of that wonderful story of his about the 'neckluss', an absolute and implicit reliance upon Mr. Pickwick's gullibility, and an inborn and ineradicable passion for chorusing.

As with the characters, so with the descriptions. One was life itself, the other was not simply word-painting, but realisation. There was the Great Storm at Yarmouth, for example, at the close of *David Copperfield*. Listening to that Reading, the very portents of the coming tempest came before us! . . . The merest fragments of it conjured up the entire scene – aided as those fragments were by the look, the tones, the whole manner of the Reader. The listener was there with him in imagination upon the beach, beside David. He was there, lashed and saturated with the salt spray, the briny taste of it on his lips, the roar and tumult in his ears – the height to which the breakers rose, and, looking over one another bore one another down and rolled in, in interminable hosts, becoming at last, as it is written in that wonderful chapter (55) of *David Copperfield*, 'most appalling!' There, in truth, the success achieved was more than an elocutionary triumph – it was the realisation to his hearers, by one who had the soul of a poet, and the gifts of an orator, and the genius of a great and vividly imaginative author, of a convulsion of nature when nature bears an aspect the grandest and the most astounding. . . .

There was . . . a sense of exhilaration in the very manner with which Dickens commenced the Reading of one of his stories, and which was always especially noticeable in the instance of [the *Christmas Carol*]. The opening sentences were always given in those cheery, comfortable tones, indicative of a double relish on the part of a narrator – to wit, his own enjoyment of the tale he is going to relate, and his anticipation of the enjoyment of it by those who are giving him their attention. Occasionally, at any rate during the last few years, his voice was husky just at the commencement, but as he warmed to his work, with him at all times a genuine labour of love, everything of that kind disappeared almost at the first turn of the leaf. The genial inflections of the voice, curiously rising, in those first moments of the Reading, at the end of every sentence, there was simply no resisting. . . .

[During their last walk together through the London suburbs, in the early summer of 1870, Dickens 'abruptly asked' Kent] 'What do you think would be the realisation of one of my most cherished day-dreams?' Adding, instantly, without waiting for any answer, 'To settle down now for the remainder of my life within easy distance of a great theatre, in the direction of which I should hold supreme authority. It should be a house, of course, having a skilled and noble company, and one in every way magnificently appointed. The pieces acted should be dealt with according to my pleasure, and touched up here and there in obedience to my own judgment; the players as well as the plays being absolutely under my command. There,' said he, laughingly, and in a glow at the mere fancy, '*that's* my daydream!'

Dickens's delighted enjoyment, in fact, of everything in any way connected with the theatrical profession, was second only to that shown by him in the indulgence of the master-passion of his life, his love of literature. The way in which he threw himself into his labours, as a Reader, was only another indication of his intense affection for the dramatic art. For, as we have already insisted, the Readings were more than simply Readings, they were in the fullest meaning of the words singularly ingenious and highly elaborated histrionic performances.

(3) [Kent recalls his saying, in 1870] to some of his own nearest and dearest – what I now, nineteen years after his death, repeat with the utmost possible deliberation – that, 'In all my recollection of him, there was not an act or a word, there was not a glance of his eye or an inflection of his voice that I would have had in any way different from what it actually was.'

. . . far beyond the ordinary run of mortals, he was charged, so to speak, from head to foot with vitality. However animated a roomful of people might be, his appearance upon the threshold gave them an instant sense of exhilaration. It was like turning the Bude light upon a half-lit chamber. Never was there, surely, at any time, such a Master of the Revels. In arranging a picnic, in presiding over a cricket-match, in conducting any out-door holiday excursion, he was unapproachable. The contagion of his high spirits infected everybody. . . .

As a host at all times he was incomparable. No guest of his, under his roof-beams, ever felt otherwise than at home. Supposing the one invited had never before partaken of his hospitality, his way of getting to his destination was mapped out for him by an elaborate itinerary. If it were an invitation to the Novelist's Kentish home, ten thousand chances to one but the visitor would be met at the Higham station by Dickens himself, who would drive him over to Gadshill in his favourite jaunting car to the chime of the musical bells on the jingling harness. And thenceforth until the guest's departure – a day, a week, a month afterwards – be sure of this, he had the happiest time of it.

As a companion he was peculiarly delightful, and this, apart from his other rare qualities, by reason in no small degree of his being so thoroughly sympathetic. For, he was no less admirable as a listener than as a talker, his assenting 'surely', or 'certainly', again and again repeated, indicating his keen and watchful attention, even to the longest explanation. If you were bent upon enjoying a chat with him to the very uttermost, and without any risk of interruption, your wisest plan was to start with him upon one of his vigorous walks, at a swinging pace, it mattered little whether in town or country. By himself, and with his companionship, by you also, they were about equally enjoyable. If in his own neighbourhood at Gad's, the ramble led you discursively among scenes with which, thanks to him, you had long ago become familiar – over Rochester-bridge where Mr. Pickwick moralized within view of the time-worn ruins of the Castle; past the Bull Inn on the staircase of which Mr. Jingle infuriated Dr. Slammer; to the rural tavern of the Leather Bottle, in the wainscoted parlour of which Mr. Tupman, then supposed to be in the last stage of depression, was found by his brother Pickwickians carousing in solitude, surrounded with all sorts of creature comforts; through Cobham Park, to which, by a pass-key, the master of Gad's Hill had the privilege of perpetual access; under the wall of the churchyard in which Pip first made the acquaintance of Magwitch; hard by the old Hall sacred to the memory of the Man who was once Haunted by his own shadow; and so, returning home through familiar streets, back again by the porch of the quaint old almshouse in which are entertained, under certain stipulated conditions, the Six Poor Travellers. If, on the other hand, you started upon a pedestrian expedition with him through the London streets, the probability was that your steps were directed by preference along those leading to the outer roads radiating from the great Metropolis. Well do I recollect that, as we started upon the last extended walk we were ever to make together through London and its south-western suburbs, immediately on our having crossed the Strand from his house in Covent Garden, we were wedged shoulder to shoulder at the corner of Wellington Street in a sudden, dense block of the foot passengers on the pavement – this trivial incident being burnt into my recollection by the fact that, during those few moments of the interrupted traffic, some Yahoo rough at our elbow rendered the very sense of hearing hideous by words so inconceivably foul and blasphemous that none could have overheard them without shuddering. It was pre-eminently characteristic of his whole nature, as it seemed to me, that anyone observing his imperturbable face while the words were being uttered and his dumb silence in their regard afterwards, must have pronounced him stone deaf as to all that had occurred. The absolute purity of his writings everybody knows. The absolute purity of his conversation is known best of all to his intimates. There was something essentially wholesome in the genius of the master humourist who was at once the manliest and yet the gentlest and tenderest of human beings.

What is especially remarkable about him is this, that from first to last he was utterly unspoilt by his long sustained and immense popularity. . . . Unless urged to do so by inquiry from some one else, he never talked about his own writings. And though he took the keenest interest at all times in anyone's appreciation of them, he habitually betrayed as little consciousness of his own fame as any great author could possibly have done. An incident strikingly illustrative of what is here remarked recurs at this moment to my recollection. Strolling westwards with him one day along the Strand, I was telling him [an anecdote about the popularity of *Pickwick*]. Listening amused to this odd testimony to the perennial freshness of his first book, Dickens did so, I observed, with a divided attention. His keen eye, while I was speaking, had taken note of a deplorable woman in the crowd with a couple of emaciated children clinging to her, all three visibly in the lowest depths of mendicancy. Furtively slipping a half-crown into the poor mother's hand at the moment of passing, he affected to be still preoccupied, with a half-quenched smile upon lips, by what I was saying – all the while evidently under the impression that I was entirely unobservant of what had just occurred. In his yearning pity for the poor, all interest in a matter that merely affected himself in a complimentary sense, had visibly and instantaneously vanished. . . .

Vividly imaginative, Dickens was at the same time gifted with so singularly clear, sound, and balanced a judgment that he took pre-eminent rank among all his friends as their wisest and most reliable adviser. The mere sight of his bright eye, the sound of his cordial voice, the grasp of his kind hand at any moment of profounder solicitude than usual, had of themselves a heartening influence to begin with. But, beyond all these merely external evidences of his sympathy, as affording solace to anyone borne down, it might chance to be, by the gravest anxiety of mind, were the wholeness and instantaneous promptitude with which he gave himself up to its consideration. Whatever the doubts brought to him might be in their character, they were surveyed in all their bearings, they were weighed to the minutest scruple, they were reduced to their intrinsic value, or, supposing them not to have any, they were utterly dissipated. Acting in this way, his common sense was like a powerful solvent.

A Reading of the *Carol*

KATE FIELD

From her *Pen Photographs of Charles Dickens's Readings*, enlarged edn (1871) pp.19–22, 28–36. Kate Field (1839–96), a vivacious American, daughter of the actor Joseph M. Field, was a journalist, lecturer, actress, and author of books on theatrical and other topics. She attended Dickens's readings in Boston and New York with great assiduity ('twenty-five of the most delightful and most instructive evenings of my life'), and wrote critiques of them in various journals. These provided the main material for her book. She wanted to publish it in England in 1868, but Anthony Trollope (who had a *tendresse* for her) reported that Dickens was 'altogether opposed' to this – for reasons unstated – and that without his co-operation the venture could not succeed – Michael Sadleir, *Trollope: A Commentary*, revised edn (1945) p. 290. The enlarged edition was published in England after his death. The book has chapters on every reading in Dickens's American repertoire.

One glance at the platform is sufficient to convince the audience that Dickens thoroughly appreciates 'stage effect'. A large screen of maroon cloth occupies the background; before it stands a light table of peculiar design, on the inner left-hand corner of which there peers forth a miniature desk, large enough to accommodate the reader's book. On the right hand of the table, and somewhat below its level, is a shelf, where repose a carafe of water and a tumbler. 'T is 'a combination and a form indeed', covered with velvet somewhat lighter in color than the screen. No drapery conceals the table, whereby it is plain that Dickens believes in expression of figure as well as of face, and does not throw away everything but his head and arms, according to the ordinary habit of ordinary speakers. About twelve feet above the platform, and somewhat in advance of the table, is a horizontal row of gas-jets with a tin reflector; and midway in both perpendicular gas-pipes there is one powerful jet with glass chimney. By this admirable arrangement, Dickens stands against a dark background in a frame of gaslight, which throws out his face and figure to the best advantage. With the book 'Dickens' stranded on the little desk, the comedian Dickens can transform a table into a stage; and had the great novelist concluded, at the last moment, not to appear before us, this ingenious apparatus would have taught us a lesson in the art of reading.

He comes! A lithe, energetic man, of medium stature, crosses the platform at the brisk gait of five miles an hour, and takes his position behind the table. This is Charles Dickens, whose name has been a household word in England and America for thirty years; whose books have been the joy and solace of many a weary heart and head. A first glance disappointed me. I thought I should prefer to have him entirely unlike himself; but when I began to speculate on how Charles Dickens *ought* to look, I gave the matter up, and wisely concluded that Nature knew her own intentions better than any one else.

Dickens has a broad, full brow, a fine head – which, for a man of such power and energy, is singularly small at the base of the brain – and a cleanly cut profile. There is a slight resemblance between him and Louis Napoleon in the latter respect, owing mainly to the nose; but it is unnecessary to add that the faces of the two men are totally different. Dickens's eyes are light-blue, and his mouth and jaw, without having any claim to beauty, possess a strength that is not concealed by the veil of iron-gray mustache and generous imperial. His head is but slightly graced with iron-gray hair, and his complexion is florid.

If any one thinks to obtain an accurate idea of Dickens from the photographs that flood the country, he is mistaken. He will see Dickens's clothes, Dickens's features, as they appear when Nicholas Nickleby is in the act of knocking down Mr. Wackford Squeers; but he will not see what makes Dickens's face attractive, the geniality and expression that his heart and brain put into it. In his photographs Dickens looks as if, previous to posing, he had been put under an exhausted receiver and had had his soul pumped out of him. This process is no beautifier. Therefore let those who have not been able to judge for themselves believe that Dickens's face is capable of wonderfully varied expression. Hence it is the best sort of face. His eye is at times so keen as to cause whoever is within its range to feel morally certain that it has penetrated to his boots; at others it brims over with kindliness. 'It is like looking forward to spring to think of seeing your beaming eye again', wrote Lord Jeffrey to Charles Dickens years ago,[1] and truly, for there is a twinkle in it that, like a promissory note, pledges itself to any amount of fun – within sixty minutes. After seeing this twinkle I was satisfied with Dickens's appearance, and became resigned to the fact of his not resembling the Apollo Belvedere. One thing is certain – if he did resemble this classical young gentleman, he never could have written his novels. Laying this flattering unction to my soul, I listen [to his reading of *A Christmas Carol*]. . . .

At the close of [its opening] paragraph the critic beside me whispers, 'Dickens's voice is limited in power, husky, and naturally monotonous. If he succeeds in overcoming these defects, it will be by dramatic genius.' I begin to take a gloomy view of the situation, and wonder why Dickens constantly employs the rising inflection, and never comes to a full stop; but we are so pleasantly and naturally introduced to Scrooge that my spirits revive. 'Foul weather didn't know where to have him. The heaviest rain and snow and hail and sleet could boast of the advantage over him in only one respect – they often "came down" handsomely, and Scrooge *never did*.' Here the magnetic current between reader and listener sets in, and when Scrooge's clerk 'put on his white comforter and tried to warm himself at the candle – in which effort, not being a man of strong imagination, he failed' – the connection is tolerably well established. I see old Scrooge, very plainly, growling and snarling at his pleasant nephew, and when that nephew invites that uncle to eat a Christmas dinner with him, and Dickens says that Scrooge said 'that he would see him – yes, I am very sorry to say he did – he went the whole length of the expression, and said he would see him in that extremity, first' – he makes one dive at our sense of humor and takes it captive. Dickens is Scrooge most decidedly – just as we have seen him in the book. There are the old features, the pointed nose, the thin lips, the wiry chin, the frosty rime on head and eyebrows, and the shrewd, grating voice. He is the portly gentleman with the conciliatory voice on a mission of charity – just the voice in which gentlemen-beggars deliver their errands of mercy; he is twice Scrooge when, the portly gentleman remarking that many poor people had rather die than go to the workhouse, he replies, 'O, well, you know, upon the whole, if they'd rather die, they had better do it and decrease the surplus population'; and thrice Scrooge when, turning upon his clerk, he says, 'You'll want all day to-morrow, I suppose?' It is the incarnation of a hard-hearted, hard-fisted, hard-voiced miser.

'If it's – if it's – quite convenient, sir.' A few words, but they denote Bob Cratchit in three feet of comforter exclusive of fringe, in well-darned, threadbare clothes, with a mild, frightened, lisping voice, so thin that you can see through it!

Then there comes the change when Scrooge, upon going home, 'saw in the knocker Marley's face!' Of course Scrooge saw it, because the expression of Dickens's face, as he rubs his eyes and stares, makes me see it, 'with a dismal light about it, like a bad lobster in a dark cellar'. There is good acting in this scene, and there is fine acting when the dying flame leaps up as though it cried, 'I know him! Marley's ghost!'

Scrooge bites his fingers nervously as he peers at the ghost, and then with infinite gusto Dickens reads that description of Marley, how, 'looking through this waistcoat, Scrooge *could see the two buttons on his coat behind*'; how Scrooge grew wondrously perplexed as to whether his old partner could sit down after undergoing such atmospheric changes; how Scrooge would persist in doubting his senses because Marley might be 'an undigested bit of beef, a blot of mustard, a crumb of cheese, a fragment of an underdone potato. There's more of gravy than of grave about you, whatever you are'; and how Scrooge finally listens to Marley, yet, believing that business habits of despatch are quite as good for the next world as for this, exclaims with comic earnestness, 'For Heaven's sake, don't be flowery, Jacob, whatever you are!' It is excellent, and at the conclusion of Stave One, my friend, the critic, and I say, 'Dickens *is* an actor'.

Nothing can be better than the rendering of the Fezziwig party in Stave Two. . . . Dickens's expression, as he relates how 'in came the housemaid with *her cousin the baker*, and in came the cook *with her brother's particular friend the milkman*', is delightfully comic, while his complete rendering of that dance where 'all were top couples at last, and not a bottom one to help them', is owing to the inimitable action of his hands. They actually perform upon the table, as if it were the floor of Fezziwig's room, and every finger were a leg belonging to one of the Fezziwig family. This *feat* is only surpassed by Dickens's illustration of Sir Roger de Coverley, as interpreted by

Mr. and Mrs. Fezziwig, when 'a positive light appeared to issue from Fezziwig's calves', and he 'cut so deftly that he appeared to wink with his legs!' It is a maze of humor. Before the close of the stave, Scrooge's horror at sight of the young girl once loved by him and put aside for gold, shows that Dickens's power is not purely comic.

Ah, but the best of all is Stave Three! I distinctly see that Cratchit family. There are the potatoes that 'knocked loudly at the saucepan lid to be let out and peeled'; there is Mrs. Cratchit, fluttering and cackling like a motherly hen with a young brood of chickens; and there is everybody. The way those two young Cratchits hail Martha, and exclaim, 'There's *such* a goose, Martha!' can never be forgotten. By some prestidigitation Dickens takes off his own head and puts on a Cratchit's; and when those two young gentlemen cry out, 'There's father coming! Hide, Martha, hide!' they not only clap their hands, but they seem to be dancing round Dickens's table. Then Bob Cratchit and Tiny Tim come in . . . and then Bob relates 'how Tiny Tim' behaved; 'as good as gold, and better. Somehow he gets thoughtful, sitting by himself so much, and thinks the strangest things you ever heard. He told me, coming home, that he hoped the people saw him in the church, because he was a cripple, and it might be pleasant to them to remember, upon Christmas day, who made lame beggars walk and blind men see.' There is a volume of pathos in these words, which are the most delicate and artistic rendering of the whole reading.

Ah, that Christmas dinner! I feel as if I were eating every morsel of it. Peter mashes the potatoes with incredible energy; Belinda sweetens the apple-sauce, and smacks her lips so loudly in the tasting as to prove that it could not be better; 'the two young Cratchits', 'cram spoons into their mouths, lest they should shriek for goose before their turn'; and Tiny Tim 'beats on the table with the handle of his knife, as he feebly cries, "Hoorray! Hoorray! Hoorray!"' in such a still, small voice. Moreover, there is that goose! I see it with my naked eye. And O, the pudding! . . . Dickens's sniffing and smelling of that pudding would make a starving family believe that they had swallowed it, holly and all. It is infectious.

What Dickens *does* is frequently infinitely better than anything he says, or the way he says it; yet the doing is as delicate and intangible as the odor of violets, and can be no better indicated. Nothing of its kind can be more touchingly beautiful than the manner in which Bob Cratchit – previous to proposing 'a merry Christmas to us all, my dears, God bless us' – stoops down, with tears in his eyes, and places Tiny Tim's withered little hand in his, 'as if he loved the child, and wished to keep him by his side, and dreaded that he might be taken from him'. It is pantomime worthy of the finest actor.

Equally clever is Bob's attempt to pacify Mrs. Cratchit, when, upon being desired to toast 'Mr. Scrooge, the Founder of the Feast', this amiable lady displays an amount of temper of which we never believed her capable. 'My dear!' says Bob, in an expostulatory tone, 'my dear! the children! Christmas day!' pointing mysteriously to each one with inimitable *naïveté*. Bob's picture ought to be taken at this moment. Indeed, now I think of it, I am astonished that artists who illustrate such of Dickens's books as are read by him do not make him their model. They can never approach his conception, they can never equal his execution, and to the virtue of truth would be added the charm of resembling the author.

Admirable is Mrs. Cratchit's ungracious drinking to Scrooge's health, and Martha's telling how she had seen a lord, and how he 'was much about as tall as Peter!' It is a charming cabinet picture, and so likewise is the glimpse of Christmas at Scrooge's nephew's. The plump sister is 'satisfactory, O, perfectly satisfactory', and Topper is a magnificent fraud on the understanding, a side-splitting fraud. I see Fred get off the sofa and *stamp* at his own fun, and I hear the plump sister's voice when she guesses the wonderful riddle, 'It's your uncle Scro-o-o-o-oge!' Altogether, Dickens is better than any comedy.

What a change in Stave Four! There sit the gray-haired rascal, old Joe, with his crooning voice, Mrs. Dilber, and those robbers of dead men's shrouds. There is something positively and Shakespearianly weird in the laugh and tone of the charwoman. 'Let the charwoman alone to be the first', she cries. 'Let the laundress alone to be the second; and let the undertaker's man alone to be the third. Look here, old Joe, here's a chance! If we have n't all three met here without meaning it!' Unconsciously the three witches of *Macbeth* arise before the imagination, which perceives by Dickens's treatment of this short but graphic scene how fine a sketch he would make did fate ever cast him for one of the sisters three.

One turn of the kaleidoscope and we stand before the body of the plundered unknown man; another, and there sit the Cratchits weeping over Tiny Tim's death, a scene that would be beyond all praise were Bob's cry, 'My little, little child!' a shade less dramatic.

Here, and only here, Dickens forgets the nature of Bob's voice, and employs all the power of his own, carried away apparently by the situation. Bob would not thus give vent to his feelings. Finally, there is Scrooge, no longer a miser, but a human being, screaming at the 'conversational' boy, the 'Itinerary of London', in Sunday clothes, to buy him the prize turkey 'that never could have stood upon his legs, that bird. He would have snapped 'em off in a minute, like sticks of sealing-wax.' There is Bob Cratchit behind time, trying 'to overtake nine o'clock' that fled fifteen minutes before; there is Scrooge poking Bob in the ribs, and vowing he will raise his salary; and there is at last happiness for all as Tiny Tim exclaims, 'God bless us, every one!'

I do not see how *The Christmas Carol* can be read and acted better. The only improvement possible is in 'The Ghosts', who are perhaps too monotonous, – a way ghosts have when they return to earth. It is generally believed that ghosts, being 'damp, moist, uncomfortable bodies', lose their voices beyond redemption and are obliged to pipe through eternity on one key. I am at a loss to see the wisdom of this hypothesis. Solemnity and monotony are not synonymous terms, yet every theatrical ghost insists that they are, and Dickens is no exception to the rule. If monotony be excusable in any one, however, it is in him; for when one actor is obliged to represent *twenty-three different characters*, giving to every one an individual tone, he may be pardoned if his ghosts are not colloquial.[2]

NOTES

1. Henry Thomas Cockburn, *Life of Lord Jeffrey* (1852) II, 465; see above, I, 89.
2. Dickens's own reading-copy of the *Carol*, containing in the margins his performance-signs and stage-directions, has been published in facsimile: *A Christmas Carol: The Public Reading Version*, ed. Philip Collins (New York, 1971). Further particulars of how Dickens performed this and other items are given in Collins's edition *Charles Dickens: The Public Readings* (1975).

A Hero to his Readings Manager

GEORGE DOLBY

(1) from his *Charles Dickens as I Knew Him: The Story of the Readings Tours in Great Britain and America (1866–1870)* (1885) pp. 8–11, 21, 30–5, 38–40, 219, 226–7, 239, 272–4, 294–6, 344–5, 360–2, 385–9, 418, 442; (2) from *Pen and Pencil*, Supplement, pp. 26–7. Dolby (died 1900) came late into Dickens's life, becoming his readings manager, on behalf of his new impresarios, Messrs Chappell, in 1866, and also managing the American tour of 1867–8. Probably through his sister, the famous contralto Madame Charlotte Helen Sainton-Dolby, who was a friend of the novelist, he had met Dickens earlier, and 'he had known me, and my reputation as a manager, for some years' (*Dickens as I Knew Him*, p. 12). But it was not until 1866 that they really became acquainted. Soon their friendship was intimate, each having a high regard for the other. Dickens was, for Dolby, 'the best and dearest friend man ever had', 'my great hero–my "Chief"– . . . and his memory is heroic now that he has gone. His death closed the brightest chapter of my life' (ibid., pp.155, vii–viii). He was a very efficient manager, large, tough and vulgar; Mark Twain called him a 'gladsome gorilla', Percy Fitzgerald said he was 'not over-refined, but loud and a little noisy': see James G. Ollé, 'Dickens and Dolby', *Dkn*, LIV (1958) 27–35. His later career was depressing, and he died a pauper in a workhouse. In the opinion of Mamie Dickens, his book on Dickens 'gives the best and truest picture of my father that has yet been written' – *Charles Dickens*, 2nd edn (1880) p. 117. It was just as well that Forster was dead when she made this pronouncement.

(1) [For the 1866 readings tour, Dickens prepared a new item, *Doctor Marigold*, derived from his recent Christmas story] and, in order to test its suitability for its purpose, a private rehearsal was given on March 18, at Southwick Place, Hyde Park, in a furnished house which Mr. Dickens had taken for the season. This audience consisted of the members of his family, and Mr. Robert Browning, Mr. Wilkie Collins, Mr. Charles Fechter, Mr. John Forster, Mr. Arthur Chappell, Mr. Charles Kent, and myself. It is hardly necessary to say that the verdict was unanimously favourable. Everybody was astonished by the extraordinary ease and fluency with which the patter of the 'Cheap Jack' was delivered, and the subtlety of the humour which pervaded the whole presentation. To those present, the surprise was no less great than the results were

pleasing; indeed, it is hard to see how it could well have been otherwise, for seldom, and but too seldom in the world's history, do we find a man gifted with such extraordinary powers, and, at the same time, possessed of such a love of method, such will, such energy, and such a capacity for taking pains. An example of this is the interesting fact that, although to many of his hearers at that eventful rehearsal of *Doctor Marigold* it was the first time it had been read, Mr. Dickens had, since its appearance as a Christmas number, only three months previously, adapted it as a Reading, and had rehearsed it to himself considerably over two hundred times – and this in addition to his ordinary work.

Great as was the success of *Doctor Marigold's Prescriptions* as a Christmas number – the sale of which exceeded 250,000 copies in the first week – *Doctor Marigold*, as a reading, more than realized the anticipations of even the most sanguine of Mr. Dickens's friends, whilst the public, and those who in various ways were more immediately interested in the Readings, were convinced that up to that time they had had but a very faint conception of Mr. Dickens's powers either as an adapter or an elocutionist. . . .

[On tour, they sometimes had an evening off.] Mr. Dickens's tastes being inclined to theatre or circus, we repaired to a circus; for, appreciative as he was of the actor's art, he had an enormous admiration for the equestrian, and never failed to visit a circus whenever the chance presented itself. . . .

[Dolby describes the Dickens of these years as] a man respectably attired in the usual lower garments, well cut and well made; over which a pea-jacket or 'reefer', Count D'Orsay cloak, or 'wrap-rascal', while a hat, soft felt of the 'wideawake' species, 'broad in the brim', and worn jauntily on one side, gave a sort of roving appearance, or 'modernized gentlemanly pirate' look, to the wearer, who was tall, upright, and sinewy; his face, adorned with a wiry moustache and grizzly beard, struck one at once; deep lined and bronzed, it was a philosopher's; the eyes, whose depths no man could fathom, were large and eloquent, and side by side lurked the iron will of a demon and the tender pity of an angel. His face had all the romance of the ancient Norseman, while his whole mien reminded one of nothing so much as a Viking. . . .

[On their travels,] first we digested the news in the daily papers, an operation never of great length with any one of the three who formed our small party [when W. H. Wills was accompanying them. On a long journey, from Aberdeen to London] Mr. Dickens undertook to provide the 'artful sandwich' and the iced gin punch by way of a 'tiffin,' whilst I arranged to provide the more substantial part of the repast. . . . For the benefit of epicures a description of the 'artful sandwich' (as Mr. Dickens was wont to call it) may not be out of place. A French roll, cut in slices and well buttered; on the buttered side place chopped parsley; and lastly, a hard-boiled egg, cut in slices, with the addition of either anchovy paste, or, better still, the anchovy fish itself. . . . Ever memorable to me will be these my journeyings and their agreeable surroundings, and I trust they will enable me to give the reader some idea of a phase in Mr. Dickens's nature, which was apparent only to a limited circle of friends with whom he felt himself quite at his ease, and to entertain whom, in that genial way of which he seemed to be sole possessor, he would take any amount of pains and trouble. In all his actions the dominant motive was a consideration for others. . . .

[During this tour, he visited Southsea, his birthplace, though they could not identify the house. Talking of his infancy and childhood] he used to say, he *always was* a puny, weak youngster, and never used to join in games with the same zest that other boys seemed to have. He never was remarkable, according to his own account, during his younger days, for anything but violent spasmodic attacks, which used to utterly prostrate him, and for indomitable energy in reading: – cricket, 'chevy', top, marbles, 'peg in the ring', 'tor', 'three holes', or any of the thousand and one boys' games, had no charm for him, save such as lay in watching others play. . . .

Returning to Southsea by another road, we suddenly found ourselves in a sort of elongated 'square', that should be called 'oblong', open at each end, such as is to be met with in Dutch towns; the houses on each side resembled a scene 'set' for the comic business of a pantomime; they were of red brick, with clean windows and white window frames, while green *jalousie* blinds of the most dazzling description added a little to the 'tone' of the place. Here the temptation to Mr. Dickens to indulge his predilections for imitating the frolics of a Clown – of the Grimaldi, Flexmore, and Tom Mathews type – presented itself. The street being entirely free from people, Mr. Dickens mounted three steps leading to one of the houses, which had an enormous brass plate on its green door; and, having given three raps on the doorpost, was proceeding to lie down on the upper step, clown fashion, when the door suddenly opened and a stout woman appeared, to the intense amusement of the 'pantaloon' (myself) and Wills, who immediately beat a retreat in the style known in pantomime as a 'rally', followed by Mr. Dickens with an imaginary policeman after him. The wind, which was very high at the time, added to the frolic, driving Mr. Dickens's hat before it, in the direction of the river, causing us to forget the situation and eagerly chase the hat to catch it ere the frolicsome blast drove it in to the water. Then, and then only, we turned to take a parting look at the scene of action, when, to our dismay, we saw every doorstep and doorway occupied by the amused tenants of the houses. There was another stampede, which was stopped by an open drain, from which emanated an odour of anything but a pleasant character, suddenly making the party pale as ghosts, and necessitating the administration, medicinally, of course, of a strong dose of brandy-and-water at the nearest hotel. . . .

What he underwent from the effects of his cold [during his American readings tour of 1867–8] it is impossible to describe. He could not sleep at night, and rarely, if ever, got up before twelve o'clock in the day. He had to abandon his breakfast, and dine at three, and could take no food until after the work of the evening was over, and then only something very light, in the shape of quail or a devilled bone. The champagne had to be given up during the Readings, and in its place I prepared an egg beaten up in sherry for him every night, to take between the parts; this seemed to do him good, and to refresh him wonderfully. . . . His spirit and determination were of the most indomitable character, and under the most trying circumstances he would be the most cheerful. On many occasions in America, I had been fearful that he would not be able to give his Readings, and but for my knowledge of him and his power of 'coming up to time' when 'time' was called, I should often have despaired of his physical capacity. It was only by a most careful observation that any one could form any idea of the extent of his sufferings, for he made it a rule, in the unselfishness of his nature, never to inflict his own inconveniences on any one else; and as for the public, he held it as a maxim that 'No man had a right to break an engagement with the public if he were able to be out of bed.' . . .

In the afternoon [of 7 February 1868, in Washington], amongst other distinguished persons who called to offer their congratulations, was Mr. Charles Sumner, who, being an old friend, was admitted into Mr. Dickens's apartments, to find him covered with mustard poultices and apparently voiceless. Mr. Sumner, turning to me, said – 'Surely, Mr. Dolby, you are not going to allow Mr. Dickens to read to-night?'

I assured him it was not a question of my 'allowing' him to do so, but a question of Mr. Dickens's determination to read if he were alive. 'I have told Mr. Dickens,' I said, 'at least a dozen times to-day, that it will be impossible for him to read; and but for my knowledge of him and of his wonderful power of changing when he gets to the little table, I should be even more anxious about him than I am.'

I was right in my conjecture, for he had not faced his audience five minutes before, as usual, his powers returned to him, and he went through his evening's task as if he had been in the most robust health. . . .

[Later in this tour, the] exertion of getting himself up to reading pitch, and the fatigue and excitement of reading, resulted in great depression of spirits, which fortunately did not last long; but it necessitated a departure from the usual routine of our Reading life, for instead of the immediate change of costume usual on these occasions with the 'rub down', it was necessary that he should lie down on the sofa in his dressing-room for twenty minutes or half an hour, in a state of the greatest exhaustion, before he could undergo the fatigue even of dressing, and taking during this time about a wineglassful of champagne to give action to his heart. These attacks of nervous depression being over, he would be himself again; and on returning to the hotel would partake of a little soup or strong beef-tea, and spend an hour or two in genial conversation with myself, and sometimes two or three friends, discussing the events of the day and the incidents of the Readings, before retiring to undergo the agonies of another sleepless night. I used to steal into his room at all hours of the night and early morning, to see if he were awake or in want of anything; always though to find him wide awake and as cheerful and jovial as circumstances would admit, never in the least complaining, and only reproaching me for not taking my night's rest. I did not express to him my own misgivings that he might break down at any moment. This caused him at times to think that I did not understand 'that the power of coming up to the mark every night with spirits and spirit may co-exist with the nearest approach to sinking under it', but in reality I did.

Our men though, and those who were not as much with him as I was . . . , could scarcely be made to understand the real state of the case with regard to his health, as they only saw him at his best. The men would receive my account of the bad way in which the Chief was, with the remark, 'It'll be all right at night, sir. The gov'nor's sure to come up smiling when you call time, and the more's wanted out of him, the more you gets.' They were very watchful and devoted to him (as he was to them), and frequently by many little acts of attention showed their love and affection for him. . . .

A favourite subject of conversation with Mr. Dickens was the art of speech-making, which he always said was one of the easiest and simplest things in the world. I remember in England on one occasion, when Mr. Wilkie Collins joined us at supper after a Reading in a small country town, the conversation at supper turned on the subject of speech-making. Mr. Wilkie Collins remarked that he had invariably felt a difficulty when called upon for a speech either at a public meeting or after dinner, adding that for important occasions his habit was to make notes of what he had to say, and keep them before him for reference during the progress of the speech.

As is well known, Mr. Dickens was one of the happiest of speakers, and on all occasions without any notes to assist him in this most difficult of arts. Declaring that to make a speech was the easiest thing in the world, he said the only difficulty that existed was in introducing the subject to be dealt with. 'Now suppose I am the president of a rowing club and Dolby is the honorary secretary. At our farewell dinner, or supper, for the season, I, as president, should propose his health in these words:'

Here he made a speech of the most flattering description, calling on the subject of it for a reply. As I did not feel equal to a response I asked Mr. Collins to try his skill first. He handed the responsibility over to Mr. Wills, who in his turn handed it back to Mr. Dickens, who then told us in a ludicrous speech what the honorary secretary ought to have said, though I am certain no ordinary honorary secretary would ever have dreamt of such a performance. Then I asked Mr. Dickens if he could explain to us his *modus operandi* of preparing an important speech, Mr. Wilkie Collins adding that it would be curious to know what (besides the speech) was passing in his mind during its delivery. He told us that, supposing the speech was to be delivered in the evening, his habit was to take a long walk in the morning, during which he would decide on the various heads to be dealt with. These being arranged in their proper order, he would in his 'mind's eye', liken the whole subject to the tire of a cart wheel – he being the hub. From the hub to the tire he would run as many spokes as there were subjects to be treated, and during the progress of the speech he would deal with each spoke separately, elaborating them as he went round the wheel; and when all the spokes dropped out one by one, and nothing but the tire and space remained, he would know that he had accomplished his task, and that his speech was at an end.

Mr. Wills suggested that if he were in this position, the wheel would whiz round with such rapidity that he would see nothing but space to commence with, and that, without notes or memoranda, in space he would be left – a conclusion in which Mr. Wilkie Collins and I fully concurred.

It was my fortune on many occasions after this to accompany Mr. Dickens when he took the chair at public dinners or meetings, and remembering on all such occasions his plan of action, I have been amused to observe him dismiss the spoke from his mind by a quick action of the finger as if he were knocking it away. . . .

[During the 'Farewell' tour in Britain, Dickens became obsessed with his new *Sikes and Nancy* item and] would listen to no remonstrance in respect of it; at the same time being impressed himself with the dangers by which the subject was beset. . . . I confess to having done all in my power to dissuade him from continuing with it. My reasons for this had reference not so much to the inappropriateness of the subject for Reading purposes – because I knew well that the sensational character of it would be a great attraction – as to the effect which the extra exertion might have on his constitution and the state of his health, which had now begun again to show signs of failing and to assume the old American form; for whether from close application to work during the summer months, or from excessive exercise in the pedestrian line at Gad's Hill, the pains had begun to return in his foot, this time in the right, instead of the left one. . . .

Taking the chances of a travelling life, such as we were in the habit of leading, and with our experiences in this respect, we felt – or thought we did – pretty secure; but there was one point on which we did not feel safe, and that was the uncertain state of health in which Mr. Dickens then was, and had been since his return from America. The pain in the foot was always recurring at inconvenient and unexpected moments, and occasionally his old enemy, the American catarrh, would assert itself; and, although he always spoke of himself as well in other respects, it was evident that these two ailments were telling greatly against him. This being the case, I was more than ever opposed to his continuing with the *Sikes and Nancy* Reading, which, in my knowledge of him, and of *it*, I always regarded as one of the greatest dangers we had to contend against.

As I knew that any further opposition to his ideas about this on my part would only make him the more determined to overcome the difficulty, I ceased talking on the subject, preferring to wait until the Reading had been given in public, when, if it should be coldly received, his own perception of the popular judgment would induce him to abandon it. Nothing but that could affect his resolve, for his idea in preparing it for reading purposes was solely to increase our coffers and to make the remainder of the tour as great a financial success as possible.

When produced in St. James's Hall on Tuesday evening, January 5th (1869), the effect of the *Sikes and Nancy* Reading was all that Mr. Dickens had anticipated from a financial point of view, and from an *artistic* point of view he had no reason to be disappointed; but in the vigour and the earnestness with which it was delivered, it was painfully apparent to his most intimate friends, and those who knew his state of health the best, that a too-frequent repetition of it would seriously and permanently affect his constitution. The terrible force with which the actual perpetration of this most foul murder was described was of such a kind as to render Mr. Dickens utterly prostrate for some moments after its delivery, and it was not until he had vanished from the platform that the public had sufficiently recovered their sense of composure to appreciate the circumstance that all the horrors to which they had been listening were but a story and not a reality.

The reception accorded to this Reading by the press was such as to create a demand for it in future Readings in London and the provinces, a fact which caused him to continue working away at it to make it as perfect for representation as were all the other Readings. The horrible perfection to which he brought it, and its novelty, acted as a charm to him and made him the more determined to go on with it come what might, and all remonstrance to the contrary was unheeded by him, notwithstanding in his own mind he knew with what danger to his constitution he was beset, and that by continuing with this additional labour he was running risks against which he was cautioned by his medical advisers and his friends. . . .

The excitement of the public in these last Scotch Readings [in February 1869] knew no bounds, and if the prices of admission had been doubled there would have been no difficulty in obtaining them. As the fame of the *Murder* Reading had reached Edinburgh, the desire to hear it was so great that not a place was to be obtained in either the first or second seats, and a few minutes after the opening of the gallery doors that portion of the house was full to overflowing.

The great interest taken in this, and the dead silence which prevailed during the delivery of it, had the effect of making Mr. Dickens more vehement, if possible, than on any previous occasion. He worked himself up to a pitch of excitement which rendered him so utterly prostrate, that when he went to his retiring-room (which he reached with difficulty), he was forced to lie on the sofa for some moments, before he could regain strength sufficient to utter a word. It took him but a short time, though, to recover, and after a glass of champagne he would go on the platform again for the final Reading, as blithe and gay as if he were just commencing his evening's work.

These shocks to the nerves were not as easily repelled as for the moment they appeared to be, but invariably recurred later on in the evening, either in the form of great hilarity or a desire to be once more on the platform, or in a craving to do the work over again. After the Edinburgh Reading, Dickens's friends in Edinburgh who had the *entrée* to his dressing-room, having regard to the state of his health, and perhaps being a little overcome and alarmed at what he used jokingly to call his 'murderous instincts', contented themselves with calling in to thank him for the pleasure he had afforded them; and, wishing him an affectionate good-night, declined all invitations to supper, so that we were left to eat this meal by ourselves. During supper he asked me for how many Readings in advance we were advertised.

I replied, 'You are advertised up to and including York on the 11th of next month.'

'That's all right,' he said; 'let us fix the Readings for the remainder of the tour.'

I went to my writing-case and produced my tour list, he at the same time producing his.

We went on with our supper, making notes the while (on our respective lists) of the Readings he had chosen for the various towns; and when we had got through about sixteen of these (a month's work), and seeing that the *Murder* was taking precedence of everything else, I ventured to remark – 'Look carefully through the towns you have given me, and see if you note anything peculiar about them.'

'No,' he replied. 'What is it?'

'Well,' I said, 'out of four Readings a week you have put down three *Murders*.'

'What of that?'

'Simply this,' I said; 'the success of this farewell tour is assured in every way, so far as human probability is concerned. It therefore does not make a bit of difference which of the works you read, for (from what I have seen) the money is safe any way. I am saying this in the interest of your health, and I feel certain that if either Tom or Arthur Chappell were here, he would endorse every word I have said, and would agree with me that the *Carol, Copperfield, Nicholas Nickleby*, or *Marigold*, will produce all the money we can take, and you will be saved the pain of tearing yourself to pieces every night for three nights a week, and to suffer unheard-of tortures afterwards, as you have to do. Reserve the *Murder* for certain of the large towns, just to keep your hand in; and if you do this you will be all the better in health, and we shall be none the worse in pocket. Even if we are, I am sure the Chappells will not regret it, but would do anything and everything to save you unnecessary fatigue.'

'Have you finished?' he said, angrily.

'I have said all I feel on that matter', was my reply.

Bounding up from his chair, and throwing his knife and fork on his plate (which he smashed to atoms), he exclaimed – 'Dolby! your infernal caution will be your ruin one of these days!'

'Perhaps so, sir', I said. 'In this case, though, I hope you will do me the justice to say it is exercised in your interest.'

I left the table, and proceeded to put my tour list in my writing-case. Turning round, I saw he was crying (my eyes were not so clear as they might be), and, coming towards me, he embraced me affectionately, sobbing the while – 'Forgive me, Dolby! I really didn't mean it; and I know you are right. We will talk the matter over calmly in the morning.'

In all my experiences with the Chief, this was the only time I ever heard him address angry words to any one, and these probably would not have been uttered had the conservation taken place under different circumstances and apart from the influence of the excitement of the evening's work. But the storm had passed, and there was an end of it.

The next day was an 'off' day, and we passed the greater portion of it indoors. The weather was too wild to permit of his going out; and even if it had been otherwise he could not have taken walking exercise, for his foot was swathed in what he used to call 'a big work of art'. He was always open to conviction, and did not disdain to defer to the judgment of another in whom he had faith, even though his own mind had been made up on any particular point; and in the frankness of his disposition he admitted that perhaps there was a little too much *Murder* in our future arrangements, and that it would be better in certain places to moderate his instincts in that respect. . . .

[During his London 'Farewell' series, in 1870, he gave three daytime performances] specially for the benefit of the theatrical profession, many of whose members had memorialized Mr. Dickens on the subject. Although these entailed on him a vast deal of additional labour and fatigue, he entered into the Readings for the players with greater zest, I think, than into any others of the course. He wanted to show them how much a single performer could do without the aid and stimulus of any of the ordinary adjuncts of the stage; how many effects of a genuinely startling character could be produced without the help of scenery, costume, limelight, or mechanical contrivancies.

He succeeded to perfection, in the presence even of so thoroughly critical an audience. They applauded every point, cheering each well-known character as the reader, by mere change of voice, manner, and action, brought forward the people of his tales. The presence of a large number of actors and actresses made these morning Readings very lively and pleasant; but the strain was great upon the reader.[2]

This he admitted himself, and in regard to the past he confessed to me at this time that it was madness ever to have given the *Murder* Reading, under the conditions of a travelling life, and worse than madness to have given it with such frequency. . . .

As often as he was in town [during his final months] I was his constant companion, and many a pleasant little dinner we discussed together, at the 'Blue Posts', in Cork Street, and elsewhere; and many a happy night we spent at the establishment, or at a theatre. But all this while I noted with pain the change that was coming over him. I missed the old vivacity and elasticity of spirit, which were always wanting, except when specially called into requisition.

(2) My last interview with Mr. Dickens was on Thursday, June 2nd, 1870, and it took place at the office of *All the Year Round* in Wellington Street, Strand. There was one remarkable feature in connection with this which I think is worth recording. . . . When

Mr. Dickens and myself were not travelling (either on business or pleasure) in London together, there was a standing arrangement to the effect that I should lunch with him at the office every Thursday. At these happy meetings the affairs of the previous week were discussed and plans laid for the coming week. On this particular occasion I was much struck by the alteration in his demeanour – not that he was less genial than usual, but that he appeared to me to be suffering from such great depression of spirits that even his gaiety of manner under these circumstances could not disguise.

The luncheon over and our other business completed I rose to take my departure, and extending my hand to him across the table where he was writing I was greatly shocked at a pained expression I detected in his features. His eyes betrayed the fact that he was suffering great mental agony, for they were becoming suffused with tears. Making an effort to cast off the cause of this emotion (whatever it might have been), he hastily rose from his place at the table and, coming to me in the centre of the room, grasped my hand, and, looking me full in the face, said, 'Good-bye, Dolby, old man'; an expression I had never known him to make, his usual parting words to me being 'Good day', or 'Good night', and these were always followed quickly by an appointment for our next meeting. The unpleasant impression produced on my mind by this circumstance was but momentary, but for days I could not help thinking of it as a singular circumstance.[1]

NOTES

1. As members of Dickens's family, and others, noted, he had a morbid dislike of saying 'Goodbye' and indeed of partings generally: cf. below, II, 357–8, his daughter Katey's account of her last farewell to him, two days before his fatal collapse. Dolby's anecdote, and Katey's, and other evidence, suggest that Dickens was quite aware, in the last weeks of his life, that he was soon to die.

2. Back in 1861 Dickens had remarked, 'I had to give up reading in public, much as I delighted in it; it took too much out of me. I had to change my clothes entirely every time, being as wet through as if I had been drenched to the skin. Writing serials is quite enough work' – Rudolph Lehmann, *An Artist's Reminiscences* (1894) p. 231.

Gad's Hill: Views from the Servants' Hall

VARIOUS

(1) from William R. Hughes, *A Week's Tramp in Dickens-Land*, revised edn (1893) pp. 370–3; (2) from Henry Woodcock, 'The Religious Side of Charles Dickens and His Sister Fanny', *Aldersgate Primitive Methodist Magazine*, Mar 1901, p. 109; (3) *Sunday Dispatch*, 20 Mar 1938. Hughes's interviews with Kentish people who remembered Dickens took place in 1888. Woodcock went to live in Gravesend in the 1860s; a keen admirer of Dickens, he sometimes met him out walking, as he reports (below). Thomas Hill, whom he records, was a local lay preacher. Another member of the Gad's Hill staff interviewed years after Dickens's death – Isaac Armatage, the pageboy – recalled him as 'the best and gentlest master man ever had' – *Dkn*, xxvii (1931) 234.

(1) We are much indebted to Mrs. Budden of Gad's Hill Place for the following interesting particulars which she obtained from Mrs. Easedown, of Higham, 'who was parlour-maid to Mr. Dickens, and left to be married on the 8th of June, the day he was seized with the fit. She says it was her duty to hoist the flag on the top of the house directly Mr. Dickens arrived at Gad's Hill. It was a small flag, not more than fourteen inches square, and was kept in the billiard-room. She says he was the dearest and best gentleman that ever lived, and the kindest of masters. She saw him after he was dead, laid out in the dining-room, when his coffin was covered with scarlet geraniums – his favourite flower. The flower-beds on the lawns at Gad's Hill in his time were always filled with scarlet geraniums; they have since been done away with. Over the head of the coffin was the oil painting of himself as a young man (probably Maclise's portrait) – on one side a picture of "Dolly Varden", and on the other "Kate Nickleby". He gave Mrs. Easedown, on the day she left his service, a photograph of himself with his name written on the back. Each of the other servants at Gad's Hill Place was presented with a similar photograph. She said he was unusually busy at the time of his death, as on the Monday morning he ordered breakfast to be ready during the week at 7.30 ("Sharp, mind") instead of his usual time, 9 o'clock, as he said "he had so much to do

before Friday." But – "Such a thing was never to be", for on the Thursday he breathed his last!'

Mrs. Wright, the wife of Mr. Henry Wright, surveyor of Higham, lived four years at Gad's Hill Place as parlour-maid. . . . She remembers, at the time of her engagement as parlour-maid, that the servants told her to let a gentleman in at the front door who was approaching. She didn't know who it was, as she had never seen Mr. Dickens before. She opened the door, and the gentleman entered in a very upright manner, and after thanking her, looked hard at her, and then walked up-stairs. On returning to the kitchen the servants asked who it was that had just come in. She replied, 'I don't know, but I think it was the master.' 'Did he speak?' they asked. 'No', said she, 'but he looked at me in a very determined way.' Said they, 'He was reading your character, and he now knows you thoroughly', or words to that effect.

As parlour-maid, it was part of her duty to carve and wait on her master specially. The dinner serviettes were wrapped up in a peculiar manner, and Mrs. Wright remembers that Lord Darley's servants were always anxious to learn how the folding was done, but they never discovered the secret. At dinner-parties, it was the custom to place a little 'button-hole' for each guest. This was mostly made up of scarlet geranium (Dickens's favourite flower), with a bit of the leaf and a frond of maidenhair fern. On one occasion in her early days, the dinner-lift (to the use of which she was unaccustomed) broke and ran down quickly, smashing the crockery and bruising her arm. Mr. Dickens jumped up quickly and said, 'Never mind the breakage; is your arm hurt?' As it was painful, he immediately applied arnica to the bruise, and gave her a glass of port wine, 'treating me', Mrs. Wright remarked, 'more like a child of his own than a servant.'

When she was married, and left Gad's Hill, she brought her first child to show her former master. He took notice of it, and asked her what he could buy as a present. She thanked him, and said she did not want anything. On leaving he gently put a sovereign into the baby's little hand, and said, 'Buy something with that.' Mrs. Wright spoke of the great interest which Dickens took in the children's treats at Higham, lending his meadow for them, providing sweets and cakes for the little ones, and apples to be scrambled for. He took great delight in seeing the scrambles. . . .

Both Mrs. Easedown and Mrs. Wright informed us (through Mrs. Budden) that 'Mr. Dickens was the best of masters, and a dear good man; that he gave a great deal away in the parish, and was very much missed; that he frequently went to church and sat in the chancel. . . . When he lived in Higham there used to be a great deal of ague, and he gave away an immense quantity of port wine and quinine.'

(2) When the writer paid his first visit to Shorne [a village near Gad's Hill], he took tea with Mr. Thomas Hill, a thoughtful and much respected local preacher, in a neat, faultessly clean and well-furnished cottage, only a few minutes' walk from Gad's Hill. 'I suppose you know Mr. Dickens?' I remarked. 'I ought to, for I have worked for him for many years, and married my wife from the Hall', was his reply, adding, with evident delight, 'Mrs. Hill nearly always assists when entertainments are given.' At the time of which we write, Mr. Dickens was, perhaps, the most popular writer in England; he was received with *éclat* in the highest circles of English society, and soon after, March, 1870, he was honoured by an interview with Her Majesty the Queen. He was often entertained by persons of the loftiest rank, and he delighted to entertain largely. Mr. Hill said, 'Mr. Dickens likes the domestic servants to share in these entertainments, and insists that they shall never be debarred from the enjoyment, except in cases of extreme necessity.' He added, 'On these occasions his humour, his kindness, his generosity, his uprightness, his consideration for the happiness of his servants, as well as his fun and frolicsomeness, are sun-clear to all who come near him. He is a grand man – a good master, I will assure you, Mr. Woodcock.'

'Oh, yes, he is a thoughtful and tender father, but he hates lying and deception as he hates the devil.' Mr. Hill continued, 'The only time I ever saw him chastise one of his sons was in the open air, and I shall never forget it.' The boy had told a lie, and his father chastised him severely. My friend was himself a tender father, and he pleaded with Mr. Dickens to spare the rod. ' "What!" exclaimed the enraged father, his breath coming in palpitating gasps, "he has told a lie! . . . He has told *me* a lie! . . . He has told *his own father a lie!* Hill! I cannot spare him!" and he did not.' Mr. Hill said, 'When I looked at the poor boy I pitied him; but when I gazed at the sorrowful face of the outraged father, my heart fairly broke down, and I turned aside to weep. The father suffered more than the child. It was a strange sight to witness, and I hope I shall never see the like again.'

(3) George Woolley was a thirteen year-old reluctant gardener-in-the-making when he went to work for Charles Dickens at Gad's Hill, Kent, in 1865 [and was interviewed in 1938 at the age of eighty-six]. 'Remember him?' cupping hand to ear, 'o' course I remember him. I have been with plenty of people since, at big houses and small ones, but I've never known a nicer gentleman to work for than Mr. Charles. He was a toff, he was; always used to wear a white bowler hat and a cutaway coat. You don't see them nowadays.

'Never known him give a cross word to anybody. Though he did like to be alone, and didn't like to be disturbed. Opposite the house was a sort of wood the master called the Wilderness. He used to go over there to write. . . . I used to hear what sounded like someone making a speech. I wondered what it was at first, and then I found out it was Mr. Dickens composing his writing out loud. He was working on *The Mystery of Edwin Drood* then. . . .

'He was a very generous gentleman. The house was always full of guests . . . and if any of his friends passed through the village without calling to see him he was really cross. . . . He had a nice laugh and always seemed good tempered. He was president of the village cricket team, and if there was a deficit in the funds at the end of the season he always used to make it up.'

The Squire of Gad's Hill

LOCAL RESIDENTS

Authorship of these items is given in the Notes. As in the previous item, W. R. Hughes's investigations are a notable source; for him and for Henry Woodcock, see the headnote to that item. Dickens disliked putting on squirearchal airs, but, as a substantial householder, besides being famous, affluent and a man of good will, he inevitably performed some such function and, at the end of his first year's residence at Gad's Hill, he told Forster that 'nothing had gratified him so much as the confidence with which his poorer neighbours treated him' (*Life*, viii, vi, 685). He was on good terms, too, with some at least of his richer neighbours and was a frequent visitor to the Chatham officers' mess – see General Sir Blinden Blood, *Four Store Years and Ten*, quoted in *Dkn*, xxx (1934) 216 – though some accounts state that, as a result of the separation scandal in 1858, 'Neighbouring

9. Portrait of Dickens in his study at Tavistock House (1859), by W. P. Frith

Frith wrote that this portrait gained 'the universal approbation of all Dickens's family and friends . . . who said "At last we have the real man"; and best satisfied of all was John Forster' (who had commissioned it). 'The picture is, indeed, all I wished – more than I dared to hope', Forster told Frith: but Dickens thought that it made him look 'a little too much as if my next door neighbour were my deadly foe, uninsured, and I had just received tidings of his house being afire; otherwise very good.'

10. Photograph of Dickens (1860s), by John Watkins

Watkins was a respected photographer, with a studio in Regent Street. Dickens sat for him a number of times between 1858 and 1866. Commenting on a particularly unsuccessful 'carte' which the family had received with 'a general howl of horror', he apologised to Watkins 'for being (innocently) a difficult subject. When I once excused myself to Ary Scheffer [the French painter] while sitting to him, he received the apology as strictly his due, and said with a vexed air: "At this moment, *mon cher* Dickens, you look more like an energetic Dutch admiral than anything else"; for which I apologised again.'

11. Photograph at Gad's Hill (1860s), by Mason & Co.

'Mr Mason, a most excellent photographic artist who came down frequently to Gad's Hill, executed . . . the portrait which formed the frontispiece to *Edwin Drood,* a very good likeness; but there was one in a family group taken some time before, in the front porch at Gad's Hill with Dickens, his two daughters and their aunt, Mr Charles Collins and Mr Chorley, which I consider admirable, and often wished it had been enlarged – I mean the single figure of Dickens himself. It is very animated, and gives a good impression of his countenance.' – Mary Boyle.

12. Photograph of Dickens (1868), by Ben Gurney

Most of the photographs of Dickens were 'so wonderfully *unlike* him', wrote
George Dolby, that during the American readings tour 'I prevailed on him to sit to
Mr Ben Gurney in New York, who succeeded in producing the only good
photograph of him in existence.' On the Gurney photographs, see *Dickensian*
(1958 and 1978).

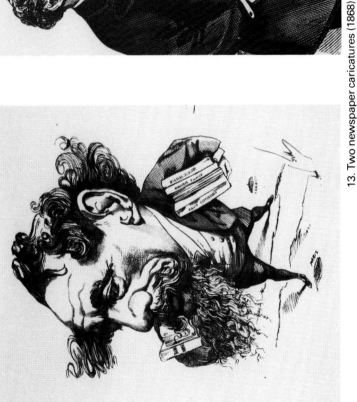

13. Two newspaper caricatures (1868)

By André Gill, *L'Eclipse*, Paris (14 June 1868). According to Percy Fitzgerald, Dickens always said that the best likeness of himself was 'one of those gigantic heads on tiny legs, a form once in high favour'. Fitzgerald mentions the one by 'Sem', another French caricaturist, but Dickens more likely had this Gill caricature in mind.

From an American newspaper, at the end of the American readings tour: George Dolby, Dickens's manager, on the right. The earnings totalled, in fact, $228,000, less $39,000 expenses.

1870.

14. Frontispiece to *Edwin Drood* (1870), engraved by J. H. Baker, from a
photograph taken in 1868 by Mason & Co.

'A very good likeness' – Mary Boyle.

15. Charles Dickens: Sketches from Memory (February 1870), by 'Spy'
(Leslie Ward)

16. Dickens with Benjamin Disraeli, Gad's Hill in the background *(The Tailor and Cutter,* 16 July 1870)

'Those who were acquainted with the personal appearance of the lamented and distinguished author, will admit that the representation is a prototype of the original, as he might have been seen shortly before his sudden and premature death. The dress consists of a frock coat of the most fashionable form, of medium length in both waist and skirt, which are also plain; the lapels are made full and bold and made to turn low down. The foreparts are cut small at the waist as the coat is not intended to button. The sleeve hands are furnished with cuffs three and a quarter inches deep, and two holes and buttons are worked in each. The vest is cut with a roll collar and to button a medium height. The trousers are of the style most appreciated by gentlemen of taste and those who are always well dressed, but never seen wearing garments possessing an extreme character.' – *Tailor and Cutter.*

gentry fell off from intimacy. Society criticised the relations existing between him and his wife's sister' – N. S. Dodge, 'Seasonable Words about Dickens', *Overland Monthly* (San Francisco), Jan 1871, p. 82, quoted by F. G. Kitton, *Dickensiana* (1886) p. 39. There are many accounts of Dickens's umpiring at local cricket matches held in the Gad's Hill field, or officiating at the Boxing Day sports there, 'acting as starter, standing upon an old wheel-barrow and using an old muzzle-loader for the purpose' –*Dkn*, xxx (1934) 117.

Mr. Henry Whitehead . . . well remembers Charles Dickens when the latter was living at Gadshill, where Whitehead was a schoolboy. In the fields near to Gadshill House Whitehead and other boys were accustomed to spend their half-holidays in scaring birds from the crops and otherwise diverting themselves. 'Dickens,' said Mr. Whitehead, 'in his gaiters, and with his stick and dog, often used to come and talk to us in the course of his walks.' On one memorable occasion he even joined the youngsters in an impromptu meal of roasted potatoes in the hedge bottom. It so happened that Whitehead was knocked down by a passing vehicle in the main road near Dickens's residence, and he still recalls with peculiar pleasure the kind way in which Dickens came out from his house and rendered 'first aid'. He took quite a fatherly interest in the progress of the lad's recovery, and constantly sent to inquire about him.[1]

The present writer [walking in the Chatham area] dogged the novelist's steps, and met him at three or four different corners, that his personality might impress itself indelibly upon memory and imagination. He was dressed in shooting attire, and looked more like a jockey than a *littérateur*. . . . When we knew him, he was worn by slowly rolling years, pale, fragile, and stooping, but his spirit was as buoyant as ever, if we might judge from the frolicsomeness of his movements. . . . We sometimes met Mr. Dickens in the most out-of-the-way places. . . . Mr. Dickens always had a few kind words and a handshake for those he met on the road and in the fields, however poor the passer-by might be. Oftener than once we had the pleasure of a chat with him, and it was a pleasure indeed to converse with so humane a man.

But our greatest pleasure was to watch him on a summer evening, after his return from London, bringing a batch of printer's proofs with him. Like most writers of books, he was as pleased with his proofs as a child with its toy, or a mother with her first-born child. With the long flying sheets flung over his left-arm, and ac-companied by Miss Hogarth (Mrs. Dickens' sister), he walked up and down the lawn in the garden, reading aloud, and making corrections.[2]

John J. Sharp . . . was from 1860 to 1900 in charge of the Rochester Post Office, and saw Mr. Dickens very, very often. While the nearest Post Office Station to Gadshill was Higham, they only had one delivery there a day, so that most of Mr. Dickens's mail was sent to Rochester, and every day Miss Georgina Hogarth, generally accompanied by Dickens's oldest daughter, Mamie Dickens, would drive to Rochester in the well-known basket carriage and stop at the Post Office for their mail. Dickens himself would frequently walk into Rochester from Gadshill, either meeting the ladies at the Post Office or immediately across the other side of the street. He was sure to come to Rochester or to Chatham, when there was a sham fight going on. He would never miss one, and while Longfellow was stopping at Gadshill, the two were invariably seen together at whatever sporting affair came off. Sharp describes Dickens as having deep lines in his face, and when walking by himself and unobserved, apparently acting some character, as you could see his face in constant motion. He always was theatrically dressed, and his voice was the most captivating possessed by any man he had ever met. Whoever heard him speak came under his spell, and, of course, everybody in Rochester knew him. . . . Mr. Sharp states that numerous names appearing in Dickens's novels were taken from Rochester people, Mr. Sharp remembering a Dorrit family very well indeed.[3]

'Yes, I was a competitor in the sports held by Charles Dickens on Boxing Day, 1869.' Thus Mr. Maunder (born 1858 and now a resident in Sydney). . . . He proceeded with his reminiscences of Dickens. 'He was in our shop frequently, and what Charles Dickens bought he paid for and what we delivered to Gadshill he settled weekly. He used to drive a wagonette, and many a time he has spoken to me as I wrapped up his parcels, and he often had long chats with my mother. . . . Remember him? Why, just as though it were yesterday. He was well known to everyone, and had a hearty word for the most humble. Why, the very dogs knew Dickens – and Dickens knew the dogs. My brother and I used to go up weekly for the laundry to Gadshill, and regularly received from Dickens two shillings to divide between us. Then again, when there was a supper party on there I was the one to open the oysters, and many a dozen I've opened, too. . . .

'Dickens was very fond of children, as you've probably heard. Well, I can vouch for this, and when I remember those Boxing Day sports down behind the old orchard, and his keen interest in them, I wonder again at the time this busy man spent over such trifles. . . . Dickens gave prizes for the winners. . . .'

Asked if he remembered Dickens's love of pet animals, he replied: – 'There were all sorts of birds at Gadshill, also cats and many dogs. Talking of dogs reminds me of the two mastiffs he had, one on each side of the back gate, chained in such a manner that they could just lick one another's noses. There was no way of getting past them, I assure you. [He tells an anecdote about Dickens's mastiff being chased off the premises by the shop's cat and dog.] I can hear his merry laugh now as I recall the incident.'[4]

We had an interesting chat [writes W. R. Hughes] with Mr. Franklin Homan, Auctioneer, Cabinet-maker, and Upholsterer of High Street, Rochester. Our informant did a good deal of work for Charles Dickens at Gad's Hill Place, and remarked 'he was one of the nicest customers I ever met in my life – so thoroughly precise and methodical. If anything had to be done, he knew exactly what he wanted, and gave his instructions accordingly. He expected every one who served him to be equally exact and punctual.'

The novelist wrote to Mr. Homan from America respecting the furnishing of two bedrooms, describing in detail how he wished them fitted up – one was maple, the other white with a red stripe. . . . The curtains separating them from the dressing-rooms were ordered to be of Indian pattern chintz. When Dickens came home and saw them complete, he said, 'It strikes me as if the room was about to have its hair cut – but it's my fault, it must be altered'; so crimson damask curtains were substituted. In the little billiard-room near the dining-room was a one-sided couch standing by the window, which did not seem to please the master of Gad's Hill Place. He said to Mr. Homan one day, 'Whenever I see that couch, it makes me think the window is squinting.' The result was that Mr. Homan had to make a window-seat instead. . . .

Upon being interrogated as to whether he knew Charles Dickens, our guide [at Rochèster Cathedral, 'the venerable verger' Mr. Miles,] immediately answers with a smile – 'Knew him! yes. He came here very often, and I knew him very well. The fact is, they want to make me out to be "Tope"'. And indeed there appears to be such a relevancy in the association, that we frequently find ourselves addressing him as 'Mr. Tope', at which he good-humouredly laughs. He further states that Dickens was frequently in Rochester, and especially so when writing *Edwin Drood*, and appeared to be studying the Cathedral and its surroundings very attentively.

The next question we put is – 'Was there ever such a person as Durdles?' to which he replies, 'Of course there was – a drunken old German stonemason, about thirty years ago, who was always prowling about the Cathedral trying to pick up little bits of broken stone ornaments, carved heads, crockets, finials, and such like, which he carried about in a cotton handkerchief, and which may have suggested to Dickens the idea of the "slouching" Durdles and his inseparable dinner bundle. He used to work for a certain Squire N——.' His earnings mostly went to 'The Fortune of War' – now called 'The Life-Boat' – the inn where he lodged.

Mr. Miles . . . considers 'Deputy' (the imp-like satellite of Durdles and the 'Kinfreederel') to be decidedly a street Arab, the type of which is more common in London than in Rochester. He thinks that the fact of the rooms over the gatehouse having once been occupied by an organ-blower of the Cathedral may have prompted Dickens to make it the residence of the choir-master. . . .

We had the pleasure of a long and interesting conversation with Mr. James Hulkes, J. P., a very near neighbour of Charles Dickens during the whole of the time that he resided at Gad's Hill Place. . . . He remarked, 'I fear I cannot be of much use to you by giving information about Mr. Dickens, as I only knew him as a kind friend, a very genial host, and a most charming companion; to the poor he was always kind – a deserving beggar never went from his house unrelieved.' . . . Mr. Hulkes spoke of the pleasant parties at Gad's Hill Place, at which he met Mr Forster, Mr. Wilkie Collins, Mr. Percy Fitzgerald, Mr. Marcus Stone, Mr. H. F. Chorley, and many others; and observed that, on the occasion of charades and private theatricals there, Charles Dickens was always in fine form. . . . In connection with charades, Mr. Hulkes alluded to Dickens's remarkable facility for 'guessing a subject fixed on when he was out of the room, in half a dozen questions'; and related the story of how at the young people's game of 'Yes and No', he found out the proper answer to a random question fixed upon by Mr. Charles Collins, one of the company, in his absence, which was, 'The top-boot of the left leg of the head post-boy at Newman's Yard, London.' . . .

We had a most interesting chat with Mr. William Stocker

Trood . . . for many years landlord of the Sir John Falstaff at Gad's Hill. He said Mr. Dickens was a very nice man to speak to, and Mrs. Dickens was a very nice lady. They were always kind and pleasant as neighbours, but Mr. Dickens did not talk much. Said Mr. Trood:–'When I was at Higham, Mr. Dickens used to say no one could put in a word; I had all the talk to myself.' The sons were all very pleasant; in fact, he liked the family very much indeed. . . .

Mrs. Master, the cheerful and obliging landlady [at the Crispin and Crispianus Inn, Strood], who has lived here thirty years, describes Dickens, when on one of his walks, as habited in low shoes not over-well mended, loose large check-patterned trousers that sometimes got entangled in the shoes when walking, a brown coat thrown open, sometimes without waistcoat, a belt instead of braces, a necktie which now and then got round towards his ear, and a large-brimmed felt hat, similar to an American's, set well at the back of his head. In his hand he carried by the middle an umbrella, which he was in the habit of constantly swinging, and if he had dogs (a not unfrequent occurrence), he had a small whip as well. He walked in the middle of the road at a rapid pace, upright, but with his eyes cast down as if in deep thought. When he called at the Crispin for refreshment, usually a glass of ale (mild sixpenny – bitter ale was not drawn in those days), or a little cold brandy and water, he walked straight in, and sat down at the corner of the settle on the right-hand side where the arm is, opposite the fire-place; he rarely spoke to any one, but looked round as though taking in everything at a glance.

Once he and a friend were sheltering there during a thunderstorm, and while Dickens stood looking out of the window he saw opposite a poor woman with a baby, who appeared very worn, wet, and travel-stained. She too was sheltering from the rain. 'Call her in here,' said Dickens. Mrs. Masters obeyed. 'Now,' said he, 'draw her some brandy.' 'How much?' she asked. 'Never mind,' he answered, 'draw her some.' The landlady drew her four-pennyworth, the quantity generally served. 'Now,' said Dickens to the woman, 'drink that up', which she did, and soon seemed refreshed. Dickens gave her a shilling, and remarked to Mrs. Masters that 'now she will go on her way rejoicing'. The story is a trivial one, but the units make the aggregate, and it sufficiently indicates his kindness of heart and thoughtfulness for others. . . . Mrs. Masters, whose recollections of Dickens are very vivid, said – 'Lor! we never thought much about him when he was alive; it was only when his death took place that we understood what a great man he was.' . . .

Our next informant was Mr. J. Couchman, master-builder and undertaker of Strood. . . . From Mr. Couchman's standpoint as a tradesman, it is interesting to record his experience of Dickens in his own words. 'Mr. Dickens,' he says, 'was always very straightforward, honourable, and kind, and paid his bills most regularly. The first work I did for him was to make a dog-kennel; I also put up the chalet at Gad's Hill. . . . '⁵ Mr. Couchman recalls an interesting custom that was maintained at Gad's Hill. There were a number of tin check plates, marked respectively 3d. and 6d. each, which enabled the person to whom they were given to obtain an equivalent in refreshment of any kind at the Sir John Falstaff. The threepenny checks were for the workmen, and the sixpenny ones for the tradesmen. The chief housemaid had the distribution of these checks to persons employed in the house, the head-gardener to those engaged in the gardens, and the coachman to those in the stables. On one occasion, our informant remembers when his men were engaged upon some work at Gad's Hill, such checks were given out to them, and that he also had one offered to him; but, recollecting that his position as a master scarcely entitled him to the privilege, he stated his objections to the housemaid, who said in reply that it was a pity to break an old custom, he had better have one. 'So,' says our informant, 'I had a sixpenny ticket with the others, and obtained my refreshment.'

Dr. Steele [the local surgeon, whose attendance on Dickens included his being summoned after the fatal collapse in 1870] had dined several times at Gad's Hill Place, and was impressed with Dickens's wonderful powers as a host. He never absorbed the whole of the conversation to himself, but listened attentively when his guests were speaking, and endeavoured, as it were, to draw out any friends who were not generally talkative. He liked each one to chat about his own hobby in which he took most interest. . . . Dr. Steele mentions a conversation once with Dickens about Gad's Hill and Shakespeare's description of it. He (the doctor) considers that Shakespeare could not have described it so accurately if he had not been there, and Dickens agreed with him in this opinion. Possibly he may have stayed at the 'Plough', which was an inn on the same spot as, or close to, the 'Falstaff'. The place must have been much wooded at that time, and Shakespeare might have been there on his way to Dover. . . .

The doctor observes that Dickens was not much of a Church-goer. He went occasionally to Higham, and used to give the vicar assistance for the poor and distressed. Dickens and Miss Hogarth asked Dr. Steele to point out objects of charity worthy of relief, and they gave him money for distribution. He remarks that Dickens did not care much about associating with the local residents, going out to dinners, etc. Most of the principal people of Rochester would have been glad of the honour of his presence as a guest, but he rarely accepted invitations, preferring the quietude of home. [Hughes here has a footnote: 'Miss Hogarth informs me that her brother-in-law frequently dined out in the neighbourhood, accompanied by his daughter and herself.'] He considered him a most genial sort of man; 'he always looked you straight in the face when speaking'. . . .

We make the acquaintance of Mr. William James Budden of Chatham, who informs us that Charles Dickens was better known there in his latter years for his efforts, by readings and otherwise, to place the Mechanics' Institute on a sound basis and free from debt. . . . [Hughes quoted the account of the 'Dullborough' Mechanics' Institute from *The Uncommercial Traveller*.]

We presently meet with another representative of the class of village labourer at Upper Higham, a cheery old man [who recalled] 'Mr. Dickens was a nice sort of man – very much liked – missed a great deal when he died – poor people and the like felt the miss of him. He was a man as shifted a good deal of money in the place. You see, he had a lot of friends – kept a good many horses, – and then there was the men to attend to 'em, and the corn-chandler, the blacksmith, the wheelwright, and others to be paid – the poor – and such-like – felt the miss of him when he died.' . . . On another occasion we met, in the same place, a third specimen of village labourer, 'a mender of roads', who knew Charles Dickens. Said our informant, 'You see, Mr. Dickens was a very liberal man; he held his head high up when he walked, and went at great strides.' The 'mender of roads' was some years ago a candidate for a vacant place as under-gardener at Gad's Hill, but the situation was filled up just an hour before he applied for it. He said Mr. Dickens gave him half-a-crown, and afterwards always recognised him when he met him with a pleasant nod, or cheerfully 'passed the time of day'. We heard in many places that Dickens was 'always kindly' in this way to his own domestics, and to the villagers in a like station of life to our intelligent friend 'the mender of roads'. A fourth villager, a groom, who had been in his present situation for twenty years, said: – 'Both the old gentleman and young Mr. Charles were very much liked in Higham. There wasn't a single person in the place, I believe, but what had a good word for them.'

Mrs. Taylor, formerly school-mistress at Higham, who came there in 1860 . . . , knew the novelist well, and used to see him almost every day when he was at home. She said, 'If I had met him and did not know who he was, I should have set him down as a good-hearted English gentleman.' He was very popular and much liked in the neighbourhood. On his return from America, in the first week of May, 1868, garlands of flowers were put by the villagers across the road from the railway station to Gad's Hill. There was a flag at Gad's (a Union Jack, she thinks), which was always hoisted when Dickens was at home. He never read at Higham, and never came to the school; but he always allowed the use of the meadow at the back of Gad's Hill Place for the school treats, either of church or chapel, and contributed to such treats sweets and what not. . . .

During our visit [to Cobham Hall, Lord Darnley's seat] we venture to ask the portly housekeeper is she remembers Charles Dickens? The ray of delight that illumines her good-natured countenance is simply magical. 'Oh,' she says, 'I liked Mr. Dickens very much. He was always so full of fun. Oh! oh! oh!' the recollection of which causes a fit of suppressed laughter, which 'communicates a blancmange-like motion to her fat cheeks', and she adds: 'He used to dine here, and was always very popular with the family, and in the neighbourhood.' . . . [6]

A few days after Dickens's death an Englishman, deeply grieved at the event, made a sort of pilgrimage to Gad's Hill – to the home of the great novelist. He went into the famous Sir John Falstaff Inn near at hand, and in the effusiveness of his honest emotions he could not avoid taking the country waiter into his confidence. 'A great loss this of Mr. Dickens,' said the pilgrim. 'A very great loss to us, sir', replied the waiter, shaking his head; 'he had all his ale sent in from this house!'[7]

NOTES

1. Arthur Humphreys, 'Links with Charles Dickens', *Dkn*, XIV (1918) 65.

2. Henry Woodcock, 'The Religious Side of Charles Dickens and the Sister Fanny', *Aldersgate Primitive Methodist Magazine*, Mar 1901, pp. 108–9.

3. Henry Alexander, 'The Postmaster of Rochester in Dickens's Days', *Dkn*, XIX (1923) 221–2.

4. 'A Sydney Man who knew Dickens', *Dkn*, IX (1913) 160–1.
5. But see p. 187 above for another chalet-erector.
6. W. R. Hughes, *A Week's Tramp in Dickens-land*, revised edn (1893) pp. 85–6, 120–1, 195–6, 207–8, 217–8, 225, 240–1, 269, 365–6, 369, 386.
7. *Tit-Bits*, 28 Jan 1882, quoted by F. G. Kitton, *Dickensiana* (1886) p. 492.

Guests at Gad's Hill

FRANCIS FINLAY AND OTHERS

[Francis D. Finlay (1832–1917), proprietor and editor of the Belfast *Northern Whig*, sent a friend this memorandum of his second visit to Gad's Hill, 9–12 June 1862.]

Monday. Left London-bridge station at 2.30 on Monday June 9, and at Higham station was met by Charles Dickens with his Irish car. Drove me over to Gad's Hill Place, where was most kindly received by Mary Dickens, Georgina Hogarth, and Mrs. Charles Collins (formerly Kate Dickens). Introduced to Charles Collins. Played several games of billiard bagatelle with C. D. and afterwards with C. C. Dinner at 6. Took in M. D. Everything very nice. Very pleasant talk. Played whist in the evening, and had a lot of chat before going to bed at 11.30. . . .

Tuesday. After breakfast walked about the grounds, chatted, wrote letters, and in the afternoon drove in to Gravesend with C. D. to meet Mr. Thos. A. Trollope, the author of *Filippo Strozzi* and other works (son of Mrs. Trollope the novelist), who lives in Italy and has been there 20 years. He is a very odd looking, but most agreeable man, very clever and forcible. Came home with him to lunch, and then we all went to play croquet on the lawn, in which we were busily engaged, with great spirit, when Mr. Fechter arrived. The game went on till dinner when Captain Goff came up from Chatham and Frank Dickens from London. Dinner exceedingly elegant, and a profusion of good talk, Fechter being admirable. After dinner croquet again until it was too dark to see any more, and then we all came in and played a most lively game of vingt-et-un until bed-time.

Wednesday. After breakfast we had croquet as usual, performed by the whole party. Mr. Trollope went away at 11, we had lunch at 1, and then Mr. Fechter went back to London, escorting Miss Dickens who was going up to the Lord Mayor's for a soirée there this evening, and to stay all night there. After they left, C. D., C. C., Miss Hogarth and I went out for a stroll, got caught in a tremendous shower, and were drenched. Came home, changed and dined (elegantly as usual) and after dinner we had some 'bounding ball' practice on the lawn, by C. D., Frank D., C. C. and myself, very good exercise indeed. Chat in the evening and whist, C. D. and I partners against Miss Hogarth and C. C. In the evening had a very long and most agreeable talk with Miss Hogarth, C. D's sister-in-law, who is a really delightful person, plain, unassuming, totally unaffected and of singularly pleasant and easy manner. After whist, a long chat, telling stories, riddles and conundrums and to bed at 11. All to break up in different directions in the morning.

Thursday. The whole pleasant party broke up. Mr. and Mrs. Collins went home to Hyde Park Gate. Miss Hogarth and Mr. C. D. to Wellington Street, and I back to Sloane Street. And so ended perhaps the pleasantest visit I ever made, or may ever make.[1]

[George Dolby, Dickens's Readings manager (see above, II, 257–68), describes life at Gad's Hill. Its entrance hall] immediately impressed one with the idea of an amount of comfort, regularity, and order not usually met with in other houses; while it also suggested a hospitality of the most genial character to come – a hospitality such as one might have been led to expect by the kindest of receptions from the host himself at the railway station of Higham, two and a half miles distant from the house. A drive through the pleasantest of the Kentish country, either on an 'outside' Irish jaunting car; or, in fine weather, in a basket carriage, with the nattiest of ponies, driven by Mr. Dickens; or, in wet weather, with a brougham drawn by the most knowing and best trained of cobs with a 'hogmain'; always escorted by three or four enormous dogs of the Mount St. Bernard, mastiff, or Newfoundland species, brought the visitor to the house. . . .

A peculiarity of the household was the fact that, except at table, no servant was ever seen about. This was because the requirements of life were always ready to hand, especially in the bed-rooms. Each of these rooms contained the most comfortable of beds, a sofa, and easy-chair, caned-bottom chairs – in which Mr. Dickens had a great belief, always preferring to use one himself – a large-sized writing-table, profusely supplied with paper and envelopes of every conceivable size and description, and an almost daily change of new quill pens. There was a miniature library of books in each room, a comfortable fire in winter, with a shining copper kettle in each fireplace; and on a side-table, cups, saucers, tea-caddy, teapot, sugar and milk, so that this refreshing beverage was always attainable, without even the trouble of asking for it. . . .

There was no specified time for the guests to be at breakfast, that meal being on the table from nine to ten, or half-past; and unless some early excursion to a place of note in the neighbourhood had been arranged, the visitors were left to do as they pleased in the morning; Mr. Dickens, as a rule, taking a turn or two round the domain to see that everything was in order outside as well as inside the house, visiting, each in its turn, the gardens, stables, kennels, and afterwards devoting himself to his literary duties and correspondence. . . .

[After dinner there] came an hour or two in the drawing-room, where Miss Dickens and Miss Georgina Hogarth held their genial court – it was all geniality at 'Gad's'. After this the gentlemen adjourned to the billiard-room, where, before going to bed, some little time was spent in the enjoyment of some excellent cigars and a walk round the table to the 'click' of the balls, either in a game at 'pool' or a 'contest' at billiards, Mr. Dickens being fond of contests, for, he used to say, 'it brings out the mettle'. Then, so far as the host was concerned, the day was done, for it was his invariable habit to retire to bed at midnight – but without imposing any condition upon his guests, that they should follow his example – the most intimate of his male friends present, if none of his sons were there, being delegated 'host' in his absence, with strict injunctions to 'see the gas out all right', and to take great care of the keys of the sideboard until morning. . . .

One of the most delightful days of [Dolby's final visit, in 1870] was occupied by a drive from Gad's Hill to Canterbury. . . . Two post carriages were turned out with postillions, in the red jackets of the old Royal Dover Road, buckskin breeches, and top-boots into the bargain. The preparations for this new pilgrimage to Canterbury were of the most lavish description, and I can see now the hampers and wine baskets . . . packed in the carriages. [Lunch was taken in a wood, and] Dickens would not let us start again until every vestige of our visit to the wood in the shape of lobster shells and other *débris* had been removed.[2]

[Charles Eliot Norton (1827–1908), the distinguished American art-historian and literary critic, met Dickens in Boston in 1868, and visited him at Gad's Hill that summer. From that 'delightful home' he wrote to his mother about Dickens's 'delightful hospitality. . . . The whole family together and individually are peculiarly attractive and pleasant, and the whole life of the house seems to be entirely sweet and affectionate and simple. . . . ' His wife Susan wrote a fuller account of their visit. Dickens had met them at the station in London] looking fresh and brisk in a suit of grey linen and felt hat to match, a flower in his buttonhole, his hands on his hips, his eyes intently fixed upon the crowd. In a moment he saw us, and gave us a welcome to England and Gad's Hill as cordial as one could wish. He had as usual, when it was possible, a carriage to himself, and when we left the Station we three were alone. . . . I looked for the 'tricks and the manners' of which I had so often heard, but my time was quite thrown away. As the train rushed on he talked with the greatest animation, described all the wonderful engineering of the roads on that side of London, people, especially the Leweses, whose genius and talents he fully appreciated, but whose 'ugliness' seemed to amuse him. 'They really are the ugliest couple in London.'[3] Then he spoke of his readings in England and America, of all the hospitality he had received there, of his great desire to go to Australia where he then had one son (now two); then the whistle blew and we got out at 'Higham by Rochester, Kent'.

A little carriage for four persons was at the Station, he jumped on to the box and we rattled off to Gad's Hill. The grounds about it are in no way particularly pretty for England. . . . On the other side of the road, opposite the house, he has a pretty bit of land and on it a Swiss Chalet, which Fechter had sent him, which he used as a summer work-room, and in order to reach it without, as it were, leaving his own grounds, he had tunnelled the Rochester high road which divided his property in two. At the back of the house was a good-sized garden separated from a fine open field by a low English wall. The views from the ground floor of the house were pleasant, and upstairs on Mr. Dickens' side, they were quite lovely – of upland Kentish meadows, somewhat leafy, and Rochester with its Cathedral and ivy covered tower.

The house itself was not in any respect pretty, but it had very pleasant things about it, and had all over, inside and out, upstairs and down, the look of a home, and a fitting home for him. . . . On the right hand side of the hall was a little library, the door of which was a sham book-case, with sham books for all of which he had painted humorous titles. On a table in the window lay the manuscript of *David Copperfield*, a perfect specimen of most careful work – there seemed the half of another 'David' in correction, but the hand never varied or became indistinct. The book shelves were full of novels, poetry, history, not suggesting a library but simply individual taste. Behind the little library was a 'billiard room'. Upstairs over the library was Mamie's bedroom, pretty and French like herself; over the drawing room Georgina's, and over the dining room Mr. Dickens's. The hall upstairs was full of engravings and books and pleasantly furnished. On a table stood a great china bowl of rose-leaves. Over the billiard room was the spare-chamber which we had, a spacious cheerful room, overlooking the garden at the back and the 'home field'.

Mamie and Georgina were in the drawing room to receive us when we arrived; the former cordial, sweet, lady-like and a little bit shy, the latter quiet, but most hospitable, and both making you like them at once. After Dickens had told them his news, and after we had had 'afternoon tea' we all separated, but before this Mrs. Collins (his youngest daughter) had come in with her husband, and [Henry Fothergill] Chorley the old musical critic. Charles and Mr. Dickens went out into the 'home field' to watch a game of cricket, and I went to my room, the perfection of comfort and exquisite freshness.

At seven o'clock we all reassembled, a large party, with other guests, among them officers from Chatham, one of them with his young wife, a stranger to everybody. Dickens, punctual to the minute, came in fresh, animated, alive to every one's interests, and in a moment had roused us completely – no one was to go to sleep there! The little lady from Chatham and I sat on either side of him at dinner – his vivacity never flagged, nor was it for one person alone. He appeared to hear what every one at the table said and turned from one end of it to the other with the utmost rapidity, told stories, talked, tête à tête, gave a toast, in short was the life of the dinner and without seeming to make any effort or ever talking in loud boisterous tones. Of course every one was likely to be silent when he talked, but then he never when liveliest was noisy.

After dinner the gentlemen soon came into the drawing room, and again Dickens seemed entirely given up to the interests of his guests, attentive to the officer's wife (a dull little woman with a decoration of lockets which amused him) and indeed to every one, the stupidest not excepted. We all stood for a time round the piano playing at words with letters. Very soon Dickens moved off to talk to the little lady who was too shy to play, but whom he evidently managed to set at her ease, and then seeing that my forces had given out he came and sat down by me taking Georgina's place and sending her off to his first charge. He talked first of our war – Georgina had been showing me a volume of photographs of Sheridan's Campaign, which had been given to him in America; he carefully avoided expressing opinions which might jar upon mine, but when I spoke of the treatment of our prisoners by the South, he expressed the utmost horror of its conduct and said that, had it not been for that, its position in spite of our success would now be very different. Then he told me much of Miss Coutts's 'refuge', or whatever it was called, for the unhappy prostitutes of London, of the Parish Refuges where by night they might expect a shelter, but which being small provided one might almost say for *none*.[4] How he had often been of a winter's night to one or other of these wretched places, and had seen the crowds of these poor starving creatures so great that there was no possibility of sheltering them. Once he had found them in such numbers outside one of these places (it was of a winter's night, and in a driving storm,) that he had gone in, confronted the keeper and insisted upon being assured with his own eyes that his house was full – he would otherwise expose him the next morning. The poor man showed the quarters and only too easily proved that the fault could not be laid upon his shoulders. Dickens established the poor women for that night, but went home, he said, feeling that it was 'hopeless'. Most of the women came from the country, often were the hop-pickers, very young girls, who when the work of a short season was over were absolutely destitute. They came to London in other cases honestly desirous of procuring work, and after *starving*, according to their individual ability, they took the only means left them of getting a crust.

Then he told me of his visits to various prisons, and how on one occasion his power of judging of character by expression had been singularly tested, and utterly routed. He had gone to a great London jail, and, having seen innumerable wretched creatures, he was shown into a cell where sat motionless, with a baby in her arms, born in the prison, a very, very young woman, 'a perfect Madonna'. He looked at her for a long time before speaking, and the more he watched her the more he was convinced that she must be innocent.

He knew no more than that she was charged with murder. He turned to the jailor after a time and said, 'There's been a great mistake made here, depend upon it.' The jailor, a good sort of man, said, 'No, sir, you're only taken in like the rest by her pretty face', and then he told her story, how she had committed a double murder in the most cold-blooded manner. Dickens could not be convinced at the time, but came to the conclusion, after taking great pains to verify all the circumstances, that the jailor's story was correct. The details I cannot remember, but the incessantly varying expression of his face and his exquisite tenderness of manner and look I shall never forget.

At the hour when the carriages were announced one unhappy officer asked in vain for his. Dickens, plainly tired, but still bright and cordial as at first, made it all easy, and his lively jokes kept us all in the best humor till a late hour when the carriage came.

The next morning we were a little late for breakfast, and found him in the breakfast room when we came down. He was evidently anxious to get to his work, but he sat at table long enough to be pleasant to us. . . . Immediately after breakfast he went to his room, his guests to books or walks, and it was not until lunch time that we all met again. He was charming as ever, and afterwards I went for the first time into his bedroom which was also his study. The furniture was simple, the walls were covered with engravings, from Hogarth; his dressing-room, which was only partitioned from the room, he had covered on the inside with wood-cuts from Leech which he had pasted on himself.[5] On his bed lay a brilliant bit of Oriental covering, part of an immense quantity which Fechter had sent with the Chalet. In the large window looking towards Rochester stood his perfectly simple unornamented leather covered writing table, on which, when he was not at work, there was never a scrap of paper to be seen; nothing but pens and ink. I went in many times and it was always the same. The neatness was perfect and his dressing room was that of a man whose personal habits were scrupulously nice without any touch of the 'dandy' which he was sometimes called.

After lunch he and Georgina and Mamie took us to drive first to the Cathedral, and then to see some fine druidical stones which interested him very much. The 'tramps', for we were on the Kent 'high road', occupied his attention constantly, and he talked a great deal about them – how futile it was to expect them to *work*, how he had often tried to persuade them to it on his own place and never succeeded, and how one day he overheard one as he looked over the wall into the garden where Dickens was standing mutter between his teeth, 'Ugly lazy devil, *he* never did a day's work in his life!'[6]

At dinner he was as animated as the day before, and told me the story with minute details of the horrible accident on the South Eastern Railway from which he escaped in a most marvellous manner. . . .

After dinner we had a great deal of lively talk and it was settled that we should all 'post' to Canterbury the next day, and then we bade good night. His children's manners to him and his to them were very sweet – he always kissed his boys just as he did Mamie and Katie. . . . When he snubbed the boys it was with so much humour that they seemed to owe him no grudge, but no one of his family seemed to enjoy his *humour* as much as Katie, and in her quick perception of it she was more like him than the others. Mamie resembled him more in her sentiment and tenderness.[7]

NOTES

1. *Dkn*, XXIX (1933) 100.
2. George Dolby, *Charles Dickens as I Knew Him* (1885) pp. 46–52, 423–5.
3. This was often said of George Eliot and G. H. Lewes.
4. Dickens had been very active in planning and running this home, Urania Cottage, from 1846, but the breakup of his marriage in 1858 ended his intimacy with Miss Coutts and his involvement in her charities. On Miss Coutts, see above, I, 20. On Urania Cottage, see his essay 'Home for Homeless Women', *Household Words*, 23 Apr 1853, repr. in *Miscellaneous Papers*, ed. B. W. Matz (1907); and Philip Collins, *Dickens and Crime* (1962) ch. 4.
5. 'Leech, he thought, was truer to life than even Hogarth': for this comparison see Lady [Constance] Russell, *Swallowfield and Its Owners* (1901) p. 307.
6. This muttering, and further anecdotes and reflections, appear in the *Uncommercial Traveller* essay entitled 'Tramps', first published in *All the Year Round*, 16 June 1860.
7. 'English Friends: From Letters and Journals of Charles Eliot Norton', ed. Sara Norton and M. A. DeWolfe Howe, *Scribner's Magazine*, XXX (1913) 500–4, 576.

Conversations in 1860

AUTHOR UNKNOWN

From Jerome Meckier, 'Some Household Words: Two New Accounts of Dickens's Conversation', *Dkn*, LXXI (1975) 5–20. These records, both headed 'Notanda', are written on Gad's Hill notepaper. Meckier writes, 'Whoever wrote these notes apparently recorded mainly the comments Dickens made. This may account for the rapid movement from topic to topic and the absence of transitions. . . . They indicate the breadth of Dickens's acquaintance, the extent and limitations of his reading, his thorough knowledge of current events, and his fondness for good anecdotes about his friends. . . . [The note printed first] can be assigned to the closing months of 1860, possibly to December. . . . The authorship of the Gad's Hill notes remains a mystery. . . . But the note-taker could not have been a perfect stranger. . . . If these two notes are indicative, conversation at Gad's Hill was lively, literary, political, and anecdotal, seldom if ever speculative, theoretical, or philosophical.' For full annotation of the many references in these notes, see Meckier's article.

Dickens had not read *Jane Eyre* and said he never would as he disapproved of the whole school. [This apropos of Miss Hogarth saying that it was an unhealthy book][1] He had not read *Wuthering Heights*. . . .[2] Spurgeon's behaviour at a German church being discussed he thought that Spurgeon was quite right in getting impatient over the doctrine of baptism and Heaven knew that he was no friend of Spurgeon's. Speaking of Sir Alexander Cockburn, Dickens said he struck one as being and looking the sharpest man I ever saw. He has most varied accomplishments – is a very good linguist, and musician has a great knowledge of horse flesh, and is very well acquainted with literature. He is a man of the world but most courteous in his demeanour and jolly as a sandboy. He was a fellow student of Bulwer's at College. [Speaking of T. K. Hervey.] He and his wife corresponded before they were married – he represented himself as most attractive. They met she shrieked and married him. His wife is always sending contributions to *All the Year Round*. Lever was a very good whist player and was an army surgeon. Talking of the Wakley action] Denman had told him that he believed Wakley's statement to be perfectly true. On his entreating Wakley to give a true account of the matter he fell down in a fit. This he took as evidence of his veracity.] Fonblanque was still writing in the *Examiner*. Savage a very inefficient manager. His theory of the Road murder] Albert Smith's last productions very poor stuff] Had himself a very queer notion of the plot of *Oliver Twist* Praised Wingrove Cooke's book – thought it superior to Russell's. Saw Peter Cunningham on the top of a coach in a very wretched condition Remarked on the price of Frith's picture. Was reserved while walking and complained of his side and sleepless nights. Read the *Arabian Nights* all one evening and made references. Preferred Smollett to Fielding. Spoke of the evident demoralisation of London since the early closing movement. He and Wilkie Collins had been walking through the Haymarket and Regent Street to Cavendish Square and had been struck by the number of street disturbances. Gave his experiences of a Police Station during the evening, and described the lock up.

Dickens spoke with great vehemence against the Chinese and their Exeter Hall sympathisers.[3] Believed that if we struck off the heads of 500 mandarins we should achieve more than by the greatest of victories. Webster who passed through the Court the other day was he believed a nephew of the comedian and had eloped with his wife. Bowlby the *Times* correspondent a good talker and a great frequenter of the Garrick Club – a man about town – Horne the author of *Orion* who had been performing on the guitar in Australia was formerly expelled from Sandhurst for insubordination. Anecdote of his recognition of Costello as a fellow student and of his contributions to *Household Words*. Marryat a fat good natured jolly fellow who used to visit him at Devonshire Terrace. M. fond of telling travellers' stories, e.g. story of 3 dogs assailing him on a bowling green and the woman 'jumping through her arm'. Had a place down in Norfolk where Stanfield's eldest son used to visit him. Possessed little or no literary talent, but had great spirits and experience of nautical affairs. Miss Marryat one of his daughters a lady of excitable disposition always sending contributions to *H. W.* undaunted by rejection and wrote the story containing the marriage of shipwrecked lovers by a priest. Discussed the history of Russell House and business matters transacted at Gads Hill. Spoke of eminent members of the Bar Brougham Palmerston Talfourd etc. Believed that much public speaking was conductive to the health.

Brougham a great drinker taking as much as 4 bottles of mulled port when he was making his speech on the Reform Bill. Spoke of the orator and his qualifications. Believes that the orator was born not made. Great attention to oneself self confidence good voice and palate were necessary. Seemed to think that self confidence was not easily acquired. The habit of attention to oneself as uncommon as that of attention to others. The speaker who concentrating his attention on his own speech spoke slowly enough, without confusion, knew how to reserve good points, took advantage of applause to strengthen himself for fresh efforts and drew fully upon his general knowledge for illustration – was quick and decided on his choice of phrases and never corrected himself and was full of Resource. This quality of resource absent with those who were possessed of great information.

NOTES

1. Square brackets in this item are *not* editorially supplied, but occur thus in the original.

2. Seven lines of manuscript are here scratched out, illegibly even by infra-red techniques. Brief identifications of the persons mentioned: Charles Spurgeon, famous and vastly popular Baptist preacher; Cockburn, Lord Chief Justice 1859–80; T. K. Hervey, editor of the *Athenaeum*; Charles Lever, novelist; Thomas Wakley MP, editor of the *Lancet*, coroner, medical reformer; Baron Thomas Denman, lawyer, and Lord Chief Justice 1832–50; Albany Fonblanque, radical journalist, and Marmion Savage were editors of the *Examiner*, 1830–47 and 1856–9 respectively; Albert Smith, entertainer and author; George Wingrove Cooke, like W. H. Russell, had written about the Crimean War; Peter Cunningham, man of letters. Dickens knew most of these men personally, some of them well. The notorious and puzzling murder at a village called Road had occurred in June 1860.

3. These notes are dated 15 December 1860. The Second China War (to open up China to European trade) had lately been vigorously conducted. Exeter Hall, always anathema to Dickens, was the centre of Evangelical and missionary activities. Of the names mentioned below, Frederic Marryat, novelist, and T. N. Talfourd, lawyer and dramatist, were friends of Dickens, as was Clarkson Stanfield, the artist. R. H. Horne and Dudley Costello were journalistic colleagues. He was acquainted with Lord Brougham. Russell House was contiguous to Dickens's London residence, Tavistock House, which he had lately sold.

His Knowledge of French Novelists

PAUL FÉVAL

From 'Charles Dickens', *Le Gaulois* (Paris), 13 June 1870; translation by Eva Searl. Féval (1816–87), popular French novelist, first met Dickens in 1862, when he was living in Paris. They met through the actor Charles Fechter, who was then performing there; Dickens wrote Fechter a notably fulsome letter about it – 'Pray tell Paul Féval that I shall be charmed to know him, and that I feel the strongest interest in making his acquaintance' (*N*, III, 313). Féval subsequently visited Gad's Hill. Dickens told him that he had 'started to feel fond of France' in 1847, being moved by the funeral of the author Frédéric Soulié, at which a widespread popular respect for literature was manifested. Féval's account of Dickens's taste in French literature is of great interest, though his accuracy is not impeccable: in passages here omitted he reports that Dickens 'died almost poor' (he left almost £100,000) and gives a garbled account of the Dickens boys' activities.

. . . Dickens admired Balzac in an uneasy and almost frightened way.[1] He found fault with him for the unchecked inflation of his ego. 'Moreover,' he added, 'this is *the* sickness of your writers. There are so many people in your country who earn their living by expressing contempt for the famous that famous men feel a constant need to wage personal attacks in retaliation. It's wrong. In Rome, conquering heroes never looked back from their chariots, to take to task the slaves who were paid to follow them hurling mud and abuse.' He continued: 'Balzac and a good few others are marked by criticism, as if it were smallpox. You see them getting over-sensitive, like horses that have been ill-treated. They start as egoists, and then the mosquito-bites of journalism make them neurotic and vicious. *I* have been spoiled the opposite way; I'm much better liked than I deserve.' He was wrong there, but he was not lying. He had nothing false in him, not even false modesty. . . .

Dickens much preferred Balzac to George Sand [but non-French readers fail to appreciate her style]. He knew us all. He had Gozlan's *Aristide Froissart* off by heart; the Indian novels of poor old Méry used to send him wild with delight.[2] I have seen him laughing and crying at once over a page of Alphonse Daudet.

Thackeray, that other departed one, used to say of Dickens that emotion ran through him as deeply and fully as blood. I once met, at Jules Simon's, Thackeray, so different from Dickens and yet almost as attractive. Dickens looked on *Vanity Fair* as an absolute masterpiece. Thackeray, with a modesty perhaps rather less genuine than his master's, used to say: 'I'm only half of Charles (and a small half, at that).' . . . It was at the instigation of both of these great spellbinders that I tried, five years ago, to import lectures and readings into France. At the end of a really successful session in the Salle Valentino, Dickens hugged me, saying that the thing was done. . . .

Dickens's house at Gad's Hill . . . is a charming place, and he himself made it so. He was very proud that he had swallows there, 'which never come to London'. He led a simple life there, but stylish, and the whole neighbourhood adored him. . . . Few people were invited to Gad's Hill after Mrs Dickens's departure. . . . Even when there were no guests, he would still dress for dinner: black suit and white neckcloth. Miss Hogarth and his daughters always dined in full evening dress. Superlatively English!

Dickens loved birds, dogs, and above all flowers. When he set off for America he was sad to be leaving behind a bunch of magnolia which he had been sent the day before. But when he reached New York the first thing he saw in his room was a huge bunch of magnolia. Miss Boyle[3] and the telegraph-system had worked this wonder.

NOTES

1. For further evidence of his knowledge of Balzac see my 'Dickens and Balzac' (forthcoming, in *Dkn*), citing Howard Paul, *Dinners with Celebrities* [1896] pp. 37–8.

2. Léon Gozlan (1816–66) was a prolific novelist and dramatist and an associate of Balzac; his *Aristide Froissart* was published in 1844. Joseph Méry (1798–1865) was a miscellaneous hack writer, and friend and collaborator of Dumas *père*: his 'Indian' novels – spoof travel books, for he had never been in India – include *La Guerre de Nizam* (1847) and *Les Damnés de L'Inde* (1858). Like Féval, and like the popular serial novelist Soulié (1800–47), mentioned above, they are all now almost forgotten. Féval's assertion that 'He knew us all' must be regarded with caution (and is ambiguous – was personally acquainted with us? knew our writings?). Had Dickens read Flaubert, for instance? – most improbable, I should guess, though *Madame Bovary* (1856–7) quickly attracted attention in England. Certainly he 'knew' personally many French writers: for example, as early as 1844 he had met

Victor Hugo, Alexandre Dumas, Théophile Gautier and others.

3. For Mary Boyle, see above, 1, 83. She arranged for a nightly gift of a nosegay to reach Dickens during his American readings tour.

He 'Always Made Me Feel Rather Afraid'

JUSTIN McCARTHY

From his *Reminiscences* (1899) 1, 32–5. McCarthy (1830–1912) was an Irish politician and novelist; also leader-writer on the *Daily News* from 1871, and author of *A History of Our Own Times* (1877) and other works. He first came to London in 1852, and his account of Dickens comes from his chapter on 'The Giants of Literature' at that time.

When I first settled in London, England was under the sway of a great literary triumvirate: Dickens, Thackeray, and Tennyson. At that time, and for long after, Browning was but the leader of a select few. Even Tennyson's popularity did not equal that of Thackeray and did not come anywhere near that of Dickens. I am not now entering into any comparison or criticism of the men as intellectual forces; I am speaking only of the hold they had on the public mind. Dickens, of course, was by far the most popular of the three; no one since his time has had anything like the same degree of popularity. No one born in the younger generation can easily understand, from any illustration that later years can give him, the immensity of the popular homage which Dickens then enjoyed. I had many opportunities of meeting Dickens, and of course I heard all of his readings and heard him deliver several after-dinner speeches. Let me say at once that he was the very best after-dinner speaker I ever heard; I do not quite know whom I should put second to him. . . . But, so far as my judgment can go, there is no difficulty about awarding the first place to Dickens. His voice was rich, full, and deep, capable of imparting without effort every tone and half-tone of emotion, pathetic, inspiriting, or humorous, that any spoken words could demand. His deep eyes seemed to flash upon every listener among the audience whom he addressed. I have no doubt that his after-dinner speeches were prepared in some fashion, but they carried with them no hint of preparation. They seemed to come from the very heart of the speaker and to go straight to the heart of the listener. I heard him make his famous speech at the dinner of the Press Fund, in which he described with so much humour and so much vividness, and with so many sudden gleams of unexpected pathos, some of his own experiences as a reporter [20 May 1865; *Speeches*, pp. 342–8]; and although most of us in that company were newspaper men in whose minds speechmaking had become somewhat too closely associated with mechanical taskwork, I think we were all of us alike carried away by the extraordinary charm of that speech. Dickens's readings seemed most of them in their way inimitable, but I generally found that I could criticise them as I could not criticise his after-dinner eloquence. I am not, however, concerned in this place to criticise Dickens as a reader any more than I should think it necessary to give my opinion of him as a writer; I am only endeavouring to recall, for the benefit of those much younger than I, some of the impressions I formed of Dickens as a speaker and as a man.

I have said that I had many opportunities of meeting Dickens; but I should say that my acquaintance with him was very slight and superficial. I used to feel very proud when he shook hands with me and remembered my name and asked me how I was getting on, or some question of that sort; but I never could pretend to have been ranked even in the outermost circle of his friends. I was not merely a young man, but a totally obscure young man, and had nothing whatever to recommend me to Dickens's notice except the fact that I belonged to the staff of a daily newspaper. To say the truth, Dickens rather frightened me; I felt uneasy when he spoke to me, and did not quite see what business I had to be speaking to such a man. His manner was full of energy; there was something physically overpowering about it, as it then seemed to me; the very vehemence of his cheery good-humour rather bore one down. From the first he appeared to me to be a man with whom I could not venture to differ on any subject. Then again, as was but natural, he was generally surrounded by a crowd of young men who sincerely worshipped him, and to whom indeed he seemed to represent all literature. I know how kind and friendly and encouraging he was to many men as young as I was, and whose very first efforts in literature received his helping hand – I knew many such young men, and they were never tired of telling me how kind he was, and how gentle, how 'quick to encourage and slow to disparage', if I may adopt certain words which I think were used by himself when speaking of another leader of literature. But I am only putting down my impressions just for what they are worth, as the phrase goes, and indeed they are worth nothing at all except as impressions, and I can only say that Dickens somehow or other always made me feel rather afraid.[1]

NOTE

1. Writing elsewhere, in his book on the *Daily News* Jubilee (1896), McCarthy remarked 'Younger people who did not know Charles Dickens, who perhaps never saw him, can have little idea of the moving power of his words, his appeals, his very presence over men. The mere thrill of his wonderful voice had a magic of persuasion in it' – quoted by F. G. Kitton, *Charles Dickens* (1902) p. 147. See also his *Portraits of the Sixties* (1903) ch. 2, 'Charles Dickens'.

America, 1867–8

VARIOUS

It is a great pleasure to see Dickens again after so many years [wrote the poet Longfellow to John Forster, a few days after his landing in Boston], with the same sweetness and flavor as of old, and only greater ripeness. The enthusiasm for him and for his Readings is immense. One can hardly take in the whole truth about it, and feel the universality of his fame. [Elsewhere, reporting his first meeting with Dickens for twenty-five years, Longfellow remarks:] He looks somewhat older, but as elastic and quick in his movements as ever.[1]

[The author and, later, novelist William Dean Howells (1837–1920) met Dickens soon after his arrival, and found him] everything in manner that his books would make you wish him to be. . . . His face is very flexible, and he is very genial and easy in talk. . . . But it was hard at the moment to remember that this man so near me was so great and had done so much to please and better the world – Everybody here [Cambridge, Mass.] is wild about the Readings. . . .²

[Another future novelist, Henry James (1843–1916), ecountered Dickens in Boston. A young man, he was invited to call after dinner at Charles Eliot Norton's house. Nearly forty years later, he recalled 'that night of Dickens, and the *emotion*, abiding that it left with me. How it *did* something for my thought of him and his work – and would have done more without the readings, the hard charmless readings (or *à peu près*) that remained with me.' His auto-biographical *Notes of a Son and Brother* (1914) contains a fuller account.]

I saw the master – nothing could be more evident – in the light of an intense emotion, and I trembled, I remember, in every limb, while at the same time, by a blest fortune, emotion produced no luminous blur, but left him shining indeed, only shining with august particulars. It was to be remarked that those of his dress, which managed to be splendid even while remaining the general spare uniform of the diner-out, had the effect of higher refinements, of accents stronger and better placed, than we had ever in such a connection seen so much as hinted. But the offered inscrutable mask was the great thing, the extremely handsome face, the face of symmetry yet of formidable character, as I at once recognised, and which met my dumb homage with a straight inscrutability, a merciless *military* eye, I might have pronounced it, an automatic hardness, in fine, which at once indicated to me, and in the most interesting way in the world, a kind of economy of apprehension. Wonderful was it thus to see, and thrilling inwardly to note, that since the question was of personal values so great no faintest fraction of the whole could succeed in *not* counting for interest. The confrontation was but of a moment; our introduction, my companion's and mine, once effected, by an arrest in a doorway, nothing followed, as it were, or happened (what *might* have happened it remained in fact impossible to conceive); but intense though the positive perception there was an immensity more left to understand – for the long aftersense, I mean; and one, or the chief, of these later things was that if our hero neither shook hands nor spoke, only meeting us by the barest act, so to say, of the trained eye, the penetration of which, to my sense, revealed again a world, there was a grim beauty, to one's subsequently panting imagination, in that very truth of his then so knowing himself (committed to his

monstrous 'readings' and with the force required for them omin-
ously ebbing) on the outer edge of his once magnificent
margin. . . .[3]

[Dickens's American début took place in Boston on 2 December
1867, with *A Christmas Carol* and *The Trial from 'Pickwick'*. Fifty
years later the wife of the journalist and editor Thomas Bailey
Aldrich wrote:] What memories unfold themselves to my vision of
that night. . . . With quick, elastic steps he takes his place. The
whole audience spring to their feet, while round after round of
applause, cheer after cheer, shout after shout of welcome greet him.
[She describes the 'wonderful evening', and then Dickens's subsequently visiting her humble abode.] A rather short, slight figure,
so he seemed to me then, without the manner that stamps the caste
of 'Vere de Vere'. He was dressed – I think dressed is the right
word – in a very light, so light that I don't know how to describe it –
I can almost say soiled white color – top coat. It was wide and short,
and stood out like a skirt, the collar of a much darker shade of velvet.
His waistcoat was velvet of another shade of brown, with brilliant
red indentations; his watch chain was buttoned into the centre
button of his waistcoat, and then it divided itself. I found myself
saying, 'How do you do', and wondering, if the watch was in one
pocket, what was at the other end of the chain in the other pocket,
and was tempted to ask him the time, in the hope that he might
make a mistake and bring out the other thing. I don't remember
what he wore on his feet, and I don't know the plaid of his trousers,
but I rather think it was a black-and-white check – what the
Englishman calls 'pepper and salt'. I don't remember any one topic
of conversation on that first visit, but I remember well the laughter
and good cheer; the charming way in which the guest made these
two young people feel that to him they really were persons of
consequence and were so regarded by this prince of strangers who
tarried within their gates.[4]

[Dickens's opening performance is described by Charles H. Taylor
in the *New York Tribune*, 2 December 1867] . . . until tonight,
Mr. Dickens has kept himself strictly secluded from all but one or
two old and intimate friends. His rooms are at the Parker House,
and there he has remained, busily engaged all day, in writing and
study, excepting when he is taking his daily eight mile
'constitutional' walk with his publisher, Fields, and steadily

declining all the invitations to breakfast, dinner, tea, supper, parties, balls, and drives, that hospitable Boston pours in upon him in an unfailing stream. Much of his time is spent in the most laborious pains-taking study of the parts he is to read. Indeed, the public has but little idea of the cost – in downright hard work of mind, and body, and voice – at which these readings are produced. Although Mr. Dickens has read, now, nearly five hundred times, I am assured, on the best authority that he never attempts a new part in public until he has spent at least two months over it in study as faithful and searching as Rachel or Cushman would give to a new character. This study extends not merely to the analysis of the text, to the discrimination of character, to the minutest points of elocution: but decides upon the facial expression, the tone of the voice, the gesture, the attitude, and even the material surroundings of the actor, for, *Acting it is, not Reading*, in the ordinary sense, at all. Mr. Dickens is so essentially an artist that he cannot neglect the slightest thing that may serve to highten the effect of what he has undertaken to do. And he is as conscientious, so strict in all his dealings – a very martinet in business and thorough man of affairs – that he will leave nothing undone, that time and labor can do, to give to the public that pays so much for the pleasure of hearing him, the full worth of its money. This is the reason why he, a man of the world, greatly delighting in society, thoroughly fitted to enjoy it himself, and to make others enjoy it – deliberately cuts himself off from it, until his task shall be done. 'I am come here,' he says, 'to read. The people expect me to do my best, and how can I do it if I am all the time on the go? My time is not my own, when I am preparing to read, any more than it is when I am writing a novel, and I can as well do one as the other, without concentrating all my powers on it until it is done.' . . . This wonderful two-hours performance – so full of varied power; brim-full, from end to end, of feeling, pathos, mirth, and fun, a sunlit shower of smiles and tears, not to be described in words, hardly to be comprehended by the mind, all this – if it be not the pure result of unremitting study, and thought, and physical labor, would, at least, not have been the perfect thing it is, without these helps. . . .

Few cities, anywhere, could show an audience of such character. Hardly a notable man in Boston, or 50 miles about, but was there, and we doubt if in London itself Mr. Dickens ever read before such an assemblage. There sat Longfellow . . . [and Oliver Wendell Holmes, James Russell Lowell, Charles Eliot Norton, Edwin

Whipple, James T. Fields and others.] Emerson's face I could not catch. Concord is far away, and snow storms no joke to travel in. Nor did Whittier come as was promised – Whittier, who has never in his life been present at an evening entertainment of any description, concert or opera, or even, strange to say, a lecture. . . .

[Emerson attended later (see below, p. 318), and so did the poet John Greenleaf Whittier (1807–92), who was greatly impressed.] I have 'made an effort' as Mrs Chick would say, & have heard Dickens. It was his last night in Boston. I found myself in the packed hall, sandwiched between Ric^d H. Dana Sen. & Longfellow with Mrs Fields one side of us & Mrs Ames the other. We waited some half hour: a slight brisk man tripped up the steps, sparkling with ring & chain – tight vested wide bosomed, short dress coat, white choker; tight pantaloons enclosing, as the Prairie girl said of Judge Douglass's – 'a mighty slim chance of legs!' Somehow a slight reminder of his own Tim Tappertit in Barnaby Rudge. Face marked with thought as well as years – head bald or nearly so – a look of keen intelligence about the strong brow, & eye – the look of a man who has seen much & is wide awake to see more. I don't think he shows the great genius that he is – he might pass for a shrewd Massachusetts manufacturer, or an active N.Y. merchant. But his reading is wonderful, far beyond my expectations. Those marvellous characters of his come forth, one by one, real personages, as if their original creator had breathed new life into them. You shut your eyes & there before you know are Pecksniff, & Sairy Gamp, Sam Weller & Dick Swiveller & all the rest. But it is idle to talk about it: you must beg, borrow, or steal a ticket & hear him. Another such star-shower is not to be expected in one's life-time.[5]

Mr Dickens does not rant, nor mouth, nor declaim, nor read after the manner of most actors and elocutionists [reported the *Hartford Daily Courant*, 19 February 1868], he talks, he converses; he never forgets that he is a gentleman of the world, relating to perfectly sensible and rational beings a simple story. There is a nameless charm in this naturalness which we could wish our public speakers of all sorts would profit by observing. [Many critics, especially in America, noted this gentlemanly 'naturalness' in the Readings. For instance, the *Nation* (New York), 12 December 1867:] The true theory of [his] performance is not that it is acting in which the actor, as much as possible, forgets himself into the very likeness of what he personates, but is rather that a gentleman dramatically tells a story among friends, indicating rather than perfectly assuming the characters of the personages brought before us; never wholly, indeed, never nearly, losing sight of his hearers and himself; never wholly, never, at any rate, for very long, getting away from the gentlemanly drawing room, with its limiting conventionalities, into the wider and freer atmosphere of the stage. Readings are simply story-telling or declaiming or the recitation of poetry with exceptionally good elocution and with occasional feats of imitation of a kind more or less subdued. . . .

[Some initial disappointment is inevitable – given Dickens's huge fame as a creator – when we see that] as he steps quickly across the stage he seems to the casual eye – if any casual eyes were there – an ordinary elderly gentleman, with steel-grey hair, thin on the top of the head and brought forward into two tufts just above the ears, with a rosy or flushed face, in evening dress, and, generally, with a dapper air rather than with a look of – what shall we say? – a great genius who is a part of the happiness of mankind henceforth. From this disappointment one soon recovers. One looks closely at the strong features, sees the mingled kindness and sharpness of the eyes, sees the whole face smiling – not the lips only, but the eyes and cheeks – at some lucky humorous stroke, and it is easy to forget some small things, and to admit that only the face before us could be the face of the Dickens whom we know. The flowers and the jewellery and the diffuse moustache and imperial seem also proper and not to be dispensed with. . . .

To pronounce judgment on Mr. Dickens as a reader we are not in all respects competent. But we may say that as we listened to him it seemed to us that in the level passages he was not extraordinarily good; that his voice is not a particularly fine one; that many of his inflections and the spirit in which he reads many passages are not at all what we should have expected or what we liked, but that wherever his admirable histrionic abilities could supplement or almost take the place of his abilities as a reader merely – then all things were done at least well, many things excellently well, and some things done so well that we have not as yet conceived of their being done better. The old judge in the trial scene seemed to us unsurpassable. . . .

All this called forth very hearty applause. But the most spontaneous and the heartiest plaudits were given when Sergeant Buzfuz said, 'Call Samuel Weller'. Evidently everybody recognized in

Samuel an old acquaintance. Everybody, too, we imagine, was a little disappointed that Sam, when he answered the call, made no more show than he did in the witness box; but when Anthony Weller disturbed the court-room by his orthographic instructions to his son, which Mr. Dickens produced in exactly the voice which we imagine as issuing from beneath the capes and coats and adipose tissue, and from among the pots of beer of a coachman of the olden time, it seemed as if the veritable Prussian Blue was himself among us in the audience.

A thousand things might be said of the impressions which Monday evening made upon Mr. Dickens's audience, most of whom saw for the first time a friend whom they had long loved. To us the most impressive thing was the burst of applause which followed the mention of Sam Weller's name. It was such an unaffected tribute of admiration as few authors have ever obtained. Mr. Dickens stood before us in the flesh – listening to that voice of human sympathy and admiration which only the posterity of most other great men hear.

[Dickens was 'a better looking man than his pictures show him to be' (*Daily Spy*, Worcester, Mass., 24 Mar 1868) and, even when feeling very ill, he bore in public a 'genial expression' of which photographs gave no idea (see above, Introduction, 1, xvii). Many critics noted this geniality and humorousness, and his tendency to join in the public's laughter at the comicalities in his readings, though in no self-praising fashion; e.g. the *Springfield Semi-Weekly Republican*, 21 Mar 1868:] He puzzles you with his complete abstraction from himself – in all his two hours' reading – save in one particular. Every one noticed that whenever Mr Dickens made a fine point, a point which made the audience laugh . . . he let down the curtain from his own face and smiled, fairly laughing, not at himself, but with the audience. Quick, curious and beautiful, that smile is the secret of the man's whole nature.

[Senator Cornelius Cole, a close friend of Abraham Lincoln, attended all four of Dickens's Readings in Washington, greatly admiring them, though also struck by the opulence – 'rather foppish' – of his evening attire: 'His neckgear was of a cut and color to be called flashy.'] The book in each case lay open before him, but he paid little or no attention to the text. It was reciting, rather than reading. He missed not a word of the passage he was giving, and delivered it in a most impressive and entertaining style, representing in voice and manner, so far as he might, the character he was quoting. It would have been an interesting occasion had he been representing some other author, but it was intensely so as Charles Dickens himself. Dickens in his numerous works has created many original characters, but not one, I should say, more interesting than himself. His manner and whole appearance struck one as exceedingly finical and yet in no degree ludicrous, a character he has apparently avoided portraying in his books. His enunciation was possibly more precise than could be expected in one who had written so much and in such haste. His dialect would be recognised as English, but there was little of the Johnny Bull about him, either in manner or diction. Where not known, Mr. Dickens might have been taken for an American, or perhaps more likely a Frenchman. In fact, I thought him about as odd a character as any he had ever drawn from his fruitful imagination.[6]

NOTES

1. Edward Wagenknecht, 'Dickens in Longfellow's Letters and Journals', in *Dickens and the Scandalmongers* (Norman, Oklahoma, 1965) p. 84; Edward F. Payne, *Dickens Days in Boston* (Boston and New York, 1927) p. 149.

2. *The Life in Letters of William Dean Howells*, ed. Mildred Howells (repr. New York, 1968) I, 122–3.

3. *The Notebooks of Henry James*, ed. F. O. Matthiesen and Kenneth B. Murdock (1947) p. 319; Henry James, *Autobiography*, ed. Frederick W. Dupee (1956) pp. 389–90.

4. Mrs Thomas Bailey Aldrich, *Crowding Memories* (Boston and New York, 1920) pp. 102–3.

5. John A. Pollard, *John Greenleaf Whittier: Friend of Man* (Boston and New York, 1949) p. 392. Dick Swiveller, however, does not appear in any of the readings. Dickens's legs, which Whittier mentions, met with widespread disapproval in America: 'as mean looking a pair of legs as I ever saw', commented Rose Eytinge ('Recollections', *New York Dramatic Mirror*, 23 Feb 1901, p. 9).

6. William Crosby Bennett, 'Dickens at Washington: Reminscences of a former United States Senator', *Dkn*, XXXIII (1937) 56.

304 DICKENS: INTERVIEWS AND RECOLLECTIONS

His Closest American Friends

JAMES AND ANNIE FIELDS

(1) from J. T. Fields, *Yesterdays with Authors* (Boston, 1872) pp. 127–9, 167, 176–7, 201–4, 209, 230–1, 233–42; (2) extracts from Annie Fields's diaries, drawn from (*a*) *James T. Fields: Biographical Notes and Personal Sketches* [ed. Annie Fields] (1881) pp. 153–5, 158, 196, 273; (*b*) *Memories of a Hostess: Drawn from the Diaries of Mrs. James T. Fields*, ed. M. A. DeWolfe Howe (1923), ch. 5, 'With Dickens in America'; (*c*) Arthur A. Adrian, *Georgina Hogarth and the Dickens Circle* (1957) pp. 111, 113–14, 126. James T. Fields (1817–81), partner in the distinguished publishing firm of Ticknor and Fields, and editor of *Atlantic Monthly*, met Dickens in 1842, and became a lifelong friend, visiting him in England, publishing many of his works in the USA, and organising his American Reading Tour in 1867–8. His second wife, Annie (1834–1915), much his junior (he had 'known her from childhood, and held her on my knee many and many a time'), was beautiful, enchanting and intelligent, and conducted a much-valued *salon* in Boston – 'so far as salons were in the old Puritan city dreamed of', remarked Henry James, who gratefully recalled both husband and wife as being 'addicted to the ingenious multiplication of such ties as could link the upper half of the title-page with the lower'. James Fields used his wife's diaries when writing these reminiscences, but material has not been repeated here. It was rumoured in Boston that Annie Fields had fallen in love with Dickens during his visit there – Susan Chitty, *The Beast and the Monk: a Life of Charles Kingsley* (1974) p. 287. He might very forgivably have returned the compliment.

(1) [James Fields opens with a contrast between the earlier and the later portraits of Dickens.] One would hardly believe these pictures represented the same man! See what a beautiful young person Maclise represents in this early likeness of the great author, and then contrast the face with that worn one in the photograph of 1869. The same man, but how different in aspect! I sometimes think, while looking at those two portraits, I must have known two individuals bearing the same name, at various periods of my own life. Let me speak to-day of the younger Dickens. How well I recall the bleak winter evening in 1842 when I first saw the handsome, glowing face of the young man who was even then famous over half the globe! He came bounding into the Tremont House, fresh from the steamer that had brought him to our shores, and his cheery voice rang through the hall, as he gave a quick glance at the new scenes

opening upon him in a strange land on first arriving at a
Transatlantic hotel. 'Here we are!' he shouted, as the lights burst
upon the merry party just entering the house, and several gentlemen
came forward to greet him. Ah, how happy and buoyant he was
then! Young, handsome, almost worshipped for his genius, belted
round by such troops of friends as rarely ever man had, coming to a
new country to make new conquests of fame and honor – surely it
was a sight long to be remembered and never wholly to be forgotten.
The splendor of his endowments and the personal interest he had
won to himself called forth all the enthusiasm of old and young
America, and I am glad to have been among the first to witness his
arrival. You ask me what was his appearance as he ran, or rather
flew, up the steps of the hotel, and sprang into the hall. He seemed
all on fire with curiosity, and alive as I never saw mortal before.
From top to toe every fibre of his body was unrestrained and alert.
What vigor, what keenness, what freshness of spirit, possessed him!
He laughed all over, and did not care who heard him! He seemed
like the Emperor of Cheerfulness on a cruise of pleasure, determined
to conquer a realm or two of fun every hour of his overflowing
existence. That night impressed itself on my memory for all time, so
far as I am concerned with things sublunary. . . .

[Fields is describing the American readings tour of 1867–8.]
Several times I feared he would be obliged to postpone the readings,
and I am sure almost any one else would have felt compelled to do
so; but he declared no man had a right to break an engagement with
the public, if he were able to be out of bed. His spirit was wonderful,
and, although he lost all appetite and could partake of very little
food, he was always cheerful and ready for his work when the
evening came round. Every morning his table was covered with
invitations to dinners and all sorts of entertainments, but he said, 'I
came for hard work, and I must try to fulfil the expectations of the
American public'. He did accept a dinner which was tendered to
him by some of his literary friends in Boston; but the day before it
was to come off he was so ill he felt obliged to ask that the banquet
might be given up. The strain upon his strength and nerves was very
great during all the months he remained in the country, and only a
man of iron will could have accomplished all he did. And here let
me say, that although he was accustomed to talk and write a great
deal about eating and drinking, I have rarely seen a man eat and
drink less. He liked to dilate in imagination over the brewing of a
bowl of punch, but I always noticed that when the punch was ready,

he drank less of it than any one who might be present. It was the sentiment of the thing and not the thing itself that engaged his attention. He liked to have a little supper every night after a reading, and have three or four friends round the table with him, but he only pecked at the viands as a bird might do, and I scarcely saw him eat a hearty meal during his whole stay in the country. . . .

The extent and variety of Dickens's [vocal] tones were wonderful. Once he described to me in an inimitable way a scene he witnessed many years ago at a London theatre, and I am certain no professional ventriloquist could have reproduced it better. I could never persuade him to repeat the description in presence of others; but he did it for me several times during our walks into the country, where he was, of course, unobserved. His recital of the incident was irresistibly droll, and no words of mine can give the *situation* even, as he gave it. He said he was once sitting in the pit of a London theatre, when two men came in and took places directly in front of him. Both were evidently strangers from the country, and not very familiar with the stage. One of them was stone deaf, and relied entirely upon his friend to keep him informed of the dialogue and story of the play as it went on, by having bawled into his ear, word for word, as near as possible what the actors and actresses were saying. The man who could hear became intensely interested in the play, and kept close watch of the stage. The deaf man also shared in the progressive action of the drama, and rated his friend soundly, in a loud voice, if a stitch in the story of the play were inadvertently dropped. Dickens gave the two voices of these two spectators with his best comic and dramatic power. . . .

We met in London [in May 1869], and I found him in capital spirits, with such a protracted list of things we were to do together, that, had I followed out the prescribed programme, it would have taken many more months of absence from home than I had proposed to myself. We began our long rambles among the thoroughfares that had undergone important changes since I was last in London, taking in the noble Thames embankments, which I had never seen, and the improvements in the city markets. . . . Among the most memorable of these London rambles was a visit to the General Post-Office, by arrangement with the authorities there, a stroll among the cheap theatres and lodging-houses for the poor, a visit to Furnival's Inn and the very room in it where *Pickwick* was written, and a walk through the thieves' quarter. Two of these expeditions were made on two consecutive nights, under the protection of police detailed for the service. On one of these nights we also visited the lock-up houses, watch-houses, and opium-eating establishments. It was in one of the horrid opium-dens that he gathered the incidents which he has related in the opening pages of *Edwin Drood*. In a miserable court we found the haggard old woman blowing at a kind of pipe made of an old penny ink-bottle. The identical words which Dickens puts into the mouth of this wretched creature in *Edwin Drood* we heard her croon as we leaned over the tattered bed on which she was lying. There was something hideous in the way this woman kept repeating, 'Ye'll pay up according, deary, won't ye?' and the Chinamen and Lascars made never-to-be-forgotten pictures in the scene. I watched Dickens intently as he went among these outcasts of London, and saw with what deep sympathy he encountered the sad and suffering in their horrid abodes. At the door of one of the penny lodging-houses (it was growing toward morning, and the raw air almost cut one to the bone), I saw him snatch a little child out of its poor drunken mother's arms, and bear it in, filthy as it was, that it might be warmed and cared for. I noticed that whenever he entered one of these wretched rooms he had a word of cheer for its inmates, and that when he left the apartment he always had a pleasant 'Good night' or 'God bless you' to bestow upon them. I do not think his person was ever recognized in any of these haunts, except in one instance. As we entered a low room in the worst alley we had yet visited, in which were huddled together some forty or fifty half-starved-looking wretches, I noticed a man among the crowd whispering to another and pointing out Dickens. Both men regarded him with marked interest all the time he remained in the room, and tried to get as near him, without observation, as possible. As he turned to go out, one of these men pressed forward and said, 'Good night, sir', with much feeling, in reply to Dickens's parting word.

Among other places, we went, a little past midnight, into one of the Casual Wards, which were so graphically described, some years ago, in an English magazine, by a gentleman who, as a pretended tramp, went in on a reporting expedition. We walked through an avenue of poor tired sleeping forms, all lying flat on the floor, and not one of them raised a head to look at us as we moved thoughtfully up the aisle of sorrowful humanity. I think we counted sixty or seventy prostrate beings, who had come in for a night's shelter, and had lain down worn out with fatigue and hunger. There was one pale young face to which I whispered Dickens's attention, and he stood over it with a look of sympathizing interest not to be easily forgotten. There was much ghastly comicality mingled with the horror in several of the places we visited on those two nights. We were standing in a room half filled with people of both sexes, whom the police accompanying us knew to be thieves. Many of these abandoned persons had served out their terms in jail or prison, and would probably be again sentenced under the law. They were all silent and sullen as we entered the room, until an old woman spoke up with a strong, beery voice: 'Good evening, gentlemen. We are all very poor, but strictly honest.' At which cheerful apocryphal statement, all the inmates of the room burst into boisterous laughter, and began pelting the imaginative female with epithets uncomplimentary and unsavory. Dickens's quick eye never for a moment ceased to study all these scenes of vice and gloom, and he told me afterwards that, bad as the whole thing was, it had improved infinitely since he first began to study character in those regions of crime and woe.

Between eleven and twelve o'clock on one of the evenings I have mentioned we were taken by Dickens's favorite Detective W——[1] into a sort of lock-up house, where persons are brought from the streets who have been engaged in brawls, or detected in the act of thieving, or who have, in short, committed any offence against the laws. Here they are examined for commitment by a sort of presiding officer, who sits all night for that purpose. We looked into some of the cells, and found them nearly filled with wretched-looking objects who had been brought in that night. To this establishment are also brought lost children who are picked up in the streets by the police – children who have wandered away from their homes, and are not old enough to tell the magistrate where they live. . . .

Dickens's admiration of Hogarth was unbounded, and he had hung the staircase [at Gad's Hill] leading up from the hall of his house with fine old impressions of the great master's best works. Observing our immediate interest in these pictures, he seemed greatly pleased, and proceeded at once to point out in his graphic way what had struck his own fancy most in Hogarth's genius. He had made a study of the painter's *thought* as displayed in these works, and his talk about the artist was delightful. He used to say he never came down the stairs without pausing with new wonder over the fertility of the mind that had conceived and the hand that had executed these powerful pictures of human life; and I cannot forget with what fervid energy and feeling he repeated one day, as we were standing together on the stairs in front of the Hogarth pictures, Dr. Johnson's epitaph, on the painter: –

> The hand of him here torpid lies,
>   That drew the essential form of grace;
> Here closed in death the attentive eyes
>   That saw the manners in the face. . . .

In his own inimitable manner he would frequently relate to me, if prompted, stories of his youthful days, when he was toiling on the London *Morning Chronicle*, passing sleepless hours as a reporter on the road in a post-chaise, driving day and night from point to point to take down the speeches of Shiel or O'Connell. He liked to describe the post-boys, who were accustomed to hurry him over the road that he might reach London in advance of his rival reporters, while, by the aid of a lantern, he was writing out for the press, as he flew over the ground, the words he had taken down in short-hand. Those were his days of severe training, when in rain and sleet and cold he dashed along, scarcely able to keep the blinding mud out of his tired eyes; and he imputed much of his ability for steady hard work to his practice as a reporter, kept at his grinding business, and determined if possible to earn seven guineas a week. A large sheet was started at this period of his life, in which all the important speeches of Parliament were to be reported *verbatim* for future reference. Dickens was engaged on this gigantic journal. Mr. Stanley (afterwards Lord Derby) had spoken at great length on the condition of Ireland. It was a long and eloquent speech, occupying many hours in the delivery. Eight reporters were sent in to do the work. Each one was required to report three quarters of an hour, then to retire, write out his portion, and to be succeeded by the next. Young Dickens was detailed to lead off with the first part. It also fell to his lot, when the time came round, to report the closing portions of the speech. On Saturday the whole was given to the press, and Dickens ran down to the country for a Sunday's rest. Sunday morning had scarcely dawned, when his father, who was a man of immense energy, made his appearance in his son's sleeping-room. Mr. Stanley was so dissatisfied with what he found in print, except the beginning and ending of his speech (just what Dickens had reported) that he sent immediately to the office and obtained the sheets of those parts of the report. He there found the name of the reporter, which, according to custom, was written on the margin. Then he requested that the young man bearing the name of Dickens should be immediately sent for. Dickens's father, all aglow with the prospect of probable promotion in the office, went immediately to his son's stopping-place in the country and brought him back to London. In telling the story, Dickens said: 'I remember perfectly to this day the aspect of the room I was shown into, and the two persons in it, Mr. Stanley and his father. Both gentlemen were extremely courteous to me, but I noted their evident surprise at the appearance of so young a man. While we spoke together, I had taken a seat extended to me in the middle of the room. Mr. Stanley told me he wished to go over the whole speech and have it written out by me, and if I were ready he would begin now. Where would I like to sit? I told him I was very well where I was, and we could begin immediately. He tried to induce me to sit at a desk, but at that time in the House of Commons there was nothing but one's knees to write upon, and I had formed the habit of doing my work in that way. Without further pause he began and went rapidly on, hour after hour, to the end, often becoming very much excited and frequently bringing down his hand with great violence upon the desk near which he stood.' . . .

Speaking of memory one day, he said the memory of children was prodigious; it was a mistake to fancy children ever forgot anything. When he was delineating the character of Mrs. Pipchin, he had in his mind an old lodging-house keeper in an English watering-place where he was living with his father and mother when he was but two years old.[2] After the book was written he sent it to his sister, who wrote back at once; 'Good heavens! what does this mean? you have painted our lodging-house keeper, and you were but two years old at that time!' Characters and incidents crowded the chambers of his brain, all ready for use when occasion required. No subject of human interest was ever indifferent to him, and never a day went by that did not afford him some suggestion to be utilized in the future.

His favorite mode of exercise was walking; and when in America, scarcely a day passed, no matter what the weather, that he did not accomplish his eight or ten miles. It was on these expeditions that he liked to recount to the companion of his rambles stories and incidents of his early life; and when he was in the mood, his fun and humor knew no bounds. He would then frequently discuss the numerous characters in his delightful books, and would act out, on the road, dramatic situations, where Nickleby or Copperfield or

Swiveller would play distinguished parts. I remember he said, on one of these occasions, that during the composition of his first stories he could never entirely dismiss the characters about whom he happened to be writing; that while the *Old Curiosity Shop* was in process of composition Little Nell followed him about everywhere; that while he was writing *Oliver Twist* Fagin the Jew would never let him rest, even in his most retired moments; that at midnight and in the morning, on the sea and on the land, Tiny Tim and Little Bob Cratchit were ever tugging at his coat-sleeve, as if impatient for him to get back to his desk and continue the story of their lives. But he said after he had published several books, and saw what serious demands his characters were accustomed to make for the constant attention of his already overtasked brain, he resolved that the phantom individuals should no longer intrude on his hours of recreation and rest, but that when he closed the door of his study he would shut them all in, and only meet them again when he came back to resume his task. That force of will with which he was so pre-eminently endowed enabled him to ignore these manifold existences till he chose to renew their acquaintance. He said, also, that when the children of his brain had once been launched, free and clear of him, into the world, they would sometimes turn up in the most unexpected manner to look their father in the face.

Sometimes he would pull my arm while we were walking together and whisper, 'Let us avoid Mr. Pumblechook, who is crossing the street to meet us'; or, 'Mr. Micawber is coming; let us turn down this alley to get out of his way'. He always seemed to enjoy the fun of his comic people, and had unceasing mirth over Mr. Pickwick's misadventures. In answer one day to a question, prompted by psychological curiosity, if he ever dreamed of any of his characters, his reply was, 'Never; and I am convinced that no writer (judging from my own experience, which cannot be altogether singular, but must be a type of the experience of others) has ever dreamed of the creatures of his own imagination. It would,' he went on to say, 'be like a man's dreaming of meeting himself, which is clearly an impossibility. Things exterior to one's self must always be the basis of dreams.' The growing up of characters in his mind never lost for him a sense of the marvellous. 'What an unfathomable mystery there is in it all!' he said one day. Taking up a wineglass, he continued: 'Suppose I choose to call this a *character*, fancy it a man, endue it with certain qualities; and soon the fine filmy webs of thought, almost impalpable, coming from every direction, we know not whence, spin and weave about it, until it assumes form and beauty, and becomes instinct with life.'

In society Dickens rarely referred to the traits and characteristics of people he had known; but during a long walk in the country he delighted to recall and describe the peculiarities, eccentric and otherwise, of dead and gone as well as living friends. Then Sydney Smith and Jeffrey and Christopher North and Talfourd and Hood and Rogers seemed to live over again in his vivid reproductions, made so impressive by his marvellous memory and imagination. As he walked rapidly along the road, he appeared to enjoy the keen zest of his companion in the numerous impersonations with which he was indulging him.

He always had much to say of animals as well as of men, and there were certain dogs and horses he had met and known intimately which it was specially interesting to him to remember and picture. . . . All animals which he took under his especial patronage seemed to have a marked affection for him. Quite a colony of dogs has always been a feature at Gad's Hill. In many walks and talks with Dickens, his conversation, now, alas! so imperfectly recalled, frequently ran on the habits of birds, the raven, of course, interesting him particularly. He always liked to have a raven hopping about his grounds, and whoever has read the new Preface to *Barnaby Rudge* must remember several of his old friends in that line. . . .

What a treat it was to go with him to the London Zoölogical Gardens, a place he greatly delighted in at all times! He knew the zoological address of every animal, bird, and fish of any distinction; and he could, without the slightest hesitation, on entering the grounds, proceed straightway to the celebrities of claw or foot or fin. The delight he took in the hippopotamus family was most exhilarating. He entered familiarly into conversation with the huge, unwieldy creatures, and they seemed to understand him. Indeed, he spoke to all the unphilological inhabitants with a directness and tact which went home to them at once. He chaffed with the monkeys, coaxed the tigers, and bamboozled the snakes, with a dexterity unapproachable. All the keepers knew him, he was such a loyal visitor, and I noticed they came up to him in a friendly way, with the feeling that they had a sympathetic listener always in Charles Dickens.

There were certain books of which Dickens liked to talk during his walks.[3] Among his especial favorites were the writings of

Cobbett, DeQuincey, the *Lectures on Moral Philosophy* by Sydney Smith, and Carlyle's *French Revolution*. Of this latter Dickens said it was the book of all others which he read perpetually and of which he never tired – the book which always appeared more imaginative in proportion to the fresh imagination he brought to it, a book for inexhaustibleness to be placed before every other book. When writing the *Tale of Two Cities*, he asked Carlyle if he might see one of the works to which he referred in his history; whereupon Carlyle packed up and sent down to Gad's Hill *all* his reference volumes, and Dickens read them faithfully. But the more he read the more he was astonished to find how the facts had passed through the alembic of Carlyle's brain and had come out and fitted themselves, each as a part of one great whole, making a compact result, indestructible and unrivalled; and he always found himself turning away from the books of reference, and re-reading with increased wonder this marvellous new growth. There were certain books particularly hateful to him, and of which he never spoke except in terms of most ludicrous raillery. Mr. Barlow, in *Sandford and Merton*, he said was the favorite enemy of his boyhood and his first experience of a bore. He had an almost supernatural hatred for Barlow, 'because he was so very *instructive*, and always hinting doubts with regard to the veracity of "Sindbad the Sailor", and had no belief whatever in "The Wonderful Lamp" or "The Enchanted Horse"'. Dickens rattling his mental cane over the head of Mr. Barlow was as much better than any play as can be well imagined.[4] He gloried in many of Hood's poems, especially in that biting 'Ode to Rae Wilson', and he would gesticulate with a fine fervor the lines,

> '. . . the hypocrites who ope Heaven's door
>   Obsequious to the sinful man of riches,–
> But put the wicked, naked, bare-legged poor
>   In parish *stocks* instead of *breeches*.'

One of his favorite books was Pepys's *Diary*, the curious discovery of the key to which, and the odd characteristics of its writer, were a never-failing source of interest and amusement to him. The vision of Pepys hanging round the door of the theatre, hoping for an invitation to go in, not being able to keep away in spite of a promise he had made to himself that he would spend no more money foolishly, delighted him. Speaking one day of Gray, the author of the 'Elegy', he said: 'No poet ever came walking down to posterity with so *small* a book under his arm.' He preferred Smollett to Fielding, putting *Peregrine Pickle* above *Tom Jones*. Of the best novels by his contemporaries he always spoke with warm commendation, and [Charles Reade's] *Griffith Gaunt* he thought a production of very high merit. He was 'hospitable to the thought' of all writers who were really in earnest, but at the first exhibition of floundering or inexactness he became an unbeliever. People with dislocated understandings he had no tolerance for.

He was passionately fond of the theatre, loved the lights and music and flowers, and the happy faces of the audience; he was accustomed to say that his love of the theatre never failed, and, no matter how dull the play, he was always careful while he sat in the box to make no sound which could hurt the feelings of the actors, or show any lack of attention. His genuine enthusiasm for Mr. Fechter's acting was most interesting. He loved to describe seeing him first, quite by accident, in Paris, having strolled into a little theatre there one night. 'He was making love to a woman,' Dickens said, 'and he so elevated her as well as himself by the sentiment in which he enveloped her, that they trod in a purer ether, and in another sphere, quite lifted out of the present. "By heavens!" I said to myself, "a man who can do this can do anything." I never saw two people more purely and instantly elevated by the power of love. The manner, also,' he continued, 'in which he presses the hem of the dress of Lucy in *The Bride of Lammermoor* is something wonderful. The man has genius in him which is unmistakable.[5]

Life behind the scenes was always a fascinating study to Dickens. 'One of the oddest sights a green-room can present,' he said one day, 'is when they are collecting children for a pantomime. For this purpose the prompter calls together all the women in the ballet, and begins giving out their names in order, while they press about him eager for the chance of increasing their poor pay by the extra pittance their children will receive. "Mrs. Johnson, how many?" "Two, sir." "What ages?" "Seven and ten." "Mrs. B., how many?" and so on, until the required number is made up. The people who go upon the stage, however poor their pay or hard their lot, love it too well ever to adopt another vocation of their free-will. A mother will frequently be in the wardrobe, children in the pantomime, elder sisters in the ballet, etc.'[6]

Dickens's habits as a speaker differed from those of most orators. He gave no thought to the composition of the speech he was to make till the day before he was to deliver it. No matter whether the effort was to be a long or a short one, he never wrote down a word of what he was going to say; but when the proper time arrived for him to consider his subject, he took a walk into the country and the thing was done. When he returned he was all ready for his task.

He liked to talk about the audiences that came to hear him read, and he gave the palm to his Parisian one, saying it was the quickest to catch his meaning. Although he said there were many always present in his room in Paris who did not fully understand English, yet the French eye is so quick to detect expression that it never failed instantly to understand what he meant by a look or an act. 'Thus, for instance,' he said, 'when I was impersonating Steerforth in *David Copperfield*, and gave that peculiar grip of the hand to Emily's lover, the French audience burst into cheers and rounds of applause.' He said with reference to the preparation of his readings, that it was three months' hard labor to get up one of his own stories for public recitation, and he thought he had greatly improved his presentation of the *Christmas Carol* while in this country. He considered the storm scene in *David Copperfield* one of the most effective of his readings. The character of Jack Hopkins in *Bob Sawyer's Party* he took great delight in representing, and as Jack was a prime favorite of mine, he brought him forward whenever the occasion prompted. He always spoke of Hopkins as my particular friend, and he was constantly quoting him, taking on the peculiar voice and turn of the head which he gave Jack in the public reading. . . .

It was said of Garrick that he was the *cheerfullest* man of his age. This can be as truly said of Charles Dickens. In his presence there was perpetual sunshine, and gloom was banished as having no sort of relationship with him. No man suffered more keenly or sympathized more fully than he did with want and misery; but his motto was, 'Don't stand and cry; press forward and help remove the difficulty.' The speed with which he was accustomed to make the deed follow his yet speedier sympathy was seen pleasantly on the day of his visit to the School-ship in Boston Harbor. He said, previously to going on board that ship, nothing would tempt him to make a speech, for he should always be obliged to do it on similar occasions, if he broke through his rule so early in his reading tour. But Judge Russell had no sooner finished his simple talk, to which the boys listened, as they always do, with eager faces, than Dickens rose as if he could not help it, and with a few words so magnetized them that they wore their hearts in their eyes as if they meant to keep the words forever. An enthusiastic critic once said of John

Ruskin, 'that he could discover the Apocalypse in a daisy'. As noble a discovery may be claimed for Dickens. He found all the fair humanities blooming in the lowliest hovel. He never *put on* the good Samaritan: that character was native to him. Once while in this country, on a bitter, freezing afternoon – night coming down in a drifting snow-storm – he was returning with me from a long walk in the country. The wind and baffling sleet were so furious that the street in which we happened to be fighting our way was quite deserted; it was almost impossible to see across it, the air was so thick with the tempest; all conversation between us had ceased, for it was only possible to breast the storm by devoting our whole energies to keeping on our feet; we seemed to be walking in a different atmosphere from any we had ever before encountered. All at once I missed Dickens from my side. What had become of him? Had he gone down in the drift, utterly exhausted, and was the snow burying him out of sight? Very soon the sound of his cheery voice was heard on the other side of the way. With great difficulty, over the piled-up snow, I struggled across the street, and there found him lifting up, almost by main force, a blind old man who had got bewildered by the storm, and had fallen down unnoticed, quite unable to proceed. Dickens, a long distance away from him, with that tender, sensitive, and penetrating vision, ever on the alert for suffering in any form, had rushed at once to the rescue, comprehending at a glance the situation of the sightless man. To help him to his feet and aid him homeward in the most natural and simple way afforded Dickens such a pleasure as only the benevolent by intuition can understand.

(2) *19 Nov 1867*. [He spoke about Lady Blessington's receptions] 'to which I thought it was the thing to go when I was a young man'. . . . He talked of the mistake it is to fancy that childhood forgot anything; it was age that forgets. [He expressed] his most cordial liking both for [the historian J. A. Froude] and his works. . . . He is by no means a man who loves to talk. His dramatic touches are peculiarly his own, but are of course more difficult to recall even than his words. Describing a little incident which happened while in New York, and seeing some doubt of the verity on the faces of his friends, he said ruefully: 'I assure you it is so! And all I can say is, how astonishing it is that I should be perpetually having things happen to me with regard to people that nobody else in the world can be found to believe.'

21 Nov. Mr. Dickens dined here. . . . Dickens bubbled over with fun, and I could not help fancying that [Oliver Wendell] Holmes bored him a little by talking at him. I was sorry for this, because Holmes is so simple and lovely, but Dickens is sensitive, very. He is fond of Carlyle, seems to love nobody better, and gave the most irresistible imitation of him. His queer turns of expression often convulsed us with laughter, and yet it is difficult to catch them, as when, in speaking of the writer of books, always putting himself, his real self, in, 'which is always the case', he said; 'but you must be careful of not taking him for his next-door neighbor'. . . . Just as we were in a tempest of laughter over some witticism of his, he jumped up, seized me by the hand, and said good-night. He neither smoked nor drank. 'I never do either from the time my readings "set in" ' he said, as if it were a rainy season.

24 Nov. He appears often troubled by the lack of energy his children show, and has even allowed James to see how deep his unhappiness is in having so many children by a wife who was totally uncongenial. He seems to have the deepest sympathy for men who are unfitly married and has really taken an especial fancy, I think, to John Bigelow, our latest minister in Paris who is here, because his wife is such an incubus.

27 Nov. What pity that these days have flown while I have been unable to make any record of them. J. has been to walk each day with Dickens, and has come home full of wonderful things he has said. His variety is so inexhaustible that one can only listen in wonder.

8 Jan 1868. . . . I have seldom sat at dinner with a gentleman more careful and fine in his choice and taste of food and drink than C. D. The idea of his ever passing the bounds of temperance is an absurdity not to be thought of for a moment. In this respect he is quite unlike Mr. Thackeray, who at times both ate and drank inordinately, and without doubt shortened his life by his careless-ness in these particulars. John Forster, C. D.'s old friend, is quite ill with gout and some other ails, so C. D. writes him long letters full of his experiences. We breakfast at half-past nine punctually, he on a rasher of bacon and an egg and a cup of tea, always preferring this same thing. Afterward we talk or play with the sewing-machine or anything else new and odd to him. Then he sits down to write until one o'clock, when he likes a glass of wine and biscuit, and afterward goes to walk until nearly four, when we dine. After dinner, reading days, he will take a cup of strong coffee, a tiny glass of brandy, and a cigar, and likes to lie down for a short time to get his voice in order. His man then takes a portmanteau of clothes to the reading hall, where he dresses for the evening. Upon our return we always have supper and he brews a marvellous punch, which usually makes us all sleep like tops after the excitement. The perfect kindliness and sympathy which radiates from the man is, after all, the secret never to be told, but always to be studied and to thank God for. His rapid eyes, which nothing can escape, eyes which, when he first appears upon the stage, seem to interrogate the lamps and all things above and below (like exclamation points, Aldrich says), are unlike anything before in our experience. There are no living eyes like them, swift and kind, possessing none of the bliss of ignorance, but the different bliss of one who sees what the Lord has done and what, or something of what, he intends. Such charity! Poor man! He must have learned great need for that. . . . He is a man who has suffered, evidently. . . . He has been a great student of Shakespeare, which appears often in his talk. . . . [He went off to his performance.] When we asked him to return to us, he said he must be loyal to 'the show', and, having three or four men with him, ought to be at an hotel where he could attend properly to the business. He never forgets the needs of those who are dependent upon him, is liberal to his servants (and to ours also), and liberal in his heart to all sorts and conditions of men.

25 Feb. [Dickens's public reading of *Doctor Marigold*] went off brilliantly. He never read better nor was more universally applauded. Mr. Emerson came down to go, and passed the night here; of course we sat talking until late, he being much surprised at the artistic perfection of the performance. It was queer enough to sit by his side, for when his stoicism did at length break down, he laughed as if he must crumble to pieces at such unusual bodily agitation, and with a face on as if it hurt him dreadfully – to look at him was too much for me, already full of laughter myself. Afterward we all went in to shake hands for a moment. When we came back home Mr. Emerson asked me a great many questions about C. D. and pondered much. Finally he said, 'I am afraid he has too much talent for his genius; it is a fearful locomotive to which he is bound and can never be free from it nor set at rest. You see him quite wrong, evidently; and would persuade me that he is a genial creature, full of sweetness and amenities and superior to his talents, but I fear he is harnessed to them. He is too consummate an artist to have a thread of nature left. He daunts me! I have not the key.' When Mr. Fields came in he repeated 'Mrs. Fields would persuade me he is a man easy to communicate with, sympathetic and accessible to his friends; but her eyes do not see clearly in this matter, I am sure.' 'Look for yourself, dear Mr. Emerson,' I answered, laughing, 'and then report to me afterward.'

1 Mar. . . . . He talked with me about Spiritualism as it is called, the humbug of which excites his deepest ire, although no one could believe more entirely than he in magnetism and the unfathomed ties between man and man. He told me many curious things about the traps which had been laid by well-meaning friends to bring him into 'spiritual' circles. But he said, 'If I go to a friend's house for the purpose of exposing a fraud in which she believes, I am doing a very disagreeable thing and not what she invited me for. . . . '

He loves to talk of Gad's Hill and stopped joyfully from other talk to tell me how his daughter Mary arranged his table with flowers. He speaks continually of her great taste in combining flowers. 'Sometimes she will have nothing but water-lilies', he said, as if the memory were a fragrance.

Some one has said, 'We cannot love and be wise.' I will gladly give away the inconsistent wisdom, for Jamie and I are truly penetrated with grateful love to C. D.

3 Mar. He is a great actor and artist, but above all a great and loving and well-beloved man. (This I cling to in memory of Mr. Emerson's dictum.)

I am deep in Carlyle's history and every little thing I hear chimes in with that. After *the* dinner (at the Parker) the other night, Mr. Dickens thought he would take a warm bath; but, the water being drawn, he began playing the clown in pantomime on the edge of the bath (with his clothes on) for the amusement of Dolby and Osgood; in a moment and before he knew where he was, he had tumbled in head over heels, clothes and all.

6 Mar. Mr. Dickens talked as usual, much and naturally – first of the various hotels of which he had late experience [and then of books]. At last they came to the book, *Ecce Homo*, in which Dickens can see nothing of value, any more than we. He thinks Jesus foresaw and guarded as well as he could against the misinterpreting of his teaching, that the four Gospels are all derived from some anterior written Scriptures – made up, perhaps, with additions and interpolations from the *Talmud*, in which he expressed great interest and admiration. Among other things which prove how little the Gospels should be taken literally is the fact that *broad phylacteries* were not in use until some years after Jesus lived, so that the passage in which this reference occurs, at least, must only be taken as conveying the spirit and temper, not the actual form of speech, of our Lord. Mr. Dickens spoke reverently and earnestly, and said much more if I could recall it perfectly.

7 Apr. Dickens . . . told Jamie the other day in walking that he wrote *Nicholas Nickleby* and *Oliver Twist* at the same time for rival magazines from month to month. Once he was taken ill, with both magazines waiting for unwritten sheets. He immediately took steamer for Boulogne, took a room in an inn there, secure from interruption, and was able to return just in season for the monthly issues with his work completed.[7] He sees now how the work of both would have been better done had he worked only upon one at a time. After the exertion of last evening he looked pale and exhausted. Longfellow and Norton joined with us in trying to dissuade him from future Readings after these two. He does not recover his vitality after the effort of reading, and his spirits are naturally somewhat depressed by the use of soporifics, which at length became a necessity. . . . *Copperfield* was a tragedy last night – less vigor but great tragic power came out of it. . . . I should hardly have known it for the same reading and reader.

10 Apr. Left home at eight o'clock in the morning, found our dearly beloved friend C. D. already awaiting us, with two roses in his coat and looking as fresh as possible. . . . I was impressed all day long with the occasional languor which came over C. D. and always with the exquisite delicacy and quickness of his perception, something as fine as the finest woman possesses, which combined itself wondrously with the action of the massive brain and the rapid movement of those strong, strong hands. I felt how deeply we had learned to love him and how hard it would be for us to part. . . .

Speaking of O'Connell [during some reminiscences of his Parliamentary reporting days], Mr. Dickens said there had been nobody since who could compare with him but John Bright, who is at present the finest speaker in England. Cobden was fond of reasoning, and hardly what would be called a brilliant speaker; but his noble truthfulness and devotion to the cause to which he had pledged himself made him one of the grandest of England's great men. . . . He said, by the way, that never since those old days when he left the House of Commons as a Reporter had he entered it again. His hatred of the falseness of talk, of bombastic eloquence, he had heard there made it impossible for him ever to go in again to hear anyone.

12 Apr. Last night we went to the circus together, C. D., J., and I. It is a pretty building. I was astonished at the knowledge C. D. showed of everything before him. He knew how the horses were stenciled, how tight the wire bridles were, etc. . . . When the young rope-dancer slipped (he was but an apprentice at the business, without wages, C. D. thought), he tried over and over again to accomplish a certain somersault until he achieved it. 'That's the law of the circus,' said C. D.; 'they are never allowed to give up, and it's a capital rule for everything in life. Doubtless this idea has been handed down from the Greeks or Romans and these people know nothing about where it came from. But it's well for all of us.'

15 Apr. [On returning from a reading in 'Steinway Hall, than which nothing could be worse for reading or speaking'] He soon came up after a little soup, when he called for brandy and lemons and made *such* a burnt brandy punch as has been seldom tasted this side of the 'pond'. As the punch blazed his spirits rose and he began to sing an old-fashioned comic song such as in the old days was given between the plays at the theatre. One song led to another until we fell into inextinguishable laughter, for anything more comic than his renderings of the chorus cannot be imagined. Surely there is no living actor who could excel him in these things if he chose to exert his ability. His rendering of 'Chrush ke lan ne chouskin!!' or a lingo which sounded like that (the refrain of an old Irish song) was something tremendous. We laughed till I was really afraid he would make himself too hoarse to read the next night. He gave a queer old song full of rhymes, obtained with immense difficulty and circumlocution, to the word 'annuity', which it appeared has been sought by an old woman with great *assiduity* and granted with immense *incongruity*. The negro minstrels have in great part supplanted these queer old English, Irish, and Scotish ballads, but they are sure to come up again from time to time. We did not separate until 12, and felt the next morning (as he said) as if we had had a regular orgy.

19 Apr. After his return [from the New York press banquet in his honour] he repeated to me from memory every word of his speech without dropping one. He never thinks of such a thing as writing his speeches, but simply turns it over in his mind and 'balances the sentences', when he is all right.

24 Apr. [Dickens has sailed for England.] He goes to the English spring, to his own dear ones, to the tenderness of the long tried love. . . . My respect for Miss Hogarth grows as I reflect upon Dickens. It is not an easy service in this world to live near such a man, to love him, to desire to do for him. He is swift, restless, impatient, with words of fire, but he is also and above all, tender, loving, strong for right, charitable and patient by moral force. Happy those who live, and bear, and do and suffer and above all love him to the end. . . . Miss Hogarth has labored for him with remarkable success and for his children. But even now he might be lonely, such is his nature. When I recall his lonely couch and lonely hours I feel he has had a strange lot. May his mistakes be expiated.

— May 1869. [At Gad's Hill: Dickens is oppressed by a 'spirit of wakefulness'; for him] sleepless nights come too often, oftener than they would to a free heart. . . . [But it is] wonderful, the flow of spirits C. D. has for a sad man.

25 Feb 1870. [Dickens's friend Fechter, the actor, remarks,] 'Yes, yes, all his fame goes for nothing since he has not the one thing. He is very unhappy in his children.' Nobody can say how much too much of this his children have to hear.

NOTES

1. ' . . . the great Detective', as Dickens calls him in a letter to Fields, 25 May 1869 (*N*, III, 727), was Inspector Charles Frederick Field, of the Metropolitan Police (here called 'W——' presumably because in some *Household Words* essays on the detective police Dickens disguises him as 'Inspector Wield'). He was the

original of Inspector Bucket in *Bleak House*: see Philip Collins, *Dickens and Crime* (1962) pp. 206–11 and *passim*.

2. Fields's – or, more probably, Dickens's – memories go awry here. In his memoranda for No. III of *Dombey*, where Mrs Pipchin is introduced, Dickens wrote: 'Mrs. Roylance – House at the seaside'. Mentioning her in his autobiographical fragment as the original of Mrs Pipchin, he records that she was 'a reduced old lady' living in Camden Town 'who took children into board, and had once done so in Brighton'. Dickens lodged with her – at the age of twelve, not two – while his father and family were in the Marshalsea Prison. When John Dickens was released, the whole family moved in on her for a while (*Life*, I, ii, 27, 33, 36).

3. For a survey, see Philip Collins, 'Dickens's Reading', *Dkn*, LX (1964) 136–51.

4. Compare his *Uncommercial Traveller* essay 'Mr Barlow', in *All the Year Round*, n. s., 1, 156–9 (16 Jan 1869).

5. Dickens contributed an essay 'On Mr. Fechter's Acting' to Fields's journal *Atlantic Monthly*, May 1869.

6. Dickens had made this the theme of an essay 'Gaslight Fairies', *Household Words*, XI, 25–8 (10 Feb 1855).

7. These novels were not written 'for rival magazines'. *Oliver Twist* was serialised in *Bentley's Miscellany*, which Dickens was editing; *Nickleby*, published in monthly parts, overlapped it for a year. There seems to be no other record of this alleged dash to Boulogne.

An Informal Call upon Dickens in 1867

G. D. CARROW

Repr. from *University* (Princeton, N. J.), winter 1965–6, in *Dkn*, LXIII (1967) 112–19. The Rev. Dr G. D. Carrow, a Methodist pastor from Philadelphia touring Europe in 1867, particularly wanted to see Dickens. At his London hotel he enquired about the possibilities, 'but the proprietors, being strict Wesleyans, did not regard Mr. Dickens with favor'. So he wrote to Dickens, who immediately invited him to call at the *All the Year Round* offices: which he did, on 9 August 1867. Dickens's remarks about *American Notes* and *Martin Chuzzlewit* may have been the more 'apologetic' because he was then carefully laying the ground for his American Readings Tour, for which he sailed in November. About the same time as Carrow met him, he was making placatory remarks in his new Prefaces to these two books.

The offices of *All the Year Round* were exceptionally plain. . . . Nowhere in the building did I see a single article of furniture excepting an oblong table and a pair of large rush bottomed armchairs in the editorial room. It was plain that even the best of friends was not expected there for the purposes of lounging or gossip. . . . Mr. Dickens had limped to the head of the stairway, and extending both hands as I approached, grasped mine and began vigorously shaking them up and down, meanwhile most heartily bidding me welcome. Then with my hands still locked in his he led me into his room and seated me in a chair immediately in front of his own.

Mr. Dickens was essentially an Englishman in appearance. My impression of his looks was as follows: head large; brow massive and projecting; hair auburn, abundant, soft and inclining to curl; cheek bones high and separated; nose prominent, straight, exceedingly expressive; eyes, the most characteristic of all his features, large, blue, full of tenderness and light, and in power of expression simply wonderful. His general bearing was earnest, frank, gracious and winning. Among his minor characteristics was that nationally English one, his exceedingly poor taste in the matter of dress. He wore a blue cloth dress coat trimmed with black velvet collar and gilt buttons, a flowered purple velvet vest and checkered cashmere pantaloons, while around his neck was the usual high shirt collar turned down in front, and the black silk tie loosely fastened with a gold ring.

As soon as we were seated knee to knee he opened upon me a very torrent of questions as to where I had been, what I had seen, what I thought of the policies of Bismarck and Louis Napoleon and how the political and social conditions of European nations impressed me as compared with those of the United States. Then, pausing a moment and looking at me with a twinkle in his eyes, he asked: 'How do you like the English? Have you found them civil and obliging? Have the police been ready to give information and to direct you in your walks about the city?'

I replied that on all these points the English had greatly exceeded my expectations; that the people seemed not only reasonably communicative but talkative to a degree that contrasted strangely with their reputation for taciturnity; and as for the police I had found them most obliging and regarded them as a model force.

'Well sir,' returned Mr. Dickens, 'I have given some attention to the municipal government of our metropolis, especially to its department of police, and you do not overrate its character for efficiency. Some members of the force would not be impaired as officers by dispensing with sundry little airs – but you know the effect of a uniform upon wiser men. Then too the fact must not be overlooked that Inspector Bucket feels himself distantly related to the Lord Mayor though he does not receive from that functionary a card to the annual banquet. Official honor is a contagious thing. As to my countrymen at large I think common fame greatly belies them; for the usual experience of strangers who visit our shores is the same as yours. John Bull closes himself up when he goes abroad not because he is afraid of strangers nor because he is ashamed of his country and himself. His opinion of his country and himself is a very comfortable one and as to being afraid – John can hardly be regarded as a coward anywhere. The explanation of his traveling manner is found in part in his sudden transfer from the narrow limit of an island home to the boundless expanse of the world.'

While talking thus, Mr. Dickens's features assumed a serio-comical expression which gave increased charm to his words. I could not, however, help reminding myself, interested though I was in these general topics, that time was passing, so I said: 'Mr. Dickens, the hour which I promised myself should your patience endure so long is already half gone. May I request then that you occupy the remainder of our interview in telling me something of yourself?' No doubt he had been watching for the Yankee in me and said within himself: 'Here he is at last!' Bending slightly forward in his chair and placing his hands upon my knees he said smiling: 'You do me great honor, sir, I am sure, in desiring me to speak of myself. But what shall I tell you? Any question that may be in your thoughts I shall be glad to answer if I can.'

I replied: 'Your American readers, through their intense interest in your works, have come to feel that they have a sort of right of property in your very being. You must therefore pardon an American's curiosity concerning your daily life and method of work. It is thought in my country that much of your work is done at night. Is that correct or erroneous?'

'Erroneous – entirely erroneous. I may state briefly what has been my invariable habit of working. I rise at seven; at eight I breakfast; until ten I walk or ride and read the morning papers; at ten precisely I go to my desk and stay there till two, and if particularly in the vein keep at it until four. Then I take the open air for exercise, usually walking. At six down to dinner and remain at table until ten, during which time I discuss domestic matters with my family or entertain such friends as may honor me with their visits. This, the great occasion of the day, over, I retire to my study, amuse myself a little with the flute, read up the reviews, or examine such original publications as may have been sent to my table; and exactly at twelve I extinguish my lights and jump into bed. So rigid is my conformity to this method of work that my family say I am a monomaniac on the subject of method.'

'And before you put out the lights,' said I, 'do you not prepare for yourself a glass of that steaming decoction with a slice of buttered toast to which Miss Betsey was so regularly addicted as she sat before her midnight fire ruminating of the fortunes and misfortunes of the Copperfield family?'

'Never a drop of the one, nor a morsel of the other,' said Mr. Dickens laughing until the frame of the rush-bottomed chair fairly creaked. 'A lunch at midnight would spoil the whole work of the next day. Yet how natural it is that the reader should infer that the author, in delineating a fictitious character, was simply portraying himself.'

Changing the subject, I asked: 'Were the descriptions of London localities contained in your works furnished from your personal observation? And if so did you make your visits incognito, or without disguise?'

'Yes, my pictures were all drawn from personal inspection. In some instances a disguise was assumed; in others concealment was unnecessary. When in the worst parts of the city my invariable precaution was to seem not to notice any person or thing in particular, I would walk along slowly, preserving an air of preoccupation, and affecting as nearly as possible the ways of a collector of house rents or of a physician going his rounds. When any scene of especial interest attracted my notice I usually halted at a crossing as if waiting for a conveyance or as if undecided which way to go. Or else I would stop and purchase some trifle, chatting with the vendor and taking my time for making a selection, or would order a glass of half-and-half, wait for the froth to subside and then consume an hour in sipping it to the bottom. In my visits to the dens of thieves and other haunts of infamy, I deemed it prudent to associate myself with a brace of policemen who were well versed in the ways of the localities I wished to examine, and who introduced me to the professionals as an old friend who was making the accustomed round with them merely for the opportunity of a talk about old times. These were what I called my field-days.[1] I suppose, sir, that I know London better than any one other man of all its millions.'

The conversation turned to books. I asked Mr. Dickens which of his various works he himself liked best. Leaning back in his chair with a humorous smile on his lips, he said: 'I am sure you would not like me to say the *American Notes* or *Martin Chuzzlewit.*' 'No,' I replied, 'an author's best performance must be one achieved on his own ground. Shakespeare could not have painted the passions and customs of another nation as he painted those of his own. The Italian, the Moor and the Jew are good portraits, but the Englishman is better.'

'You reason correctly, sir' returned the novelist, and then he proceeded to recount the circumstances of his first visit to the United States, and the conditions under which the *American Notes* and *Martin Chuzzlewit* were composed. His explanation was apologetic in its character, and I observed that the bitter criticisms of the American press had been received as partially merited and had left no resentment rankling in his heart. Then he glided into a lively running comment upon his more elaborate works, alluding to the circumstances that had suggested their plots and shaped the personalities of their characters. It was plain that these reminiscences rekindled much of the interest and enthusiasm that had attended their original creation, and that the author regarded his fictitious heroes and heroines as if they had been so many groups of friends. Returning at length from the sparkling review on which my question had started him, he said: 'You wish to know which of my fictitious children I love the best. I will say – Copperfield!'

The confession was made with a peculiar smile which obviously indicated recollections of Mr. Micawber – the old smile so frequently noted by the author's most intimate friends and which so wonderfully expressed that intuitive perception of human weakness and the power to make it diverting in which he excelled.

It was at this stage of our interview that I made allusion to the pleasure I had experienced in reading his works and to their influence on my judgment of humanity, and seemed to fairly startle him by a compliment.

'Mr. Dickens,' I said. 'Providence seems to have endowed you with an insight into the heart of woman, never to my mind possessed in an equal degree by any other save that wonderful Galilean who knew the heart of all. You have sometimes in a single paragraph laid open the heart of a woman as Sir Walter Scott has failed to do in his whole Waverley series.'

Had I fired a pistol in his ear he could not have seemed more surprised. 'Why my dear sir!' he said. Then he called up in quick succession a goodly array of Sir Walter's most graphic characters, meanwhile expatiating upon and eulogizing his genius as though the wizard of the north had in dying committed to him the defense of his reputation.

'Yes', I returned, 'You must read him as I cannot; but it should be remembered that Sir Walter was a man of but one passion – that of ambition to found a family. Whereas, I hold that a man must have really loved a woman if he would fully interpret the secrets of a woman's heart.'

'You are correct again, sir,' replied Mr. Dickens smiling. 'But to what particular character in my works have you alluded?' The question drew him more closely to me; and replacing his hands on my knees, he added, 'Do me favor to explain yourself.' His smile was expressive of curiosity as well as of pleasure, and showed that he was saying to himself, 'I wonder if this Yankee clergyman does truly comprehend me?'

I answered: 'Various characters might be advanced in support of my opinion; but I shall take the first one occurring to me at this moment.' And I rapidly sketched the incidents of that famous scene in *Bleak House* where the 'little woman' accepts her guardian's proposal of marriage. While I did so, the face of the great artist took on a pensive, tender aspect, and when I had concluded he seized both my hands exclaiming: 'I see you understand me! I see you understand me! And that is more precious to the author than fame or gold.'

Thus far only such topics had been touched on as enabled me to address Mr. Dickens in the language of just and honest admiration. I now ventured a little adverse criticism. I had in view but one feature of his work and at that I wished to hear his explanation, so I said: 'Mr. Dickens, my great pleasure in your works has en-countered one set-back, exciting almost pain in my mind.'

'Pray sir, what was that?' he enquired with astonishment.

'I fear that the satirical dress,' I continued, 'with which you have clothed some of your religious characters will lead many persons, especially the young and uncultivated, to treat the strictest types of Christian conduct with suspicion. The characters to whom I chiefly allude are Stiggins, Chadband and Mrs. Clennam. While I am sure that I understand your motives myself I have often feared lest certain shallow-minded people confound genuine examples of Christian earnestness with the dunces whom I have just named and whose hypocrisy you so justly exposed.'

I can never forget his words of reply, uttered with an air of protestation and a solemnity of tone strongly indicative of his sincerity. 'Some of the criticisms to which you have referred,' he remarked, 'I have seen. My view has been to make transparent the design of my writings, and my belief is that by my readers generally I am perfectly understood. Ours is an age of great religious activity. There is much zeal for the common cause of Christianity, but more for the success of particular denominations. Rivalry added to zeal has led to the employment of improper persons as Christian teachers. To endeavor to check this tendency seemed to me could not be otherwise than good service to the real truth; and as for Mrs. Clennam, her example will the sooner make way for a piety more consonant to the gentle spirit of the New Testament. I have been accustomed to regard my books as weekday gospel for the poor. My chief interest has been to elevate and improve the condition of the masses. I now make this statement frankly to you because of the interest you have expressed in me and in the work of my life. Nothing sir, could give me so great pain as to know that any word of mine had for one moment diverted a human soul from the path of rectitude.'

There was a pause. The last sand of my hour had fallen and propriety recognized the parting moment. Simultaneously we rose from our chairs; then taking both my hands in his, Mr. Dickens said, 'I'm sure you'll permit my lameness to excuse me for taking leave of you where I stand. I thank you most heartily for your visit – I wish you a safe return to your country and home. I pray God to bless you and give you many years to live!'

NOTE

1. Carrow, forgivably, did not realise that Dickens was punning here, in this reference to his expeditions under the guidance and protection of Detective-Inspector Field (see above, II, 202, note 1).

Dickens's Characters, Talents and Limitations

EDWARD BULWER-LYTTON

From Sibylla Jane Flower, 'Charles Dickens and Edward Bulwer-Lytton', *Dkn*, LXXIX (1973) 89. Edward George Earle Lytton Bulwer Lytton, first Baron Lytton (1803–73), novelist and politician, had known Dickens since the 1830s and been a close friend from the late 1840s, collaborating with him on the Guild of Literature and Art, contributing to *All the Year Round*, and being associated with him in various other ways. The two novelists admired each others' work and often visited each others' houses. In 1869, when he was sorting through his papers, Lytton endorsed his collection of Dickens letters with this character sketch.

His work need no eulogies from me. In his own way he is unrivalled and that way is one which leads to the widest range of popularity. My intercourse with him has always been constant and friendly – tho' the writers of the Periodical Press most under his influence have spoken of me with vehement abuse or contemptuous depreciation – as if they thought that would please him. He has been fortunate in escaping the envy of fellow writers and has aided this good fortune by very skilful care of his own fame – watching every occasion to refresh it – in times when it has seemed to fade a little and maintaining a corps of devoted parasites in the Press. He understands the practical part of Authorship beyond any writer – W. Scott not excepted.

His nature is good and genial – but from his study of popularity – he a little overparades his goodness – An admirable actor, he is not without theatrical arts off the stage. He can even be insincere but unconsciously so. His power of observation on minute points of humour and character are marvellous – he detects oddities and out of them invents original creations by a pleasing exaggeration of the salient points, so that his most humorous characters have a touch of caricature. He fails in characters of intellectual depth or refinement nor can he describe the struggle of the grander passions. He is no metaphysician – nor could he have made a poetic dramatist. He hit upon that which he could do better than any other man and is only less than himself where he deviates from it. Certainly, on the whole, one of the greatest geniuses in fiction the world has produced.

'Such a Man!'

SIR ARTHUR HELPS

(1) from John R. DeBruyn, 'Charles Dickens Meets the Queen: A New Look', *Dkn*, LXXI (1975) 87–8; (2) from Arthur Helps, 'In Memoriam', *Macmillan's Magazine*, XXII (1870) 236–40. Queen Victoria, having met 'Mr. Dickens, the celebrated author', at Buckingham Palace on 9 Mar 1870, recorded in her journal that 'He is very agreeable, with a pleasant voice and manner. He talked of his latest works, of America, the strangeness of the people there, of the division of classes in England, which he hoped would get better in time. He felt that it would come gradually.' That the meeting took place, only just in time – for Dickens was dead two months later – was probably due to Arthur Helps (1813–75), Clerk to the Privy Council since 1860 and occasional author, knighted 1875, a 'very close friend indeed' of Dickens by this time, as Professor DeBruyn argues. Extract (1) consists of advice tendered by Helps to Her Majesty. DeBruyn notes that one courtier reported that Dickens was 'a conversational failure at the Palace'. Maybe so; but it is difficult to envisage Dickens failing in such intellectually unexacting circumstances, and his own account sounds more cheerful – George Dolby, *Dickens as I Knew Him* (1885) pp. 454–8. They talked, he said, about the 'servant question', the 'price of provisions, the cost of butchers' meat, and bread' – matters on which he was unlikely to be nonplussed by Her Majesty's stock of knowledge. Extract (2) is from Helps's obituary tribute. John Forster particularly commended it in the *Life* and, indulging in the sincerest form of flattery, silently stole or adapted passages from it. See also letters from W. L. Pollock and George Grove, praising this essay and amplifying points in it – *Correspondence of Sir Arthur Helps*, ed. E. A. Helps (1917), pp. 175–7.

(1) *4 Mar 1870*. Mr. Helps presents his humble duty to Your Majesty; & encloses a letter which he has received from Mr. Dickens. Mr Helps thinks the Queen will be pleased with this letter. It really would be right that the author, whose name will hereafter be closely associated with the Victorian era, should have been presented to Queen Victoria. And Your Majesty would like the man: he, too, has the most anxious desire to raise what we call 'the lower classes'; & would sympathize with Your Majesty in many of the Queen's views and aspirations.

5 Mar 1870. Mr. Helps presents his humble duty to Your Majesty, and has received the Queen's letter of yesterday's date. First, as regards Mr. Dickens. His Christian name is Charles. Mr. Helps forgets which is his last work; but he will ascertain that point before he sees Your Majesty. One of his best works is *David Copperfield*: and it is supposed that it gives or at least gives a hint of the narrative of the author's early life. Your Majesty might naturally say that Your Majesty's many cares and duties have prevented your reading all the works of your most eminent authors, & might, playfully, ask Mr. Dickens's advice whether *David Copperfield* would be the work of his which he would wish Your Majesty to read next. The Queen might also allude to his readings; and reading is a subject which, in Mr. Helps judgment, the Queen thoroughly understands. The Queen might naturally say that she would like to have a pleasure which so many of her subjects have enjoyed, & might ask him whether he would read to her at Windsor. If this were to be done, Your Majesty might have an opportunity of treating this really eminent man as a guest and not merely as a reader. But all these suggestions are merely submitted for Your Majesty's better judgment in such matters. Mr. Helps has no doubt whatever that Your Majesty will manage the interview very well. The Queen always does go through those things well.

(2) There will be few households that will not desire to possess some portrait of Mr. Dickens; but alas, how little can any portrait tell of such a man! His was one of those faces which require to be seen with the light of life. What portrait can do justice to the frankness, kindness, and power of his eyes? They seemed to look through you, and yet only to take notice of what was best in you and most worthy of notice. And then his smile, which was most charming! And then his laughter – not poor, thin, arid, ambiguous laughter, that is ashamed of itself, that moves one feature only of the face – but the largest and heartiest kind, irradiating his whole countenance, and compelling you to participate in his immense enjoyment of it.

He was both witty and humorous, a combination rarely met with; and, both in making and appreciating fun – which we may perhaps define as a happy product of humour and geniality, upborne by animal spirits – I never met his equal.

It need hardly be said that his powers of observation were almost unrivalled; and therein, though it is a strange comparison to make, he used to remind me of those modern magicians whose wondrous skill has been attained by their being taught from their infancy to see more things in less time than any other men. Indeed, I have said to myself, when I have been with him, he sees and observes nine facts for any two that I see and observe.

As is generally the case with imaginative men, I believe that he lived a great deal with the creatures of his imagination, and that they surrounded him at all times. Such men live in two worlds, the actual and the imaginative; and he lived intensely in both. I am strongly confirmed in this opinion by a reply he once made to me. I jestingly remarked to him that I was very superior to him, as I had read my *Pickwick* and my *David Copperfield*, whereas he only wrote them. To which he replied that I did not know the pleasure he had received from what he had written, and added words, which I do not recollect, but which impressed me at the time with the conviction that he lived a good deal with the people of his brain, and found them very amusing society.

He was of a commanding and organizing nature – a good man of business – frank, clear, decisive, imperative – a man to confide in, and look up to, as a leader, in the midst of any great peril. This brings me to another part of his character which was very remarkable. He was one of the most precise and accurate men in the world; and he grudged no labour in his work. Those who have seen his MSS. will recollect what elaborate notes, and comments, and plans (some adopted, many rejected), went to form the basis of his works. To see those manuscripts would cure anybody of the idle and presumptuous notion that men of genius require no forethought or preparation for their greatest efforts, but that these are dashed off by the aid of a mysterious something which is comprehended in the word 'genius'. It was one of Mr. Dickens's theories, and I believe a true one, that men differ hardly in anything so much as in their power of attention; and certainly, whatever he did, he attended to it with all his might.

Mr. Dickens was a very good listener, paying the greatest attention to the person who was speaking (that is, if he was saying anything worth attending to), and never interrupting, except perhaps by uttering, if he approved of what was being said, the words 'Surely, surely', which was a favourite expression of his. He was very refined in his conversation, at least what I call 'refined'–for he was one of those persons in whose society one is comfortable from the certainty that they will never say anything which can shock other people, or hurt their feelings, be they ever so fastidious or sensitive.[1]

I have hardly spoken enough of his punctilious accuracy. As a curious instance of this, I may mention that where most men use figures, he would use words – for example, in his letters, writing the day of the month always in full. He had a horror of being misunderstood, and grudged no labour to be 'understanded of the people'.

His love of order and neatness was almost painful. Unpunctuality made him unhappy. I am afraid, though, some people would hardly have called him punctual, for he was so anxious to be in time that he was invariably before time. The present writer has this same fault, if fault it be, which was once the cause of a droll circumstance that occasioned some amusement to our friends. We were going to a railway station together. I planned to be a quarter of an hour before the time; and he, who had the final ordering of the carriage, and who had not a proper belief in my punctuality, added another quarter of an hour of his own; so that our conjoint prepunctualities brought us to the station a good half-hour before the time. The time, however, that we spent together on that occasion, was well spent by me in listening to him as he discoursed upon the beautiful forms of clouds.

At home, and as a host, he was delightful. I think I have observed that he looked at all things and people dramatically. He assigned to all of us characters; and in his company we could not help playing our parts.

He had the largest toleration. I had not intended to say anything about his works; but I must do so now, as I see that they afford a singular instance of this toleration. Think of this precise, accurate, orderly, methodical man depicting so lovingly such a disorderly, feckless, reckless, unmethodical character as that of Dick Swiveller, and growing more enamoured of it as he went on depicting! I rather think that in this he was superior to Sir Walter Scott, for in almost all Scott's characters there appear one or the other, or both combined, of Scott's principal characteristics, namely, nobility of nature and shrewdness. . . . Mr. Dickens's own kindness of nature is visible in most of his characters. He could not well get rid of that, as a general rule, by any force of fiction. Still there are a few characters, such as that of Jonas Chuzzlewit, in which he has succeeded in denuding the character of any trait belonging to himself.

We doubt whether there has ever been a writer of fiction who took such a real and living interest in the actual world about him. Its many sorrows, its terrible injustice, its sufferings, its calamities, went to his heart. Care for the living people about him – for his 'neighbour', if I may so express it – sometimes even diminished his power as an artist; a dimunition of power for which, considering the cause, we ought to love his memory all the more.

I have sometimes regretted, perhaps unwisely, that he did not take a larger part – or shall I say a more prominent part? – in public affairs. Not for our own sakes, but for his. Like all men who see social evils very strongly and clearly, and also see their way to remedies (to be, as they think, swiftly applied), he did not give enough weight, I think, to the inevitable difficulties which must exist in a free State to prevent the rapid and complete adoption of these remedies. 'Circumlocution' is everywhere – in the Senate, at the Bar, in the Field, in ordinary business, as well as in official life; and men of Mr. Dickens's temperament, full of ardour for the public good and somewhat despotic in their habits of thought, find it difficult to put up with the tiresome aberrations of a freedom which will not behave itself at once in a proper way, and set to work to provide immediate remedies for that which ought to be remedied. When you come close to any great man, you generally find that he has somewhat of a despotic nature in this respect. . . .

Mr. Dickens was simple in his ways of living, in his tastes, in his ambition. Probably, in the inevitable imitation of a great man, there will, for some time, be a run upon simplicity of this kind. But there are many persons whom such simplicity does not suit, or become. Now, if Mr. Dickens had possessed a love for what is not simple; if he had been devoted to what is grand, and gorgeous, and resounding, we should have known it, because *he* would have known it, and would have been the first person to have told himself of it, and would, to use an official phrase, have 'governed himself accordingly'. That exquisite sincerity of nature which produces such a result was most manifest in him. He was very dramatic in his imagination, and brought all that he saw and felt into a magic circle of dramatic creation. But he never dramatized himself to himself. . . .

Mr. Dickens loved the poor. He understood them. He was wise enough to see how very needful recreation is for them; and I shall never forget the delight with which he described to me, giving it with all those details that were with him fine touches of art, an entertainment that he had provided for the neighbouring poor in his own fields; and how he had rejoiced at their orderliness and good behaviour. He ardently desired, and confidently looked forward to, a time when there would be a more intimate union than exists at present between the different classes in the State – a union embracing alike the highest and the lowest.

It always seemed to me that he had a power of narration which was beyond anything even which his books show forth. How he would narrate to you, sitting on a gate or on a fallen tree, some rustic story of the people he had known in his reighbourhood! It was the very perfection of narrative. Not a word was thrown away, not an adjective misused; and I think all those who have had the good fortune to hear him recount one of these stories will agree with me, that it was a triumph – an unconscious triumph – of art.

He was one of those men who almost invariably speak well of others behind their backs – one of the truest of friends, and very little given to resent any injury that concerned himself alone. In that respect he often put me in mind of Lord Palmerston, though he was not equal to that statesman in supreme serenity of temper. There was, however, a considerable resemblance between these two remarkable men in several points. They had both a certain hearty bluffness of manner. There was a sea-going way about them, as of a captain on his quarter-deck. They were both tremendous walkers, and took interest in every form of labour, rustic, urban, or commercial. Then, too, they made the most and the best of everything that came before them: stood up sturdily for their own way of thinking; and valued greatly their own peculiar experiences.

Mr. Dickens delighted to praise; and there were few persons who appreciated more fully than he did the works of his contemporaries. His criticisms on the literary works of others were given in that frank, friendly, helpful way which makes criticism most effective. I know a brother author of his who received such criticism from him very lately, and profited by it. Mr. Dickens, seeing that the said author was much perplexed in finding a good title for a work which he was preparing, took the greatest interest in aiding his friend; and, during the last few weeks of his life, amidst all his own labours, would write sometimes more than one letter a day to make fresh suggestions about this troublesome, but most important, thing, the title of a work.[2] These are small traits to mention; but they are very significant.

Everybody has heard of Mr. Dickens's pre-eminence as an actor, but perhaps it is not so generally known what an admirable speaker he was. The last speech, I believe, that he ever made was at the Academy dinner; and I think it would be admitted by every one, including those who also made excellent speeches on that occasion, that Mr. Dickens's was the speech of the evening. He was herein greatly aided by nature, having that presence, conveying the idea of courage and honesty, which gives much effect to public speaking, and also possessing a sweet, deep-toned, audible voice, that had exceeding pathos in it. Moreover, he had most expressive hands – not beautiful, according to the ordinary notions of beauty, but nervous and powerful hands. He did not indulge in gesticulation; but the slight movements of these expressive hands helped wonderfully in giving additional force and meaning to what he said, as all those who have been present at his readings will testify. Indeed, when he read, or when he spoke, the whole man read, or spoke.

NOTES

1. Cf. Sir George Russell: 'Dickens was eminently pure-minded. . . . In the course of a long and intimate friendship of many years I never heard him say a word which might not have been spoken in the society of ladies' – Lady Russell, *Swallowfield and Its Owners* (1901) p. 305.
2. The correspondence extant (in $\mathcal{N}$) throws no light on the identity of this author.

Glimpses

VARIOUS

A medley of impressions of the later Dickens, chiefly by people who did not know him well, followed by accounts of his final weeks.

Dickens was at dinner and he and I fraternised [wrote the Revd Charles Kingsley (1819–75) in April 1855, after their only known meeting]. He is a really genial lovable man, with an eye like a hawk. Not high bred but excellent company, and very sensible. But Mrs. Dickens! Oh the fat vulgar vacancy![1]

[Dickens and his wife are reported on, second-hand, by another novelist, Nathaniel Hawthorne (1804–64), who was then U. S. Consul in Liverpool. He had been dining out in London.] Speaking of Dickens, last evening, Mrs. Milnes[2] mentioned his domestic tastes, how he preferred home-enjoyments to all others, and did not willingly go into society. Mrs. Bennoch, too, the other day, told us how careful he was of his wife, taking upon himself all possible trouble as regards his domestic affairs, making bargains at butchers and bakers, and doing, as far as he could, whatever duty pertains to an English wife. There is a great variety of testimony, various and variant, as to the character of Dickens. I must see him before I finally leave England.[3]

[In 1857, Hans Christian Andersen (1805–75) was staying at Gad's Hill, and was fretting over a recent bad review. Dickens comforted him, saying:] 'You should never read the papers, except what you have yourself written. I have not for 24 years read criticism about myself!' – He had brought with him a Mr. Shirley Brooks, one of the foremost contibutors to *Punch*; it was he had written that article about me. Afterwards Dickens embraced me and said, 'Never allow yourself to be upset by the papers, they are forgotten in a week, and your book stands and lives. God has given you so very much, go your own way and give what you have in you, go your way, you are head and shoulders above all the little men!' – And while we were walking in the road he wrote with his foot in the sand, 'That is criticism,' he said and wiped it out, 'thus it is gone. – A work which is good lives by itself, you have tested it before; see what the result is!' [Andersen greatly appreciated this sympathy. 'The family life seems so harmonious' he wrote at this time, Dickens himself being 'like the best in his books; affectionate, lively, cheerful and cordial.' Indeed, 'Take the best out of all Dickens's writings, make from them the picture of a man, and you have Charles Dickens.' He was 'throughout all the weeks I stayed there, always radiating good health, happy and full of sympathy'. He stayed for five weeks – which, Dickens commented, 'seemed to the family AGES!'][4]

Having known Charles Dickens for a long period, I feel that I am justified in speaking of his personal characteristics [wrote Henrietta Ward. Her husband E. M. Ward, RA (1816–79) met Dickens in 1851 and painted his portrait in 1853–4, and Dickens 'became one of our most cherished friends'.] The most remarkable [characteristic] was, undoubtedly, his extreme sympathy for the suffering, and for those who needed sympathy. On one occasion my husband met with an accident to his hand, which necessitated the attendance of Dr. Elliotson. Before the arrival of the medical man Dickens took charge of the patient himself, doing everything that was necessary – bathing the injured part with vinegar, binding it up, and performing to perfection the combined functions of surgeon and nurse. He even appeared on the scene at midnight, provided with medicines and liniments ordered by the doctor to be administered at that hour, and, feeling perhaps that no one else could be trusted, thus ventured to continue his kind attention to the grateful invalid. I could give many instances of this extraordinary sympathy on the part of our friend if I thought further corroboration necessary.[5]

Charles Dickens? Not an attractive man to the casual eye but, when you became friendly with him, delightfully attractive [replied Sir Mountstuart E. Grant Duff (1829–1906), politician, diarist and bookman, to an enquirer. In his diary for 1861 he records their first meeting, at the cottage of Professor (later Sir) Richard Owen.[6]] I had not seen Dickens before, and thought his look singularly unprepossessing. The first unfavourable impression, however, very soon wore off, and I did not detect any thing in his conversation that at all answered to his appearance. He talked to me . . . about Gore House and Count D'Orsay, of whom he spoke with great regard, [and] of Holland House. . . . [7]

While dining with Fauntleroy at Verey's, saw Charles Dickens [wrote the American author and journalist John R. Thompson (1823–73) in his journal, 25 May 1865]. He looked very little like a gentleman, and to our amazement, took out a pocket-comb and combed his hair and whiskers, or rather his goatee, at the table. And yet this is the celebrated man that ridiculed the manners of the Americans! [Two days later, at Verey's] . . . saw Charles Dickens again with a repetition of the comb performance. [The following year, Thompson went to one of the readings, which he greatly enjoyed.] Dickens would have made an admirable actor. His rapid change of voice and manner in the impersonation of character was almost like what we read of the elder Mathews. Much as I liked the entertainment, however, I could not avoid thinking it *infra dig* for the acknowledged Master of Fiction to come down to

'Mrs. Raddle'. Fancy Thackeray giving us imitations of 'Becky Sharp', or Bulwer-Lytton assuming the air and style of 'Augustus Tomlinson!' . . . [8]

Dickens's strong sympathy gave him an extraordinary memory even for trifles [writes the actor Charles Brookfield (1857–1913), son of Thackeray's friend the Revd W. H. Brookfield]. When my father was given the living of Somerby, near Grantham, both my mother and he rather dreaded the monotony of life in a small country village. Dickens did his best to cheer my mother on the subject. 'Are there *no* old friends living anywhere in the neighbourhood of Somerby?' he inquired. 'Surely there must be *somebody* you know within ten miles or so?' 'No,' replied my mother mournfully, 'not a single soul. Oh! I think there *is* one acquaintance of my husband's,' she suddenly recollected. 'A Mr. Maddison, I fancy the name is. But he is not an intimate friend. William knows him only very slightly.' 'Ah, but that's all right!' exclaimed Dickens, his whole face brightening. 'You'll find Maddison a delightful resource. You'll discover there's a lot more in Maddison than you ever dreamed there was. Maddison will become a very important factor in your life. Yes, I'm glad you've got Maddison.' And, wringing her heartily by the hand, he went his way. It so happened that my mother did not meet Dickens again for three or four years, till one evening at a crowded party she caught his eye at the other end of the room. His face immediately lit up with a humorous expression, and he picked his way through the crush until he reached her side. 'Well,' he inquired, in an eager undertone, 'and *how's Maddison?*'[9]

[Sir William Hardman (1828–90), lawyer, and editor of the *Morning Post*, was acquainted with Catherine Dickens, and much disapproved of 'the great Charles [who] has so shamefully separated' from her. In February 1864 he records:] Poor Mrs. Charles Dickens is in great grief at the loss of her second son, Walter Landor Dickens, who has died with his regiment in India. . . . Her grief is much enhanced by the fact that her husband has not taken any notice of the event to her, either by letter or otherwise. If anything were wanting to sink Charles Dickens to the lowest depth of my esteem, *this* fills up the measure of his iniquity. As a writer, I admire him; as a man, I despise him.[10] [Another friend of Catherine's, Jane Panton, writes that she has] always stood up for Mrs. Dickens. She was a kind, good woman, good in every sense of

the word, and when she left her husband's house, she left her heart
behind her.

I well recollect being in a box at the theatre one evening with my
mother and Mrs. Dickens: the latter burst into tears suddenly and
went back into the box. Charles Dickens had come into the opposite
box with some friends, and she could not bear it. My mother took
her back to her house in Gloucester Road, Regent's Park, telling me
to sit quietly until she returned. When she did she said nothing to
me, but I heard her tell Papa about it, and add, 'I thought I should
never be able to leave her; that man is a brute.' Papa shrugged his
shoulders and said nothing.[11]

I was delighted to find that Charles Dickens was sound upon the
Gospel [wrote the Evangelical philanthropist George Moore (1806–
76) after staying several days at Gad's Hill]. I found him a true
Christian without great profession. I have a great liking for him.[12]

On November 2, 1867, a dinner was given in Freemasons' Hall to
Charles Dickens, about to visit America [writes the American
author and divine, Moncure D. Conway (1832–1907)]. Most of the
men who were carrying on the literary, dramatic, and artistic work
of London were present.[13] . . . When Dickens arose [to speak] he
had to stand long while the shouts stormed upon him. Men leaped
on chairs, tossed up napkins, waved glasses and decanters over their
heads – and there was a pressing up from the lower tables until
Dickens was girt about by a solid wall of friends. As he stood there
silent I watched his face; it was flushed with excitement, and those
wonderful eyes flamed around like a searchlight. Had Tennyson
been there a poem might have been written more pathetic than the
address of Ulysses to his brave companions who had 'toiled and
wrought' with him, when his purpose held 'to sail beyond the
sunset'. Dickens saw before him authors, actors, artists, with whom
in early days he had partaken humblest fare: Horace Mayhew,
Mark Lemon, Walter Thornbury, Westland Marston, Tom Taylor,
Buckstone, Edmund Yates, G. H. Lewes, the sons of Jerrold and
Tom Hood, his own sons stood near, as if witnesses to the career
whose victories they had followed from the lowly beginning to this
culmination.

When the storm of enthusiasm had quieted, Dickens tried to
speak, but could not; the tears streamed down his face. As he stood

there looking on us in silence, colour and pallor alternating on his face, sympathetic emotion passed through the hall. When he presently began to say something, though still faltering, we gave our cheers, but felt that the real eloquence of the evening had reached its climax in the silent tears of Dickens.[14]

Dickens often expressed a longing for sudden death, and he was not the man to assert an opinion for mere word's sake [wrote his early biographer R. Shelton Mackenzie (1809–80)]. A friend has told us that walking across Kensington Gardens one day with Dickens, a thunder storm suddenly came. As the rain began to descend, the great Novelist proposed shelter beneath the trees. 'No,' said his heroic but timid friend, 'that is too dangerous. Many people have been killed beneath trees from the effects of lightning.' 'Well,' said Dickens, turning and looking earnestly at his friend, 'of all the fears that harrass a man on God's earth, the fear of sudden death seems to me the most absurd, and why we pray against it in the Litany I cannot make out. A death by lightning most resembles the translation of Enoch.' He then quoted the lines from Byron's *Corsair*, commencing:

> Let him who crawls enamored of decay,
> Cling to his Couch, and sicken years away;
> Heave his thick breath, and shake his palsied head;
> Ours – the fresh turf, and not the feverish bed;
> While, gasp by gasp, he falters forth his soul,
> Ours with one pang – one bound – escapes control.[15]

I had met him in May [1870], at Charing Cross [writes Blanchard Jerrold (1826–84), journalist, and contributor to Dickens's weeklies], and had remarked that he had aged very much in appearance. The thought-lines of his face had deepened, and the hair had whitened. Indeed, as he approached me I thought for a moment I was mistaken, and that it could not be Dickens: for that was not the vigorous, rapid walk, with the stick lightly held in the alert hand, which had always belonged to him. It was he, however: but with a certain solemnity of expression in the face, and a deeper earnestness in the dark eyes. However, when he saw me and shook my hand, the delightful brightness and sunshine swept over the gloom and sadness; and he spoke cheerily, in the old kind way – not in the least about himself – but about my doings, about Doré, about London as a subject (and who ever knew it half so well as he, in all its highways and byeways?) – about all that could interest me, that occurred to him at the moment. And he wrung my hand again, as we parted, and the cast of serious thought settled again upon the handsome face, as he turned, wearily I thought for him, towards the Abbey.[16]

NOTES

1. Susan Chitty, *The Beast and the Monk: a Life of Charles Kingsley* (1974) p. 174.

2. Wife of the politician and man of letters, Richard Monckton Milnes, later Baron Houghton (1809–85). Dickens was friendly with the Milneses and, as his letters show, was on close terms with Mrs Milnes. Mrs Bennoch, referred to below, was the wife of the merchant Francis Bennoch (1812–90), 'the man to whom I owed most in England', as Hawthorne wrote. The Bennochs moved in literary circles, but there is no evidence of their knowing Dickens.

3. *The English Notebooks by Nathaniel Hawthorne*, ed. Randall Stewart (1941) p. 379. This is the final entry about Dickens in the *Notebooks*; Hawthorne seems never to have seen or met him. Earlier entries – one is quoted above (see I, 109) – mostly report hostile tittle-tattle, and describe someone as being 'of the Dickens school, a little flashy and rowdyish' (p. 326).

4. Elias Bredsdorff, *Hans Andersen and Charles Dickens: a Friendship and its Dissolution* (Cambridge, 1956) pp. 70, 94, 109; Gladys Storey, *Dickens and Daughter* (1939) p. 22.

5. *Pen and Pencil*, Supplement, pp. 11–13. Mrs. E. M. Ward's *Memories of Ninety Years* (1926) contains further reminiscences of Dickens, including such titbits as that he had a favourite cat which he kept in his study while writing (p. 255) and that he used to stay at a hostelry in Slough for several days at a time (p. 158) – maybe during the period when Ellen Ternan lived there? – see Felix Aylmer, *Dickens Incognito* (1959).

6. Dickens first met Owen in 1843, and they became friends. Owen contributed to *Household Words*, and described Dickens as 'a handsome man – but much more – there is real goodness and genius in every mark of his face, and the lines in it are very strongly marked'. Later, however, he thought Dickens had spoiled his face by adding a beard (Rev. Richard Owen, *Life of Richard Owen* (1894) I, 391; II, 131).

7. James Milne, *Memoirs of a Bookman* (1934) p. 20; Mountstuart E. Grant Duff, *Notes from a Diary 1851–1872* (1897) I, 195.

8. John R. Robinson, 'London Diary of 1863–66', in J. G. Wilson (ed.), *Criterion* (New York, 1901), quoted in James Grant Wilson, *Thackeray in the United States* (1903) I, 267.

9. Charles H. E. Brookfield, *Random Reminiscences* (1911 edn) pp. 22–3.

10. *The Letters and Memoirs of Sir William Hardman: Second Series, 1863–1865*, ed. S. M. Ellis (1925) p. 147. Dickens wrote only three brief letters to Catherine during the 1860s, and none on the occasion of Walter's death. He and Catherine never met after their separation.

11. Jane Panton, *Leaves from a Life* (1908) p. 143. Her 'papa' was the painter W. P. Frith (on whom see above, 1, 48–51).

12. Samuel Smiles, *George Moore, Merchant and Philanthropist* (1880) p. 274. For Dickens's involvement in charities dear to Moore, see *Speeches*, Index, p. 452.

13. Public and social life were equally well represented, by the Lord Chief Justice, the Lord Chief Baron, the Lord Mayor of London, prominent politicians and members of the aristocracy, leading journalists, etc. See *Speeches*, pp. 368–74, which quotes the *New York Tribune* report, 18 Nov 1867: it was 'a high historical event. . . . Nothing like it has ever before occurred in London. . . . The company that assembled to honour Dickens, represented humanity.'

14. Moncure D. Conway, *Autobiography, Memories and Experiences* (1904) II, 128–9.

15. R. Shelton Mackenzie, *Life of Charles Dickens* (Philadelphia, 1870) p. 245. On Mackenzie, see above, 1, xxvi, 110.

16. Blanchard Jerrold, 'Charles Dickens: In Memoriam', *Gentlemen's Magazine*, n.s. v (1870) 239–40. Blanchard Jerrold was the son of Dickens's old friend Douglas Jerrold, and it was probably Dickens's kindness to the bereaved Jerrold family that he was recalling when he described his energetic practical help to a widow moving into new premises – Dickens in shirt-sleeves up a ladder, hanging up pictures etc. This comes in *A Day with Charles Dickens* (1871), pt 1 of a series, *The Best of All Good Company*. Besides recording personal memories, Jerrold there reprints various other people's recollections of Dickens, e.g. R. H. Horne's that he 'scarcely ever looked direct at anything. . . . He had no need. His was one of those gifted visions upon which objects photographed themselves on the retina in rapid succession' (p. 8).

Advice to a Beginner

CONSTANCE CROSS

From her 'Charles Dickens: A Memory', *New Liberal Review*, Oct 1901, pp. 392–8. Constance Cross (1846–?) was, as she says, 'an obscure girl-author' when she had her only meeting with Dickens, six weeks before his death. Her *No Guiding Star: A Novel* had appeared in 1868, and she later published other tales and verses, some of them under the auspices of the Religious Tract Society. A few days after their meeting, having read a story of hers in manuscript, Dickens sent her a severe and detailed critique: 'feeble matter' treated in 'a worn out way that never was a very firm one. . . . You will get nowhere by the road you are now pursuing', etc., though he recognised that she was 'modest and earnest' in her aspirations, and sent her this discouraging advice 'most unwillingly' (*N*, III, 774–5). She met Dickens through Bulwer Lytton, 'who had encouraged me from very early days to tread the paths of literature' and around whom she had 'cast a halo of romance which the nature of his works seemed to justify'. For Dickens she felt no such ardour – until she met him. Her account, though inaccurate in some details, provides some unique information (about his intention to live in Germany and master the language) and, with his letter to her of 4 May 1870, shows him, very creditably, taking a responsible interest in the efforts and prospects of a not very promising beginner.

. . . I remember arriving at 5, Hyde Park Place, Mr. Dickens's town residence, in the soft sundown hour of an April day. The windows of the room in which we sat overlooked the Marble Arch and the spacious Park beyond. I never see this particular locality but I am reminded of that conversation, of somewhat over an hour, in which I learned, as it were, to unlearn myself. For it is quite needless to observe that Mr. Dickens had no sympathy with the romantic element in my character, and was at infinite pains to impress on me the necessity of cutting and pruning the exuberance of my fancy, and to direct me to lofty aims in the art I desired to cultivate.

The characteristic of this great writer which appealed to me most strongly was his perfect naturalness. I might have known him all my life – it was so easy to tell him my inmost thoughts, to find myself interesting him by my freedom of speech, a freedom in which I had never indulged with Lord Lytton. I found him gentle, kindly, friendly; and I remember he spoke in a low, subdued voice, and with an earnestness and truthfulness that appealed to something higher in my nature than the mere desire to achieve literary success. We conversed on various subjects – fiction, history, poetry – and he deprecated the poetical tendency of my style. 'You are on a path,' he said, 'that will lead you nowhere.' Then he rather abruptly asked me if I had studied any modern languages. When I told him French and German, he exclaimed: 'Ah! German – I thought so; a story of yours to which Lytton drew my attention indicated as much. In it you have quite adopted the German manner, and with success. But do not continue that manner; it is unreal, it could not always be adapted to subjects in every sense prosaic.' Then we talked of Schiller and Goethe and Lessing, and he seemed pleased to find that I had not been attracted or influenced by Heine.[1] He questioned me as to the method by which I had arrived at what knowledge I possessed of German, and then confided to me (rather to my surprise after our conversation) that he was contemplating a stay of two years in Germany, in order that he might acquire the language colloquially, as was ever his custom before studying the construction of any foreign tongue. He told me he had decided to go, accompanied by his daughter, to Thuringia, and that he was much looking forward to the accomplishment of his plan. He was, however, prevented by death from carrying out this intention.

Then we talked of his work, of the creations of his brain, and the room became peopled somehow with those creations, for, as we named them, he spoke as if they were living beings, the friends and companions of his everyday life. He asked me which of all his works I liked the best, and when I replied *David Copperfield*, I could see that I had afforded him the greatest possible delight. 'I am rejoiced to hear you say that,' he exclaimed, 'for it is the one of all my books that I love the most. I suppose it is because so many of the experiences related in it have been my own'; and he looked sad and thoughtful for a moment or two.

'I am told that *Nicholas Nickleby* and *Martin Chuzzlewit* are considered your greatest works,' I ventured to observe. 'Yes,' he replied, 'I believe they are; but they do not touch your heart like the other, do they?' . . .

After this he told me a little of his early life, and asked me if I had ever seen Gadshill. I replied that I had not. 'I love it,' he said thoughtfully; and then he recounted the story which I think is pretty generally known [about his childhood ambition 'to be rich and buy this house': *Life*, I, i, 2–3]. I remember his relation of this incident the more vividly because, as he was speaking, a wistful look stole into his eyes, his gaze went far beyond me, over the Marble Arch, over the Park glades, piercing, or striving to pierce, as it were, the great golden haze of the setting sun; and he said in tones as of one communing with his own soul, 'Yes, I love the dear old place; and I hope – when I come to die – it may be there.' Just six weeks later to the day of the week, the hour of the evening, he had his hope fulfilled. . . .

But Mr. Dickens discoursed on other subjects than himself. He spoke of Thackeray with undisguised admiration and affectionate regard; he deplored Lord Lytton's attitude towards him, observing that Thackeray came too near him in greatness. . . . Mr. Dickens evidently desired to modify the impression I might have received concerning Thackeray without undermining my loyalty to Lord Lytton. 'When you are older, and have seen more of life,' he said, 'you will be able to form your own judgment of the merits of these two great writers; you will find there was room for both – yet we shall not see another Thackeray this century.'

'George Eliot' also at this time was but a name to me, but I mentioned to Mr. Dickens Lord Lytton's contempt for her writings. 'Yes,' he said, 'I know; he will not allow genius to either Thackeray or George Eliot, and to the latter not even a lofty intellect.' 'But you do,' I interposed. 'I? Indeed I do. The manuscript of *Adam Bede* was sent to me for my opinion as to the sex of the writer. I decided that it was the work of a woman. The manuscript showed the intellect of a man, but the heart of a woman; and I was not mistaken.[2] I am a very great admirer of George Eliot.'

I could only listen; my mind had yet to grow up to the greatness of the writers he admired, and so I was naturally more impressed by the charm of Mr. Dickens's manner, by the quite way in which he interested me in his home life, describing how he passed his evenings, which seemed to be generally in the society of a much-loved daughter, to whom he often affectionately referred.

I remember the room in which we sat was in blue and white, and looked inhabited. In no way did it remind me of the lonely grandeur of Lord Lytton's residence. And, of course, so young an observer as I then was would be much struck by the amazing contrast the two men afforded, and my wonder excited at the strong friendship I knew existed between them. The born aristocrat, the man who never seemed able to escape the influences of his blue blood, yet became and felt as a brother to this man of the people; for, setting aside Mr. Dickens's social status, he was by the very nature of his genius a man of the people. He would have said so himself; he would have gloried in it.

I found Mr. Dickens very practical. He spoke a great deal of the pecuniary advantages to be derived from his profession. 'Good literature will always command its price', he said. He then told me that a short story was the best test of capacity for writing fiction. 'It is an art to be cultivated,' he said, 'and in its way it is a higher art than the long story or novel.' He gave expression to much the same opinions respecting the relation between authors and publishers as those to which we are now accustomed in the organ of the Society of Authors.

Mr. Dickens also said: 'I have certainly been very successful; but, whatever amount I have received for my works, my publishers have made double that amount.' It appeared to me that he looked very much on the commercial side of literature. It was this, I fancy, more than anything else, that made him appear to me such a complete contrast to Lord Lytton. The latter, I do not doubt, was as sensible as Mr. Dickens of the advantages accruing from substantial returns for his brainwork; but the romantic halo I had cast about him, and which he always seemed to like to retain, perhaps deterred him from descending to the sordid details of pounds, shillings, and pence. Or it may have been his class, his order; for he was as impregnated with all the characteristics of that order as Charles Dickens was with those of the more commonplace sections of humanity. Lord Lytton never once mentioned money to me as a desirable and probable return for an outlay of intellect. It was fame – always fame – to go down to posterity as a great writer. Moreover, I do not think he would have liked to mix up the acquisition of gain with the lofty ideals presented by Cervantes and Spenser, which ideals he had begged me to make the supreme study of my life. Mr. Dickens proposed no ideals for my contemplation. Human nature as we found it, he said, should be the model of all good work; there must be no 'painting men as they ought to be'. And he gave expression to much the same sentiment as Longfellow has so well formulated in one of his Fireside verses:

> That is best which lieth nearest;
> Shape from that thy work of art

But although Mr. Dickens sent me to the fountain-head for observation of the great drama of life, he at the same time suggested a course of reading which I am inclined to think was intended to counterbalance the romantic and unpractical tendency of my mind, and which indeed had that effect. I remember so well his careful enumeration of authors and their respective works – Buckle's *Civilisation*, Mr. Froude's writings, Macaulay's *History* and *Essays* – especially the *Essays* – books of travel, biographies, no fiction. They afforded a striking contrast to Lord Lytton's list. And then he gave me kindly words of encouragement, and expressed the hope that he should see me again.

During the interview I ventured to ask him what method he pursued in the composition of his works, and if they were all completed before going to press. 'By no means,' he replied; 'they are not written beyond the part that is to be published at a given time; but the plot, the motive of the book, is always perfected in my brain for a long time before I take up my pen. I add a great deal to the original idea as I work on, but, as I always know the end from the beginning, I can safely commit my work in parts to the press.'

'But suppose,' I stammered . . . , 'suppose you died before all the book was written?' 'A-h!' he said, and paused; then added, 'That has occurred to me – at times', and again the long, future-piercing look seemed to be penetrating the golden haze. Then he turned his kindly glance on me, and said cheerfully: 'One can only work on, you know – work while it is day.'

NOTES

1. It is surprising to find Dickens expressing an antipathy – or any other response – to Heine, there being so little evidence of his knowing or caring about German culture. His intention to live in Germany and learn the language, mentioned below, is similarly unpredictable.

2. Constance Cross's memory, or Dickens's, was at fault here. He had not been shown the manuscript of *Adam Bede* but had immediately guessed George Eliot's sex while reading her first book, *Scenes of Clerical Life*, a copy of which she had sent him. He enormously admired *Adam Bede*, and much wanted George Eliot to write a serial for *All the Year Round*; see above, 1, 112.

At Lady Molesworth's

LADY DOROTHY NEVILL AND LORD REDESDALE

(1) from *The Reminiscences of Lady Dorothy Nevill*, ed. Ralph Nevill (1906) pp. 146–7; (2) from Lord Redesdale, *Memories* (1915) II, 517–18. Lady Dorothy Nevill (1826–1913) was a well-known hostess, and author of several volumes of reminiscences; Lord Redesdale (1837–1916), diplomatist and author, was at Eton with Dickens's son Charley (see above, 1,167). Lady Molesworth was, as Redesdale puts it, 'a great figure-head in London society. At her house were to be met all the prominent personages in the great world, from the Prince of Wales downwards, and there was always a goodly leaven of Art and Literature' (*Memories*, 11, 518). Bishop Wilberforce remarked that, 'if the King of the Cannibal Islands were to come to England, within twenty-four hours he would be dining with Lady Molesworth' (*Reminiscences of Lady Dorothy Nevill*, p. 147). Dickens's letter to her about these engagements, dated 5 May 1870, is subscribed 'Ever affectionately yours' (*N*, III, 775).

(1) Lady Molesworth, indeed, although by no means brilliantly intellectual herself, possessed a mysterious power of drawing out clever people and making them talk – a social quality of the highest possible value. . . . She used to give two different kinds of dinner-

parties, some large, of from fifteen to twenty people, mostly drawn from the fashionable world, and others small, at which some six or eight of the best brains in London could exchange ideas. Bishop Wilberforce, Dr. Quin (a celebrated wit of that day), Lord Houghton, and Sir Edwin Landseer, were amongst the many clever men whom one met constantly at her entertainments. I remember an occasion on which Lady Waldegrave, being anxious to have Charles Dickens as one of her guests, had persuaded Mr. Bernal Osborne [MP] to bring the great novelist to dine, the latter's aversion to fashionable society having with difficulty been overcome. A number of very fashionable people were present, and all agog as to how amusing Dickens would be, as is the wont of many of their kind who imagine clever men are going to turn intellectual somersaults in consideration of being dragged into a society which is quite incapable of either understanding or appreciating their genius. In due course Mr. Bernal Osborne and his captive arrived, and we all sat down; but things did not turn out as expected, for the author of *Pickwick* merely uttered a few commonplace remarks and nothing more. Mr. Bernal Osborne said to me afterwards: 'I feared this; once he imagines he is being trotted out, he won't say a word!'

A short time afterwards Lady Molesworth asked me to dine to meet the same great writer; we were to be but six – our hostess, Mr. Dickens, Lord Torrington, a great musical critic, another literary man, and myself. That evening was one of the most agreeable I have ever known; Dickens simply bubbled over with fun and conversation, talking in a way which resembled nothing so much as some of the best passages in his own books. He laughed and chaffed, telling me, I remember, that he had a great scheme for writing a cookery-book, and I believe the poor man really meant it, but, alas! his death, which occurred very shortly after, prevented the realization of the idea.[1]

(2) One night towards the end of May [1870] I was at the theatre with Charles Dickens and old Lady Molesworth. Just we three in a private box. Between the acts we had great fun. Dickens was in high spirits, brim-full of the *joie de vivre*. His talk had all the sparkle of champagne, and he himself kept laughing at the majesty of his own absurdities, as one droll thought followed another. He was not always in such a vein, for if he thought he was being lionized he would sit mumchance; but he really liked the old lady and of course

I did not count; so he was at his ease and at his very best, so bright, so merry and – like his books – so human.

During the evening Lady Molesworth insisted on his naming a night to go and dine with her. The date was fixed and on the following day the invitations came out for a day in June. Alas! That dinner never came off, for on the 9th of June, two or three days before the night agreed upon, the whole English-speaking world was stricken with grief. Dickens was lying dead at his beloved Gad's Hill. It seemed impossible. He had been so brilliant that night. He was only fifty-eight years of age, twenty years younger than I am at this time of writing, and though we knew that he suffered terribly from exhaustion after his readings, which seemed to sap all his energy, undermined as it had been by the strain of many troubles, added to hard and incessant work, he was at times still so young and almost boyish in his gaiety that it was an unspeakable shock.[2]

Those murderous readings which killed him were enthralling. Never shall I forget the effect produced by his reading of the death of Steerforth; it was tragedy itself, and when he closed the book and his voice ceased the audience for a moment seemed paralysed, and one could almost hear a sigh of relief.

Had he, as he was once minded to do, taken up acting as a profession he would have been as famous as Garrick. Would the gaiety of nations have been as darkly eclipsed as it was when he died and *Edwin Drood* remained a mystery?

NOTES

1. Dickens was at Lady Molesworth's on 29 May 1870, eleven days before his death.

2. For Redesdale's memories of Dickens twenty years earlier, see above, 1, 167.

One Week before his Death

HERMAN MERIVALE

(1) from *Pen and Pencil*, Supplement, pp. 30–1; (2) from his letter to *The Times*, published 8 Feb 1883; (3) from Percy Fitzgerald, *Memoirs of an Author* (1894) 1, 13–14. Merivale (1839–1906), playwright, novelist, and contributor to *All the Year Round*, had been performing in 'a tremendous melodrama', *Carlmilhan*, with one of Dickens's daughters, at a country house. Dickens, hearing about this, was fired to propose an amateur production of a French drama, *The Prima Donna*, in London; he intended to take part, but his lameness prevented this. He directed it, however; both his daughters took part, and Millais – who a week later was to draw Dickens's deathbed portrait – designed the scenery. The performance took place at Cromwell House, the home of Mr and Mrs (later Sir Charles and Lady) Freake, on 2 June 1870. George Dolby had seen Dickens that morning, and 'it was painfully evident to me that he was suffering greatly both in body and mind' – *Charles Dickens as I Knew Him* (1885) p. 464. But when an early biography (A. W. Ward's) remarked how ill Dickens was in these final weeks, Merivale was moved to protest that 'There is no need to surround a national loss and all its infinite sadness with a fictitious gloom': Dickens had been very sprightly that evening – his last theatrical venture. See also Merivale's 'About Two Great Novelists' [Dickens and Thackeray], *Temple Bar*, LXXXIII (1888) 188–204.

(1) C. D. was very nice to me all those days – bright-eyed and cheery – always interested in me as an old contributor whom he had only known by correspondence; as an old friend of his daughters, and most for my connection with the stage, of which he loved of all things to discourse. He had nearly half-an-hour a day of it with me before we began rehearsing, and was great upon *Carlmilhan*. At rehearsal he was all business and attention – a martinet, and threw himself into every part in turn – either low comedian or old man – with instant versatility I never saw surpassed. I never saw any sign of illness except that his foot was always in a slipper, and he on a stick (which alone prevented his taking part in the play himself). . . .

Dickens enjoyed *Carlmilhan*, at second-hand, like a boy, the more as he said he had fancied that he knew the name of every new play that had been acted for years (melodrama of the higher kind was his pet passion), but that this strange-named pirate was entirely new to him. So much, however, did the train of thought suggested fire the old play-spirit in the man, that it came about that the last months of his life were to be associated once more with the art he had loved and practised so well.

(2) I was at his house in Hyde Park Place almost every day for some hours, for the rehearsals. . . . Charles Dickens undertook the entire stage management; and, though he was suffering from his lameness, directed all the rehearsals with a boy's spirit, and a boy's interest in his favourite art; 'coaching' us all with untiring kindness, marking his 'prompt book' as he marked his readings, and acting all the parts *con amore* one after another, passing from the 'old man' to the 'young lover' with all his famous versatility and power. The performance came off at Cromwell House on the 2nd of June. The later rehearsals took place there; and, like the performance, on the drawing-room floor, under Dickens's active personal direction. On the night (a stifling one) he was behind the scenes as prompter and stage-manager, ringing all the bells and working all the lights, and went through the whole thing with infectious enjoyment.

(3) I think I may have had one glimpse of Dickens that night [writes Percy Fitzgerald], but he kept himself secluded and shrouded from observation. After the play was over, as I have been assured by our hostess, he could not for a few moments be found, and was discovered by his son-in-law [Charles Collins] behind the scenes, seated in a corner in a dreamy state and abstracted. He thought, he said, he was at home. He was wearied out: yet insisted on returning that night to Gadshill, and, I believe did so. That was Thursday, June 2, and on the Wednesday following he was dead.[1]

NOTE

1. Percy Fitzgerald, who gives a full account of the evening's proceedings ('That night was long remembered. A brilliant company was assembled . . . ') , mentions that Dickens was also thinking, at this time, of revising and playing in the old Adelphi melodrama, *The Wreck Ashore* (*Memoirs of an Author*, I, 14–15). Fitzgerald is mistaken in his belief that Dickens returned to Gad's Hill that night; he slept at the *All the Year Round* office and worked there – most unusually, on a Friday – the next morning (see Charley Dickens, above, I, 138).

A Few Days before his Death

KATE DICKENS PERUGINI

(1) and (3) from her '*Edwin Drood* and the Last Days of Charles Dickens', *Pall Mall Magazine*, XXXVII (1906) 648, 652–4; (2) from Gladys Storey, *Dickens and Daughter* (1939) pp. 132–4. There is an unimportant conflict on dates: Katey says that she arrived at Gad's Hill on Saturday 4 June, but Gladys Storey says that it was on the Sunday.

(1) That my father's brain was more than usually clear and bright during the writing of *Edwin Drood*, no one who lived with him could possibly doubt; and the extraordinary interest he took in the development of this story was apparent in all that he said or did, and was often the subject of conversation between those who anxiously watched him as he wrote, and feared that he was trying his strength too far. For although my father's death was sudden and unexpected, the knowledge that his bodily health was failing had been for some time too forcibly brought to the notice of those who loved him, for them to be blind to the fact that the book he was now engaged in, and the concentration of his devotion and energy upon it, were a tax too great for his fast ebbing strength. Any attempt to stay him, however, in work that he had undertaken was as idle as stretching one's hands to a river and bidding it cease to flow; and beyond a few remonstrances now and again urged, no such attempt was made, knowing as we did that it would be entirely useless. And so the work sped on, carrying with it my father's few remaining days of life, and the end came all too soon, as it was bound to come, to one who never ceased to labour for those who were dear to him, in the hope of gaining for them that which he was destined never to enjoy. And in my father's grave lies buried the secret of his story. . . .

I had gone down to Gad's Hill on Saturday, June 4th, to see him. He had only returned to the country a week before, as he had been staying in Hyde Park Place for his Readings, and to give my sister a little gaiety during the London season.

I had been with him constantly in town, and was therefore

unprepared to find him looking a good deal changed. This was so noticeable on the Sunday afternoon, when he came in from a short walk, that I spoke of his altered appearance to my aunt and sister, who were the only other members of our family at home. They assured me that he was really better than he had been, and would probably, after he had rested a little, be more like himself; and they were right, for at dinner he appeared less worn, and was very cheerful and talkative. In the evening we went for a stroll in the garden, but soon returned to the house, as he was fatigued; and then he said that he would like to sit in the dining-room, for he took so much pleasure in the new conservatory, that had been finished during his absence, that he preferred to be where he could see the flowers.[1]

There was a matter of some little importance to myself that I wished to consult him upon. This I told him, and he said that later in the evening, when my aunt and sister went to bed, we would talk of it together. My sister then played and sang, and her voice, which was very sweet and thrilling, reached us from the drawing-room, where she sat alone. My father enjoyed her music, as he always did, and was quite happy, although silent now, and looking very pale, I thought. At about eleven o'clock my sister and aunt retired; the servants were dismissed, and my father and I remained seated at the table: the lamps which had been placed in the conservatory were now turned down, but the windows that led into it were still open. It was a very warm, quiet night, and there was not a breath of air: the sweet scent of the flowers came in through the open door, and my father and I might have been the only creatures alive in the place, so still it was.

I told him of what was on my mind, and for a long time he gave his close attention to it, helping and advising me to come to a decision. It was very late when I at last rose from my seat and said that I thought it was time for him to rest, as he looked so tired; but he bade me stay with him for a little, as he had much to say. He was silent, however, for some minutes after this, resting his head upon his hand, and then he began talking of his own affairs, telling me exactly how he stood in the world, and speaking, among other things, of *Edwin Drood*, and how he hoped that it might prove a success – 'if, please God, I live to finish it'.

I must have turned to him, startled by his grave voice, for he put his hand upon my arm and repeated, 'I say *if*, because you know, my dear child, I have not been strong lately.' Again he was silent, gazing wistfully through the darkened windows; and then in a low voice spoke of his own life, and many things that he had scarcely ever mentioned to me before. I was not surprised, nor did it seem strange at the time, that he should be speaking thus; but what greatly troubled me was the manner in which he dwelt upon those years that were gone by, and never, beyond the one mention of *Edwin Drood*, looked to the future. He spoke as though his life were over and there was nothing left. And so we sat on, he talking, and I only interrupting him now and then to give him a word of sympathy and love. The early summer dawn was creeping into the conservatory before we went upstairs together, and I left him at his bedroom door. But I could not forget his words, and sleep was impossible . . . .

(2) [Katey gave Gladys Storey fuller particulars of this conversation with her father. She had gone to Gad's Hill to talk to him] about going on the stage as a means of earning a little extra money. Mr. Wigan (who had seen her act in *The Frozen Deep*) had offered to give her an engagement should she decide to take the step.[2] When she broached the subject to her father, he replied: 'We will talk about it when the others have gone to bed.' . . . At dinner . . . all kinds of topics were discussed; he asked her about her painting, a subject in which he always showed great interest, and enquired about her husband's health. It was a lively meal accompanied by merry laughter. Afterwards, he smoked his customary cigar and strolled into the conservatory on a further tour of inspection. The good-nights having been said, he turned to the subject referred to. 'Now tell me all about it,' he said.

'I shall never forget that talk!' Mrs. Perugini said to the author. 'With great earnestness my father dissuaded me from going on the stage. "You are pretty and no doubt would do well, but you are too sensitive a nature to bear the brunt of much you would encounter. Although there are nice people on the stage, there are some who would make you hair stand on end. You are clever enough to do something else." He finally dismissed the subject by saying, "I will make it up to you." He went on to speak of other subjects – with regret. He wished, he said, that he had been "a better father – a better man." He talked and talked, *how* he talked, until three o'clock in the morning, when we parted for bed. I know things about my father's character,' continued Mrs. Perugini, 'that no one else ever knew; he was not a good man, but he was not a fast man,

but he was wonderful! He fell in love with this girl, I did not blame
her – it is never one person's fault.'

Mrs. Perugini was of the opinion that had her father married
Maria Beadnell or Ellen Ternan, the ultimate result would have
been the same, for he 'did not understand women'.[3] It would have
been impossible to eradicate one 'fault' from the make-up of Charles
Dickens and have left him the 'uncanny genius' that he was, for each
'fault' contributed in some way to the great result.

(3) [Next morning] when I went down to breakfast he had already
gone over to the Châlet, where he worked during the warm
weather. I felt extremely uneasy, and told my sister and aunt the
cause of my anxiety. My aunt promised to write the next day and
give us news of him, for my sister was returning to town with me that
morning, and we could not be at Gad's Hill until the following
Saturday. My father disliked partings, so I merely left him my dear
love, and intended to go away without any farewell; but as we sat in
the porch waiting for the carriage that was to take us to the station,
an uncontrollable desire to see him once again came upon me, and
was too strong to be resisted. I told them I must go to him for one
short moment, and hurried across to the Châlet, that stood hidden
by trees at the back of the shrubbery, and after mounting the little
outside staircase found my father in the upper room, which he had
converted into a summer study. His head was bent low down over
his work, and he turned an eager and rather flushed face towards me
as I entered. On ordinary occasions he would just have raised his
cheek for my kiss, saying a few words, perhaps, in 'the little
language' that he had been accustomed to use when we were
children; but on this morning, when he saw me, he pushed his chair
from the writing-table, opened his arms, and took me into
them.[4] . . .

I hastened back to the house, repeating to myself, 'I am so glad I
went – I am so glad', though why I was so glad it would have been
difficult to tell, for I was to see him soon again. He certainly looked
better, was more cheerful, and full of interest in his work; and surely
there was nothing to fear! We had good accounts of him too on
Wednesday morning from my aunt, and a letter came written by
himself; but alas! on the evening of that day, the third after we had
left Gad's Hill, we were summoned to return home at once, as my
father had been taken seriously ill. . . . He died peacefully, the next
evening.

NOTES

1. He had supervised its construction, and it was, as he 'laughingly' – but all too truly – told Katey, 'positively the last improvement' (Storey, *Dickens and Daughter*, p. 133).

2. The brothers Alfred and Horace Wigan were actor-managers; either could be intended here. For *The Frozen Deep*, see above, II, 241. Katey was doubtless inclined to accept this offer now because her husband Charles Collins was very ill and unable to do much work, and it was expected that he would soon die, though he survived until 1873.

3. Gladys Storey is here requoting Katey's remark (p. 100) 'My father did not understand women.'

4. 'Mrs. Perugini went to the chalet to say good-bye to her father, who always had a horror of those two words. She found him at work on *Edwin Drood*. To his girls he was in the habit of offering his cheek to be kissed; on this occasion he kissed *her* very affectionately' (Storey, *Dickens and Daughter*, p. 134). As Katey told G. B. Shaw in 1897, her father was 'most extraordinarily reticent for a man who was supposed to be so full of frankness and geniality' (*P*, I, XIV).

Suggestions for Further Reading

John Forster's *The Life of Charles Dickens* (1872–4) remains the most useful biography. J. W. T. Ley's annotated edition (London: Cecil Palmer, 1928) is difficult to obtain; the only available reprint is the two-volume Everyman's Library edition, ed. A. J. Hoppé (London: Dent, 1966). The standard modern biography is Edgar Johnson's *Charles Dickens: His Tragedy and Triumph* (London: Gollancz, 2 vols, 1953; 1 vol., revised and abbreviated, Harmondsworth: Penguin, 1978). Biographies between these dates which contain valuable material or interpretations include those by F. G. Kitton (1890), Percy Fitzgerald (2 vols, 1905), Ralph Straus (1928), Edward Wagenknecht (1929, revised 1965), Thomas Wright (1935) and Una Pope-Hennessy (1945). Edmund Wilson's biographical and critical essay 'Dickens: the Two Scrooges', in *The Wound and the Bow* (London: W. H. Allen, 1941), offered a very influential re-interpretation. More recent biographical studies of special merit are K. J. Fielding's *Charles Dickens: a Critical Introduction* (London: Longmans, 1958, revised 1965), Angus Wilson's *The World of Charles Dickens* (London: Secker & Warburg, 1970), and Norman and Jeanne Mackenzie's *Dickens: A Life* (London: Oxford University Press, 1979).

Few of the items in the present collection are reprinted in their entirety, and readers may wish to pursue particular enquiries by consulting the contexts from which items are derived. Books on special aspects of Dickens's life and career include Robert Langton's *The Childhood and Youth of Charles Dickens* (London: Hutchinson, 1883, revised 1891, 1912), William Glyde Wilkins's *Charles Dickens in America* (London: Chapman & Hall, 1911), W. J. Carlton's *Charles Dickens, Shorthand Writer* (London: Cecil Palmer, 1926), Gladys Storey's *Dickens and Daughter* (London: Frederick Muller, 1939), Ada Nisbet's *Dickens and Ellen Ternan* (Berkeley and Los Angeles, Calif.: University of California Press, 1952), A. A. Adrian's *Georgina Hogarth and the Dickens Circle* (London: Oxford University Press, 1957), Christopher Hibbert's *The Making of Charles Dickens* (London: Longmans, 1967), Raymund Fitzsimons's *The Charles*

Dickens Show: An Account of the Public Readings (London: Geoffrey Bles, 1970), Fred Kaplan's *Dickens and Mesmerism* (Princeton, N. J.: Princeton University Press, 1975) and Robert L. Patten's *Charles Dickens and his Publishers* (London: Oxford University Press, 1978).

Dickens's letters are vivid, numerous and of enormous biographical interest: see the List of Abbreviations for particulars of the main editions. There is no available selection from them, unfortunately. K. J. Fielding's edition of the *Speeches* (Oxford: Clarendon Press, 1960) and Philip Collins's edition of the *Public Readings* (Oxford: Clarendon Press, 1975) give much information about these aspects of Dickens's career.

Biographical materials are surveyed by K. J. Fielding in his British Council booklet *Charles Dickens* (London: Longmans, 1953, revised 1960, 1963) and by Michael Slater in his contribution to *The English Novel: Select Bibliographical Guides*, ed. A. E. Dyson (London: Oxford University Press, 1974). For more detailed listings and discussion see the Dickens sections by Ada Nisbet in *Victorian Fiction: A Guide to Research*, ed. Lionel Stevenson (New York: MLA, 1964), and by Philip Collins in *The New Cambridge Bibliography of English Literature*, vol. 3, ed. George Watson (Cambridge: Cambridge University Press, 1969), and *Victorian Fiction: A Second Guide to Research*, ed. George Ford (New York: MLA, 1978).

Index

Danson, Dr Henry, on C.D., 5–7
Danson, John Towne, on C.D., 75–9
Darnley, Lord, 116, 208, 280
Daudet, Alphonse, 292
Davey, E., on C.D., 129–31
Deichmann, Baroness, on C.D., 111–12
Delane, John T., 80, 106, 207–8
Denman, Baron Thomas, 107, 289–90
De Quincey, Thomas, 313
Dexter, Henry, 58
Dickens, Alfred, on C.D., 155–8, 175
Dickens, Catherine (née Hogarth), on
  C.D., xxii, 16–17; 2, 35, 39, 52–3,
  68, 79, 89, 130, 139, 152, 154, 156,
  191, 196, 207, 233, 277, 317, 337,
  340–1, 343. See also Dickens,
  Charles, as a husband.
Dickens, Charles

PERSONAL QUALITIES, TASTES, ETC.
actor, might have been a professional, 29, 134, 190, 205, 236, 351.
  See also theatricals, amateur.
appearance, 5, 8, 10, 11, 14, 20, 48–9,
  52–6, 71, 98, 100, 117, 182–4, 199,
  200–1, 205–6, 222, 225, 233, 240,
  251, 300, 304–5, 324, 339. See also
  dress, eyes, face.
art, taste in, 184, 189, 201, 203, 240
benevolence, kindness, 23, 26, 29, 40,
  60, 73, 162, 182, 243, 248, 249,
  271, 277, 279, 286, 307, 315–16,
  318, 339
boyhood, xxii, 2–9, 13, 131, 162, 259
business, aptitude for, xiv, 18, 63, 64,
  71, 96, 101, 104, 212, 217, 222,
  226, 229, 249, 299, 330, 333, 347
charm, xiii, 26, 42, 73, 95–6, 113,
  114, 116, 170, 216, 224, 227, 243
children, love of, xviii, 13, 31–2, 142,
  196, 273, 275. See also father, as a.
Christmas, enjoyment of, 146–8, 162,
  186
circus, delight in, 209, 258, 321
conjuror, as a, 61–2, 81, 143
conversation, 19, 26, 34, 37, 52, 66,
  70, 85, 110–19, 130–1, 148, 157,
  160, 166, 170, 174, 176, 191–2,
  194, 201, 209, 216, 219, 232, 234,

248, 278, 284, 289–92, 312, 316,
  317, 331, 333, 336, 342, 350–1. See
  also purity in speech.
dancing, love of, 35–6, 62, 71, 85,
  133, 240
dogs, fondness for, 139, 148, 275, 282,
  312
dreams, 27, 311
dress, xviii–xix, 5, 11, 13, 14, 20, 34,
  41, 52, 54, 55, 72, 111, 113, 117,
  143, 194, 196, 199, 234, 240, 258,
  272, 273, 274, 277, 297, 298, 300,
  302, 324; Plate 16
eating and drinking, 112, 123, 145,
  194, 196, 204, 208, 219–20, 277,
  305–6, 317–18, 326
editor, as a, 75–80, 192–232
egoism, 26, 152, 207
energy, vitality, xiv, 18, 20, 24, 115,
  117, 133, 140, 159,.166, 168, 182,
  210, 212, 229, 239, 247, 258, 295
English, typically, 203, 303, 324
eyes, 11, 18, 33, 39, 41, 42, 47, 53, 54,
  56, 57, 65, 71–2, 74, 85, 89, 95, 96,
  98, 113, 117, 157, 183, 189, 205–6,
  214, 219, 225, 232, 233–4, 252,
  258, 294, 297, 300, 301, 318, 324,
  332, 337
face, xix, 11, 18, 20, 40, 42, 47, 52, 53,
  54, 55–6, 58, 65, 71, 74, 82, 98,
  100, 115, 117, 138–9, 141, 157,
  167, 170, 182–3, 189, 191, 197,
  206, 228, 245, 251–2, 258, 297,
  332, 343
father, as a, 94, 131–65, 196, 240,
  271, 288, 317, 322, 356
final days, 137–8, 267–8, 269–70,
  342, 350–8
finances, 14, 63, 68, 88, 219, 222, 347
flowers, love of, 139, 143, 148, 269,
  293, 319, 355
foreigners, views on, 45, 163, 203–4,
  221, 237, 290, 345
friend, as a, 22, 32, 83, 118, 212, 218,
  257
fun, xvi–xvii, 20, 34, 38, 42, 70, 74,
  78, 82, 91, 93, 113, 115, 117, 164,
  165, 167, 170, 216, 259–60, 280,
  305, 310, 315, 317, 350